MCP Mathematics

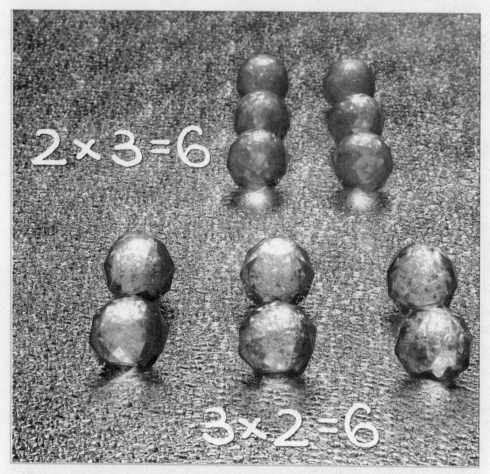

Richard Monnard • Royce Hargrove

Project Staff

Art & Design: Robert Dobaczewski, Kathleen Ellison, Senja Lauderdale, David Mager, Jim O'Shea, Angel Weyant

Editorial: Stephanie P. Cahill, Gina Dalessio, Phyllis Dunsay, Mary Ellen Gilbert, Dena Kennedy, Theresa McCarthy, Marilyn Sarch Doug Falk, Clare Harrison

Marketing:

Production/ Manufacturing: Irene Belinsky, Lawrence Berkowitz, Louis Campos, Pamela Gallo, Leslie Greenberg, Suellen Leavy, Ruth Leine, Michele Uhl

Publishing Operations: Carolyn Coyle, Richetta Lobban

SAVVAS
LEARNING COMPANY

ISBN-13: 978-0-7652-6060-4
ISBN-10: 0-7652-6060-3
19 2021

1-800-848-9500
Savvas.com

Contents

Chapter 14   Division

Chapter 15   Fractions and Probability

Chapter 16   Decimals

Addition and Subtraction Facts

Addition Facts Through 10

Patsy walks from home to school along Oak Street and Maple Street. How many blocks does she walk to school?

We are looking for the total number of blocks Patsy walks.

Patsy walks _____ blocks on Oak Street.

She then walks _____ blocks on Maple.

To get the total, we add _____ and _____.

_____ + _____ = _____ or

addend   addend   sum

☐ addend

+ ☐ addend
―――――
☐ sum

Patsy walks _____ blocks to school.

Getting Started _____

Complete each number sentence.

1. 4 + 3 = _____   2. 1 + 7 = _____   3. 4 + 0 = _____   4. 9 + 1 = _____

5. 2 + 2 = _____   6. 4 + 4 = _____   7. 3 + 5 = _____   8. 6 + 4 = _____

Find each sum.

9. 3 + 2	10. 5 + 5	11. 4 + 0	12. 2 + 7	13. 1 + 5	14. 0 + 9
15. 6 + 2	16. 2 + 3	17. 8 + 1	18. 7 + 3	19. 4 + 5	20. 3 + 6

Practice

Complete each number sentence.

1. $6 + 2 = \underline{\hspace{1cm}}$ 2. $0 + 2 = \underline{\hspace{1cm}}$ 3. $1 + 2 = \underline{\hspace{1cm}}$ 4. $8 + 2 = \underline{\hspace{1cm}}$

5. $4 + 6 = \underline{\hspace{1cm}}$ 6. $3 + 1 = \underline{\hspace{1cm}}$ 7. $4 + 3 = \underline{\hspace{1cm}}$ 8. $3 + 6 = \underline{\hspace{1cm}}$

9. $3 + 3 = \underline{\hspace{1cm}}$ 10. $0 + 0 = \underline{\hspace{1cm}}$ 11. $2 + 0 = \underline{\hspace{1cm}}$ 12. $7 + 2 = \underline{\hspace{1cm}}$

Find each sum.

13. $\begin{array}{r} 7 \\ + 0 \\ \hline \end{array}$ 14. $\begin{array}{r} 1 \\ + 4 \\ \hline \end{array}$ 15. $\begin{array}{r} 2 \\ + 4 \\ \hline \end{array}$ 16. $\begin{array}{r} 0 \\ + 9 \\ \hline \end{array}$ 17. $\begin{array}{r} 1 \\ + 1 \\ \hline \end{array}$ 18. $\begin{array}{r} 3 \\ + 4 \\ \hline \end{array}$

19. $\begin{array}{r} 0 \\ + 3 \\ \hline \end{array}$ 20. $\begin{array}{r} 6 \\ + 3 \\ \hline \end{array}$ 21. $\begin{array}{r} 2 \\ + 2 \\ \hline \end{array}$ 22. $\begin{array}{r} 7 \\ + 1 \\ \hline \end{array}$ 23. $\begin{array}{r} 3 \\ + 2 \\ \hline \end{array}$ 24. $\begin{array}{r} 0 \\ + 6 \\ \hline \end{array}$

25. $\begin{array}{r} 4 \\ + 0 \\ \hline \end{array}$ 26. $\begin{array}{r} 2 \\ + 7 \\ \hline \end{array}$ 27. $\begin{array}{r} 4 \\ + 4 \\ \hline \end{array}$ 28. $\begin{array}{r} 2 \\ + 1 \\ \hline \end{array}$ 29. $\begin{array}{r} 2 \\ + 3 \\ \hline \end{array}$ 30. $\begin{array}{r} 9 \\ + 1 \\ \hline \end{array}$

31. $\begin{array}{r} 7 \\ + 3 \\ \hline \end{array}$ 32. $\begin{array}{r} 0 \\ + 7 \\ \hline \end{array}$ 33. $\begin{array}{r} 1 \\ + 7 \\ \hline \end{array}$ 34. $\begin{array}{r} 8 \\ + 1 \\ \hline \end{array}$ 35. $\begin{array}{r} 1 \\ + 6 \\ \hline \end{array}$ 36. $\begin{array}{r} 4 \\ + 2 \\ \hline \end{array}$

Now Try This!

This machine is programmed to add 5. Write the missing sums on the Out cards. Write the missing addends on the In cards.

Lesson 1-1 • Addition Facts Through 10

Addition Facts Through 18

Bill earned 7 quarters raking leaves on Monday. His father gave him 6 more on Tuesday when he finished the job. How many quarters did Bill have in all?

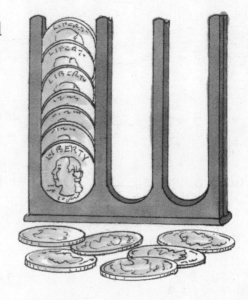

We need to find the total number of quarters Bill earned.

Bill earned _____ quarters on Monday.

His father paid him _____ more quarters when he finished the job.

To get the total, we add _____ and _____.

_____ + _____ = _____ or

$$\begin{array}{r} \square \\ + \ \square \\ \hline \square \end{array}$$

Bill earned _____ quarters in all.

Getting Started

Complete each number sentence.

1. 3 + 9 = _____

2. 8 + 8 = _____

3. 4 + 7 = _____

4. 9 + 8 = _____

5. 8 + 7 = _____

6. 7 + 7 = _____

7. 6 + 9 = _____

8. 6 + 8 = _____

Find each sum.

9.   7
    + 4

10.   9
     + 6

11.   8
     + 4

12.   9
     + 9

13.   7
     + 8

14.   3
     + 8

15.   8
     + 8

16.   7
     + 5

17.   8
     + 9

18.   9
     + 2

19.   7
     + 7

20.   4
     + 9

Practice

Complete each number sentence.

1. $9 + 9 =$ _____   2. $4 + 6 =$ _____   3. $7 + 8 =$ _____   4. $6 + 7 =$ _____

5. $7 + 9 =$ _____   6. $8 + 5 =$ _____   7. $7 + 4 =$ _____   8. $8 + 4 =$ _____

9. $5 + 5 =$ _____   10. $2 + 9 =$ _____   11. $4 + 9 =$ _____   12. $8 + 6 =$ _____

13. $3 + 8 =$ _____   14. $8 + 9 =$ _____   15. $7 + 6 =$ _____   16. $5 + 9 =$ _____

Find each sum.

17. $\begin{array}{r} 7 \\ + 5 \\ \hline \end{array}$
18. $\begin{array}{r} 6 \\ + 6 \\ \hline \end{array}$
19. $\begin{array}{r} 8 \\ + 3 \\ \hline \end{array}$
20. $\begin{array}{r} 9 \\ + 7 \\ \hline \end{array}$
21. $\begin{array}{r} 2 \\ + 8 \\ \hline \end{array}$
22. $\begin{array}{r} 3 \\ + 7 \\ \hline \end{array}$

23. $\begin{array}{r} 9 \\ + 4 \\ \hline \end{array}$
24. $\begin{array}{r} 6 \\ + 8 \\ \hline \end{array}$
25. $\begin{array}{r} 9 \\ + 7 \\ \hline \end{array}$
26. $\begin{array}{r} 5 \\ + 6 \\ \hline \end{array}$
27. $\begin{array}{r} 9 \\ + 6 \\ \hline \end{array}$
28. $\begin{array}{r} 5 \\ + 8 \\ \hline \end{array}$

29. $\begin{array}{r} 9 \\ + 3 \\ \hline \end{array}$
30. $\begin{array}{r} 7 \\ + 7 \\ \hline \end{array}$
31. $\begin{array}{r} 5 \\ + 8 \\ \hline \end{array}$
32. $\begin{array}{r} 4 \\ + 7 \\ \hline \end{array}$
33. $\begin{array}{r} 9 \\ + 5 \\ \hline \end{array}$
34. $\begin{array}{r} 5 \\ + 7 \\ \hline \end{array}$

Complete each table.

35.

Add 8	6	3	4	7	5	8	0

36.

Add 9	3	6	2	5	7	4	9

Problem Solving

Solve each problem.

37. Frank has 9 plants left to sell. His sister has only 3. How many plants do they have left to sell altogether?

38. Dina rode her bike 6 miles on Monday, doing her paper route. On Tuesday, she rode 8 miles so she could deliver more papers. How many miles did she ride both days?

Subtraction Facts Through 10

If Raoul uses 4 of his stamps to mail letters to his friends, how many stamps will he have left?

We need to find the number of stamps Raoul has left.

Raoul has _____ stamps.

He uses _____ stamps to mail his letters.

To get the number left, we subtract _____ from _____

$$\underline{\qquad} - \underline{\qquad} = \underline{\qquad}$$ or

minuend   **subtrahend**   **difference**

☐ **minuend**

− ☐ **subtrahend**

☐ **difference**

Raoul will have _____ stamps left.

Getting Started

Complete each number sentence.

1. 7 − 3 = _____   2. 4 − 2 = _____   3. 6 − 5 = _____   4. 9 − 7 = _____

5. 8 − 2 = _____   6. 7 − 1 = _____   7. 10 − 3 = _____   8. 10 − 5 = _____

Find each difference.

9. 2
  − 0
  _____

10. 6
  − 3
  _____

11. 9
  − 2
  _____

12. 8
  − 7
  _____

13. 5
  − 5
  _____

14. 4
  − 3
  _____

15. 9
  − 4
  _____

16. 3
  − 1
  _____

17. 8
  − 3
  _____

18. 7
  − 0
  _____

19. 6
  − 2
  _____

20. 2
  − 2
  _____

Practice

Complete each number sentence.

1. $10 - 5 =$ _____
2. $1 - 0 =$ _____
3. $2 - 2 =$ _____
4. $7 - 4 =$ _____

5. $0 - 0 =$ _____
6. $10 - 9 =$ _____
7. $5 - 1 =$ _____
8. $4 - 3 =$ _____

9. $7 - 3 =$ _____
10. $5 - 5 =$ _____
11. $6 - 0 =$ _____
12. $6 - 3 =$ _____

Find each difference.

13. $\begin{array}{r} 5 \\ -4 \\ \hline \end{array}$
14. $\begin{array}{r} 10 \\ -6 \\ \hline \end{array}$
15. $\begin{array}{r} 3 \\ -3 \\ \hline \end{array}$
16. $\begin{array}{r} 10 \\ -1 \\ \hline \end{array}$
17. $\begin{array}{r} 5 \\ -2 \\ \hline \end{array}$
18. $\begin{array}{r} 2 \\ -1 \\ \hline \end{array}$

19. $\begin{array}{r} 7 \\ -5 \\ \hline \end{array}$
20. $\begin{array}{r} 7 \\ -7 \\ \hline \end{array}$
21. $\begin{array}{r} 5 \\ -3 \\ \hline \end{array}$
22. $\begin{array}{r} 7 \\ -1 \\ \hline \end{array}$
23. $\begin{array}{r} 1 \\ -1 \\ \hline \end{array}$
24. $\begin{array}{r} 4 \\ -2 \\ \hline \end{array}$

25. $\begin{array}{r} 6 \\ -4 \\ \hline \end{array}$
26. $\begin{array}{r} 7 \\ -6 \\ \hline \end{array}$
27. $\begin{array}{r} 4 \\ -4 \\ \hline \end{array}$
28. $\begin{array}{r} 10 \\ -3 \\ \hline \end{array}$
29. $\begin{array}{r} 4 \\ -1 \\ \hline \end{array}$
30. $\begin{array}{r} 6 \\ -1 \\ \hline \end{array}$

Complete each wheel.

31.

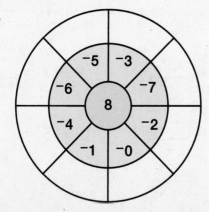

32.

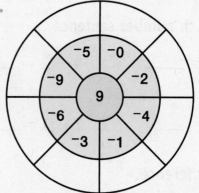

Problem Solving

Solve each problem.

33. Kyle's cat had 9 kittens. He gave 6 kittens to his uncle. How many kittens does he have left?

34. Maria walked for 3 miles in the morning. After lunch, she walked another 4 miles. How far did she walk in all?

Lesson 1-3 • Subtraction Facts Through 10

Subtraction Facts Through 18

Ling and Nancy both collect stickers.
How many more stickers does Ling
have than Nancy?

> We want to know how many more
> stickers Ling has than Nancy.
>
> Ling has ____ stickers.
>
> Nancy has ____.
> To find the difference, we subtract ____ from ____.
>
> ____ – ____ = ____ or
>
>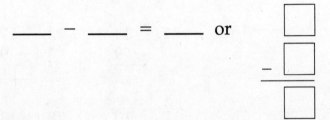
>
> Ling has ____ more stickers than Nancy.
>
> Use addition to check your subtraction.
>
> If **14 – 9 = 5**, then **5 + ____ = 14**.

Getting Started _____

Complete each number sentence. Use addition to check.

1. 16 – 8 = ____
2. 14 – 5 = ____
3. 12 – 4 = ____
4. 18 – 9 = ____

5. 11 – 7 = ____
6. 13 – 6 = ____
7. 15 – 9 = ____
8. 17 – 8 = ____

Find each difference. Use addition to check.

9. 12
   – 7

10. 11
   – 3

11. 16
   – 7

12. 13
   – 9

13. 11
   – 5

14. 12
   – 3

15. 15
   – 6

16. 12
   – 6

Practice

Complete each number sentence. Use addition to check.

1. $12 - 8 =$ _____   2. $14 - 7 =$ _____   3. $11 - 2 =$ _____   4. $12 - 7 =$ _____

5. $11 - 9 =$ _____   6. $11 - 4 =$ _____   7. $12 - 3 =$ _____   8. $12 - 6 =$ _____

9. $13 - 6 =$ _____   10. $15 - 9 =$ _____   11. $16 - 8 =$ _____   12. $15 - 6 =$ _____

13. $13 - 4 =$ _____   14. $14 - 6 =$ _____   15. $13 - 5 =$ _____   16. $12 - 5 =$ _____

Find each difference. Use addition to check.

17.	18.	19.	20.	21.	22.
18 − 9	11 − 7	15 − 7	10 − 3	14 − 9	17 − 9

23.	24.	25.	26.	27.	28.
11 − 6	13 − 9	13 − 8	11 − 5	10 − 8	13 − 7

29.	30.	31.	32.	33.	34.
16 − 9	10 − 5	14 − 8	11 − 8	16 − 7	17 − 8

Complete each table.

35.

Subtract 8	11	14	17	16	12	15

36.

Subtract 7	14	11	13	15	12	16

Problem Solving

Solve each problem.

37. Cassie has $18 to spend on a CD for her brother's birthday. The CD costs $9. How much money will Cassie have left?

38. Mitch has 5 crickets and 12 grasshoppers in his collection. How many more grasshoppers than crickets does Mitch have?

Basic Properties

Adding and subtracting are easy if we remember some important rules.

Order or Commutative Property

We can add in any order.

$$\begin{array}{r} 3 \\ + 4 \\ \hline \square \end{array} \qquad \begin{array}{r} 4 \\ + 3 \\ \hline \square \end{array}$$

$3 + 4 =$ ____

$4 + 3 =$ ____

Grouping or Associative Property

We can group any two addends.

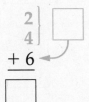

$(2 + 4) + 6 = ?$

____ $+ 6 =$ ____

$2 + (4 + 6) = ?$

$2 +$ ____ $=$ ____

Zero or Identity Property

Adding zero does not affect the answer.

$$\begin{array}{r} 5 \\ + 0 \\ \hline \square \end{array} \qquad \begin{array}{r} 0 \\ + 5 \\ \hline \square \end{array}$$

$5 + 0 =$ ____

$0 + 5 =$ ____

Subtracting zero does not affect the answer.

$$\begin{array}{r} 9 \\ - 0 \\ \hline \square \end{array}$$

$9 - 0 =$ ____

Inverse or Opposite Operations

We can check addition by subtracting.

$$\begin{array}{r} 9 \\ + 6 \\ \hline \square \end{array} \qquad \begin{array}{r} 15 \\ - 6 \\ \hline \square \end{array}$$

$9 + 6 =$ ____

$15 - 6 =$ ____

We can check subtraction by adding.

$$\begin{array}{r} 14 \\ - 6 \\ \hline \square \end{array} \qquad \begin{array}{r} 8 \\ + 6 \\ \hline \square \end{array}$$

$14 - 6 =$ ____

$8 + 6 =$ ____

Practice

Find each sum. Add in any order.

1. 7
   + 5

2. 6
   + 3

3. 2
   + 7

4. 7
   + 4

5. 4
   + 5

6. 9
   + 6

7. 6
   + 7

8. 3
   + 4

9. 4
   + 9

10. 7
    + 7

11. 8
    + 6

12. 5
    + 9

Find each sum by grouping any two addends.

13. 3
    2
    + 4

14. 7
    1
    + 2

15. 6
    3
    + 4

16. 4
    4
    + 2

17. 2
    4
    + 5

18. 7
    4
    + 3

19. 5
    4
    + 5

20. 2
    8
    + 3

21. 6
    2
    + 3

22. 3
    5
    + 4

23. 5
    3
    + 6

24. 8
    1
    + 6

Find each sum or difference.

25. 6
    − 0

26. 7
    + 0

27. 5
    − 0

28. 4
    + 0

29. 9
    − 0

30. 3
    + 0

Add and check by subtracting.

31.
    4
    + 7

    − □
    □

32.
    5
    + 8

    − □
    □

33.
    6
    + 7

    − □
    □

Subtract and check by adding.

34.
    14
    − 6

    + □
    □

35.
    12
    − 7

    + □
    □

36.
    16
    − 9

    + □
    □

Lesson 1-5 • Basic Properties

Name _____

Problem Solving:
Use a Four-Step Plan

Luis and Pedro decide to buy a planter
and a card for their parents' anniversary.
Luis has saved $8 and Pedro has saved $7.
How much will they spend? How much money
will they have left?

 SEE

A planter costs _____. A card costs _____.

Luis has saved _____. Pedro has saved _____

We need to find
   the total cost of a planter and card.
   the combined savings of the two boys.
   the difference between these two amounts.

 PLAN

To find how much the planter and card cost
together, we add _____ and _____.

To find out how much money the boys saved,
we add _____ and _____. To find the amount they
have left, we subtract their total costs from the
amount of money they saved.

 DO

$$\begin{array}{r} \$8 \\ +\ 7 \\ \hline \end{array} \qquad \begin{array}{r} \$12 \\ +\ 2 \\ \hline \end{array} \qquad \begin{array}{r} \boxed{} \\ -\ \boxed{} \\ \hline \end{array}$$

The boys will spend _____ and have _____ left over.

 CHECK

$$\begin{array}{r} \$14 \\ +\ 1 \\ \hline \end{array}$$

Picture labels: CARDS... $2   PLANTERS $12

Apply

Solve each problem. Remember to use the four-step plan.

1. Nathan's stamp album can hold 18 stamps. He had 6 stamps and a friend gave him 3 more. How many more stamps does he need to fill his album?

2. Sharon's pie recipe calls for 16 graham crackers. She has 2 packets of crackers with 6 crackers in each. How many more crackers does she need?

3. A 4-ounce box of nails costs $2, and a 2-ounce box costs $1. How much do 10 ounces of nails cost?

4. Jason has 10 new books. He read 2 books on Saturday and 3 on Sunday. How many books does he have left to read?

5. Jackson wants to buy a backpack that is marked $15. The sale sign says that $3 will be taken off the marked price. How much change will Jackson get back if he gives the clerk $15?

6. An artist had 14 paintings to sell. The first week in November he sold 7 large paintings and 2 small paintings. How many paintings does he have left to sell?

7. What if the sale sign in Exercise 5 said that $2 will be taken off the marked price? How much change would Jackson get back then?

8. Read Exercise 4 again. Rewrite the exercise so that the number of books Jason has left to read is 6.

9. In the United States, Thanksgiving Day is the fourth Thursday in November. What are the earliest and the latest dates on which this holiday can fall?

10. In Canada, Thanksgiving Day is the second Monday in October. What are the earliest and the latest dates on which this holiday can fall?

Find each sum.

1.
$\begin{array}{r} 0 \\ +8 \end{array}$ $\begin{array}{r} 9 \\ +2 \end{array}$ $\begin{array}{r} 8 \\ +8 \end{array}$ $\begin{array}{r} 7 \\ +4 \end{array}$ $\begin{array}{r} 9 \\ +3 \end{array}$ $\begin{array}{r} 9 \\ +6 \end{array}$ $\begin{array}{r} 5 \\ +3 \end{array}$ $\begin{array}{r} 4 \\ +0 \end{array}$ $\begin{array}{r} 2 \\ +6 \end{array}$ $\begin{array}{r} 5 \\ +4 \end{array}$

2.
$\begin{array}{r} 4 \\ +6 \end{array}$ $\begin{array}{r} 2 \\ +5 \end{array}$ $\begin{array}{r} 0 \\ +9 \end{array}$ $\begin{array}{r} 9 \\ +0 \end{array}$ $\begin{array}{r} 7 \\ +2 \end{array}$ $\begin{array}{r} 3 \\ +7 \end{array}$ $\begin{array}{r} 1 \\ +1 \end{array}$ $\begin{array}{r} 2 \\ +4 \end{array}$ $\begin{array}{r} 8 \\ +3 \end{array}$ $\begin{array}{r} 4 \\ +7 \end{array}$

3.
$\begin{array}{r} 4 \\ +5 \end{array}$ $\begin{array}{r} 8 \\ +6 \end{array}$ $\begin{array}{r} 1 \\ +8 \end{array}$ $\begin{array}{r} 3 \\ +0 \end{array}$ $\begin{array}{r} 7 \\ +0 \end{array}$ $\begin{array}{r} 2 \\ +3 \end{array}$ $\begin{array}{r} 1 \\ +9 \end{array}$ $\begin{array}{r} 7 \\ +8 \end{array}$ $\begin{array}{r} 4 \\ +4 \end{array}$ $\begin{array}{r} 2 \\ +0 \end{array}$

4.
$\begin{array}{r} 7 \\ +6 \end{array}$ $\begin{array}{r} 3 \\ +6 \end{array}$ $\begin{array}{r} 2 \\ +8 \end{array}$ $\begin{array}{r} 4 \\ +3 \end{array}$ $\begin{array}{r} 0 \\ +0 \end{array}$ $\begin{array}{r} 5 \\ +1 \end{array}$ $\begin{array}{r} 0 \\ +3 \end{array}$ $\begin{array}{r} 3 \\ +5 \end{array}$ $\begin{array}{r} 6 \\ +2 \end{array}$ $\begin{array}{r} 5 \\ +6 \end{array}$

5.
$\begin{array}{r} 8 \\ +7 \end{array}$ $\begin{array}{r} 1 \\ +7 \end{array}$ $\begin{array}{r} 6 \\ +0 \end{array}$ $\begin{array}{r} 1 \\ +5 \end{array}$ $\begin{array}{r} 0 \\ +4 \end{array}$ $\begin{array}{r} 3 \\ +2 \end{array}$ $\begin{array}{r} 7 \\ +7 \end{array}$ $\begin{array}{r} 3 \\ +1 \end{array}$ $\begin{array}{r} 5 \\ +0 \end{array}$ $\begin{array}{r} 4 \\ +9 \end{array}$

Find each difference.

6.
$\begin{array}{r} 2 \\ -2 \end{array}$ $\begin{array}{r} 9 \\ -6 \end{array}$ $\begin{array}{r} 6 \\ -3 \end{array}$ $\begin{array}{r} 5 \\ -0 \end{array}$ $\begin{array}{r} 7 \\ -2 \end{array}$ $\begin{array}{r} 9 \\ -4 \end{array}$ $\begin{array}{r} 9 \\ -7 \end{array}$ $\begin{array}{r} 7 \\ -1 \end{array}$ $\begin{array}{r} 6 \\ -5 \end{array}$ $\begin{array}{r} 2 \\ -1 \end{array}$

7.
$\begin{array}{r} 6 \\ -0 \end{array}$ $\begin{array}{r} 2 \\ -0 \end{array}$ $\begin{array}{r} 4 \\ -1 \end{array}$ $\begin{array}{r} 6 \\ -1 \end{array}$ $\begin{array}{r} 4 \\ -3 \end{array}$ $\begin{array}{r} 1 \\ -0 \end{array}$ $\begin{array}{r} 4 \\ -2 \end{array}$ $\begin{array}{r} 9 \\ -5 \end{array}$ $\begin{array}{r} 9 \\ -9 \end{array}$ $\begin{array}{r} 12 \\ -8 \end{array}$

8.
$\begin{array}{r} 8 \\ -1 \end{array}$ $\begin{array}{r} 7 \\ -5 \end{array}$ $\begin{array}{r} 9 \\ -3 \end{array}$ $\begin{array}{r} 10 \\ -5 \end{array}$ $\begin{array}{r} 13 \\ -6 \end{array}$ $\begin{array}{r} 7 \\ -0 \end{array}$ $\begin{array}{r} 6 \\ -4 \end{array}$ $\begin{array}{r} 8 \\ -2 \end{array}$ $\begin{array}{r} 15 \\ -7 \end{array}$ $\begin{array}{r} 11 \\ -3 \end{array}$

9.
$\begin{array}{r} 11 \\ -4 \end{array}$ $\begin{array}{r} 8 \\ -3 \end{array}$ $\begin{array}{r} 8 \\ -5 \end{array}$ $\begin{array}{r} 1 \\ -0 \end{array}$ $\begin{array}{r} 7 \\ -3 \end{array}$ $\begin{array}{r} 3 \\ -3 \end{array}$ $\begin{array}{r} 16 \\ -7 \end{array}$ $\begin{array}{r} 8 \\ -4 \end{array}$ $\begin{array}{r} 5 \\ -2 \end{array}$ $\begin{array}{r} 13 \\ -8 \end{array}$

10.
$\begin{array}{r} 8 \\ -0 \end{array}$ $\begin{array}{r} 8 \\ -6 \end{array}$ $\begin{array}{r} 5 \\ -5 \end{array}$ $\begin{array}{r} 9 \\ -2 \end{array}$ $\begin{array}{r} 9 \\ -1 \end{array}$ $\begin{array}{r} 6 \\ -6 \end{array}$ $\begin{array}{r} 17 \\ -9 \end{array}$ $\begin{array}{r} 18 \\ -9 \end{array}$ $\begin{array}{r} 15 \\ -8 \end{array}$ $\begin{array}{r} 14 \\ -8 \end{array}$

Circle the letter of the correct answer.

1 $9 + 7$
a. 16
b. 18
c. 13
d. 9

2 $6 + 6$
a. 6
b. 12
c. 10
d. 15

3 $5 + 4$
a. 5
b. 6
c. 9
d. NG

4 $7 + 6$
a. 11
b. 12
c. 13
d. NG

5 $\begin{array}{r} 9 \\ + 2 \end{array}$
a. 12
b. 14
c. 16
d. NG

6 $\begin{array}{r} 5 \\ + 8 \end{array}$
a. 11
b. 12
c. 13
d. NG

7 $\begin{array}{r} 9 \\ 2 \\ + 3 \end{array}$
a. 14
b. 13
c. 12
d. NG

8 $5 + 0$
a. 8
b. 5
c. 17
d. NG

9 $9 - 3$
a. 6
b. 8
c. 10
d. NG

10 $18 - 9$
a. 6
b. 7
c. 8
d. NG

11 $\begin{array}{r} 15 \\ - 6 \end{array}$
a. 8
b. 7
c. 9
d. NG

12 $\begin{array}{r} 4 \\ - 0 \end{array}$
a. 0
b. 4
c. 8
d. NG

13 $8 + 6 = 14$
$14 - 6 = \square$
a. 7
b. 6
c. 8
d. NG

14 $12 - 5 = 7$
$7 + 5 = \square$
a. 12
b. 8
c. 10
d. NG

$\square$ **score**

STOP

Place Value

Tens and Ones

Fred and Joel played the tens-rod game at recess. Fred was taking his turn when the bell rang. What were each of their scores?

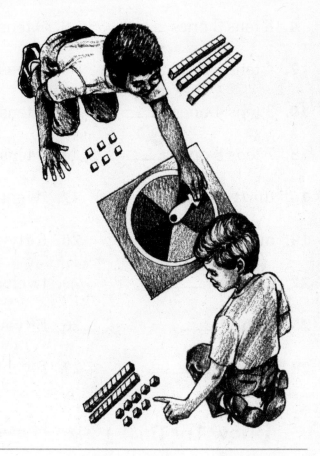

Fred had _____ tens and _____ ones.

He scored _____ + _____ or _____ points.

His score was **thirty-six**.

Joel had _____ tens and _____ ones.

He scored _____ + _____ or _____ points.

His score was **twenty-eight**.

Getting Started

Write each number.

1. _____

2. _____

3. _____

4. 2 tens 6 ones _____

5. sixty _____

6. 1 ten and 9 ones _____

7. 4 tens 8 ones _____

8. thirty-three _____

9. fourteen _____

10. 5 tens 0 ones _____

11. eighty-one _____

12. 7 tens 7 ones _____

Practice

Write each number.

1. ▊▊▊▊ ▦ _____

2. ▊ ▦ _____

3. ▊▊▊▊ _____

4. 8 tens 3 ones _____
5. 3 tens 8 ones _____
6. 1 ten 5 ones _____

7. 4 tens 0 ones _____
8. 5 tens 7 ones _____
9. 6 tens 8 ones _____

10. 3 tens 4 ones _____
11. 5 tens 5 ones _____
12. 8 tens 0 ones _____

13. 7 tens 8 ones _____
14. 9 tens 3 ones _____
15. 2 tens 0 ones _____

16. thirty-six _____
17. twenty-one _____
18. eight _____

19. ninety-five _____
20. forty-four _____
21. seventy-seven _____

22. eighteen _____
23. twelve _____
24. seventy-nine _____

25. eighty _____
26. fifty-seven _____
27. forty-three _____

28. ninety-six _____
29. seventeen _____
30. sixty-two _____

Now Try This!

On Paradise Island a 🪨 stands for one. Ten rocks are the same value as one 🌴.
Ten trees are written as a ☀.

 means **10 + 10 + 6** or **2 tens and 6 ones** or **26.**

1. What does  equal? _____

2. Write 217 as a Paradise Island number.

3. Are these Paradise Island numbers equal? _____

Hundreds

The third-grade class at Halston School held a beanbag toss. What was Room 10's score?

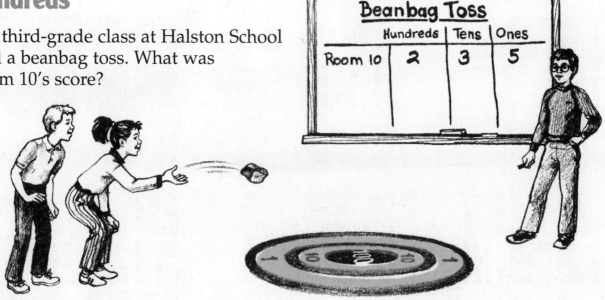

Beanbag Toss			
	Hundreds	Tens	Ones
Room 10	2	3	5

Room 10 scored _____ hundreds, _____ tens, and _____ ones.

They scored _____ + _____ + _____. We write this as _____.

Its word name is **two hundred thirty-five**.

Room 10's score was _____.

Getting Started

Write each number.

1. 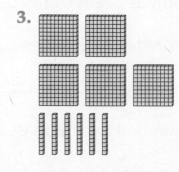 _____

2. _____

3. _____

4. 3 hundreds 1 ten 5 ones _____

5. 9 hundreds 2 tens 9 ones _____

6. two hundred eight _____

7. four hundred twenty-seven _____

8. 5 hundreds 3 tens 7 ones _____

9. seven hundred eleven _____

Practice

Write each number.

1.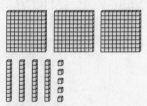

2. 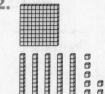 _____

3.  _____   _____

4. 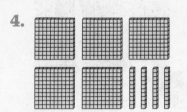 _____

5. 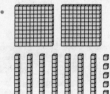 _____

6. 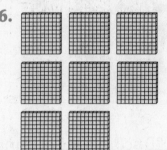 _____

7. 9 hundreds 4 tens 3 ones _____

8. 6 hundreds 4 tens 3 ones _____

9. 4 hundreds 0 tens 2 ones _____

10. 9 hundreds 7 tens 0 ones _____

11. 8 hundreds 2 tens 6 ones _____

12. 1 hundred 5 tens 9 ones _____

13. 5 hundreds 0 tens 0 ones _____

14. 7 hundreds 6 tens 3 ones _____

15. 2 hundreds 5 tens 6 ones _____

16. 4 hundreds 9 tens 1 one _____

17. 6 hundreds 4 tens 3 ones _____

18. 3 hundreds 9 tens 0 ones _____

19. 1 hundred 0 tens 1 one _____

20. 9 hundreds 0 tens 9 ones _____

21. one hundred twenty-five _____

22. six hundred eight _____

23. four hundred fifty-two _____

24. nine hundred seventy-five _____

25. three hundred forty _____

26. five hundred seventeen _____

27. two hundred thirty-nine _____

28. eight hundred ninety-nine _____

29. three hundred seventy-five _____

30. one hundred ninety _____

Lesson 2-2 • Hundreds

Money

During the move to her new house,
Wanda's penny bank is broken.
She decides to exchange her 123
pennies at the bank. How
much has Wanda saved?

Wanda has _____ pennies. She exchanges these

pennies for _____ dollar and _____ dimes.

She has _____ pennies left.

We read this as **one dollar and twenty-three cents**.

We write it as _____.

Wanda has saved _____.

REMEMBER Amounts less than one dollar can also
be written with a dollar sign and a decimal point.

We can write **53 cents** as **$0.53**.
We can write **5 cents** as **$0.05**.

Getting Started

Write each amount. Use a dollar sign and a decimal point.

1.

2.

_____

3.

_____

4.

_____

Practice

Write each amount. Use a dollar sign and a decimal point.

1.

_____

2.

_____

3.

_____

4.

_____

5.

_____

6.

_____

7.

_____

8.

_____

Lesson 2-3 • Money

Name _____

Lesson 2-4

Counting Money

How much money does Georgio have?

Coins and Bills	We count:
	one dollar
	two dollars and
	twenty-five
	fifty
	seventy-five
	eighty
	eighty-five
	eighty-six
	eighty-seven
	eighty-eight cents

Georgio has _____ dollars and _____ cents or _____.

Getting Started

Write each amount. Use a dollar sign and a decimal point.

1.

   _____

2.

   _____

Practice

Write each amount. Use a dollar sign and a decimal point.

1.

_____

2.

_____

3.

_____

4.

_____

5.

_____

6.

_____

7.

_____

8.

_____

Making Change

Tanya bought a game with a ten-dollar bill.
How much **change** did she get?

SALE
puzzles $3.75
games $7.59
books $2.75
stamp $8.42
kits

We want to know how much change Tanya
got. The game cost _____.

Tanya paid for the game with a _____.

Start by counting on from _____.

Coins and Bills	We count:
	$7.60
	$7.70
	$7.75
	$8.00
	$9.00, $10.00

Tanya's change was 2 one-dollar bills, 1 quarter, 1 dime,
1 nickel, and 1 penny, or _____.

Getting Started

Use the sign at the top of the page to answer Exercises 1 and 2.

1. Juan bought a puzzle with 1
   five-dollar bill. How much
   change did he get? Name the
   coins and bills he received and
   write the total amount in dollars
   and cents.

   _____

   _____

2. Marsha bought a stamp kit with
   a ten-dollar bill. How much
   change did she get? Name the
   coins and bills she received and
   write the total amount in
   dollars and cents.

   _____

   _____

Practice

**Use the sign in the School Store to answer Exercises 1 through 5.
Try to use the fewest coins and bills.**

notebooks	$2.78
pencil cases	$1.55
pencil sharpener	$0.63
box of markers	$3.35
calculator	$7.37

1. Janell bought a box of markers with 1 five-dollar bill. How much change did she get? Name the coins and bills she received and write the total amount in dollars and cents.

_____

2. Eric bought a notebook with 1 ten-dollar bill. How much change did he get? Name the coins and bills he received and write the total amount in dollars and cents.

_____

3. Elena bought a pencil sharpener with 1 five-dollar bill. How much change did she get? Name the coins and bills she received and write the total amount in dollars and cents.

_____

4. Abdul bought a pencil case with 1 ten-dollar bill. How much change did he get? Name the coins and bills he received and write the total amount in dollars and cents.

_____

5. Sara bought a calculator with 2 five-dollar bills. How much change did she get? Name the coins and bills she received and write the total amount in dollars and cents.

_____

Now Try This!

Use logical reasoning to solve each problem.

1. Megan bought a stapler at the School Store for $4.65 with 1 five-dollar bill. Write three ways you could make change for Megan. Which way uses the fewest coins?

2. Sam has 4 dimes, 2 nickels, and 1 quarter. What is the fewest coins he could trade for this amount?

Lesson 2-5 • Making Change

Rounding to the Nearest Ten

Beth is using a number line to help
round her numbers to the nearest ten.

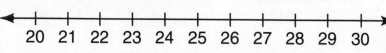

Beth's numbers are _____ and _____

The number 24 is between _____ and _____.

It is closer to _____.

The number 26 is between _____ and _____.

It is closer to _____.

To round to the nearest ten,
look at the ones digit.

If the ones digit is 0, 1, 2, 3, or 4, the
tens digit stays the same, and the
ones digit is replace by zero.

Beth rounds 24 to _____.

If the ones digit is 5, 6, 7, 8, or 9, the
tens digit is raised one, and the ones
digit is replaced by zero.

Beth rounds 26 to _____.

Getting Started

Round each green number or amount of money to the nearest ten. Circle the answer.

1. 60   62   70

2. 60¢   66¢   70¢

3. 40   43   50

4. 90   96   100

5. 40   41   50

6. 30¢   35¢   40¢

Round each number or amount of money to the nearest ten.

7. 77 _____

8. 19¢ _____

9. 68 _____

10. 45 _____

11. 38¢ _____

12. 27 _____

Practice

Round each green number or amount of money to the nearest ten. Circle the answer.

1. 50   53   60

2. 40¢   46¢   50¢

3. 10   17   20

4. 20¢   28¢   30¢

5. 80   81   90

6. 70   73   80

7. 40   45   50

8. 90¢   93¢   100¢

9. 20   26   30

10. 70   77   80

11. 40   42   50

12. 50¢   55¢   60¢

Round each number or amount to the nearest ten.

13. 48 _____

14. 51 _____

15. 19¢ _____

16. 87¢ _____

17. 62 _____

18. 35¢ _____

19. 11 _____

20. 68¢ _____

21. 98¢ _____

22. 33¢ _____

23. 79 _____

24. 71 _____

25. 9 _____

26. 57 _____

27. 75¢ _____

28. 43 _____

[Now Try This!]

Choose the number from the jar that is closest to, but less than, the middle number. Write this number in the first column. In the last column, write the number that is closest to, but greater than the middle number. Finally, round the middle number and circle the answer in the first or last column.

Less than		Greater than
_____	236	_____
_____	143	_____
_____	27	_____
_____	83	_____
_____	125	_____
_____	108	_____

Numbers in jar: 230 80 20 27 100 150 90 30 236 125 83 120 130 140 110 240 143 108

Rounding to the Nearest Hundred

Rinaldo wants to round his
numbers to the nearest hundred.

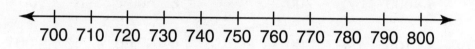

700 710 720 730 740 750 760 770 780 790 800

Rinaldo's numbers are _____ and _____.

The number 746 is between _____ and _____.

It is closer to _____.

The number 769 is between _____ and _____.

It is closer to _____.

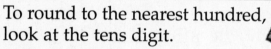 

To round to the nearest hundred,
look at the tens digit.

268

If the tens digit is 0, 1, 2, 3, or 4, the
hundreds digit stays the same, and
the tens and ones digits are replaced
by zeros.

If the tens digit is 5, 6, 7, 8, or 9, the
hundreds digit is raised one, and the
tens and ones digits are replaced by
zeros.

Rinaldo rounds 746 to _____.

Rinaldo rounds 769 to _____.

Getting Started

**Round each green number or amount of money to the nearest hundred or dollar.
Circle the answer.**

1. 500   583   600

2. 900   909   1,000

3. $6.00 $6.30 $7.00

4. 100   147   200

5. 700   750   800

6. 300   329   400

Round each number or amount of money to the nearest hundred or dollar.

7. 429 _____

8. 650 _____

9. $9.81 _____

10. 807 _____

11. 196 _____

12. $5.83 _____

Practice

Round each green number or amount of money to the nearest hundred or dollar. Circle the answer.

1. 300   *356*   400

2. 200   *212*   300

3. $6.00   *$6.28* $7.00

4. $1.00   *$1.07* $2.00

5. 600   *675*   700

6. 800   *850*   900

7. 200   *283*   300

8. 100   *196*   200

9. $7.00   *$7.57* $8.00

10. $4.00   *$4.12* $5.00

11. 900   *985*   1,000

12. 300   *349*   400

Round each number or amount of money to the nearest hundred or dollar.

13. 736 _____

14. $4.27 _____

15. 385 _____

16. 150 _____

17. 226 _____

18. $8.57 _____

19. $5.35 _____

20. 929 _____

21. 599 _____

22. $6.09 _____

23. $3.15 _____

24. 950 _____

25. 468 _____

26. 815 _____

27. $2.12 _____

28. 777 _____

29. 286 _____

30. $7.45 _____

Now Try This!

Now you try it. Make a prediction before you pick.

Lesson 2-7 • Rounding to the Nearest Hundred

Thousands

Recess is over and Nadia is putting
the place-value blocks away. Simon asks,
"What is the total value of your blocks?"

Thousands	Hundreds	Tens	Ones
3	6	4	5

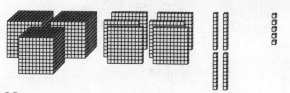

Nadia has _____ thousands,

_____ hundreds, _____ tens, and _____ ones.

Nadia writes _____.

She says, "The total value of my blocks is _____."

Getting Started

Write each number.

1. _____

2. _____

3. _____

4. _____

5. three thousand, six hundred six _____

6. nine thousand, two hundred fifty-five _____

7. six thousand, two hundred twelve _____

8. one thousand, nineteen _____

What is the value of the 3 in each number?

9. 4,329 _____   10. 3,291 _____   11. 6,430 _____

Practice

Write each number.

1. 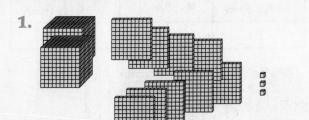 _____

2. 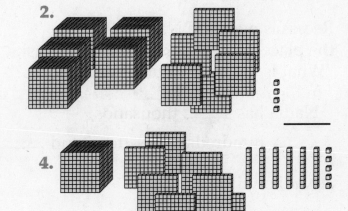 _____

3. 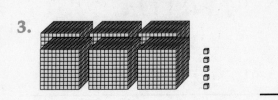 _____

4. _____

5. four thousand, five hundred twenty-five _____

6. six thousand, two hundred seventy-nine _____

7. one thousand, eight hundred four _____

8. seven thousand, seven hundred _____

9. nine thousand eighty-three _____

10. three thousand nineteen _____

11. five thousand, one hundred thirty-three _____

12. two thousand, six hundred twelve _____

13. eight thousand four hundred nintey _____

14. six thousand, five hundred ninety-five _____

15. four thousand one _____

16. one thousand, one hundred eleven _____

What is the value of the 6 in each number?

17. 6,521 _____

18. 3,621 _____

19. 4,006 _____

20. 3,609 _____

21. 9,467 _____

22. 6,975 _____

Lesson 2-8 • Thousands

Ten Thousands and Hundred Thousands

On July 20, 1969, Neil Armstrong walked on the Moon. About how far was he from Earth?

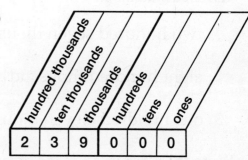

hundred thousands	ten thousands	thousands	hundreds	tens	ones
2	3	9	0	0	0

In the number of miles, there are ____ hundred thousands, ____ ten thousands, ____ thousands, ____ hundreds, ____ tens, and ____ ones.

We write _____ .

We say **two hundred thirty-nine thousand**.

Neil Armstrong was about _____ miles from Earth.

Getting Started

Write each number.

1. three hundred fifty-nine thousand _____

2. six hundred twenty-three thousand _____

3. seven hundred fifty thousand _____

4. five hundred seventy-six thousand _____

Write the place value of the green digit.

5. 369,450 _____

6. 692,056 _____

7. 687,291 _____

8. 405,000 _____

9. 37,580 _____

10. 209,376 _____

Fill in each blank.

11. 335,921 = ____ hundred thousands ____ ten thousands ____ thousands ____ hundreds ____ tens ____ one

Write each number.

1. two hundred seven thousand _____

2. eight hundred thousand _____

3. one hundred eleven thousand _____

Write the place value of the green digit.

4. 156,231 _____   5. 475,300 _____

6. 717,241 _____   7. 395,750 _____

8. 249,309 _____   9. 525,000 _____

Fill in each blank.

10. 596,015 = ____ hundred thousands ____ ten thousands
____ thousands ____ hundreds ____ tens ____ one

(Now Try This!)

Use these Roman numeral values to help you answer the questions about this news event in early Roman times.

I = 1   V = 5   X = 10   L = 50   C = 100   D = 500   M = 1,000

Chariot races were held in the Roman Coliseum yesterday. There were MMDLX seats filled with cheering spectators. There were XVIII chariots paced against each other. The winner was awarded CCL gold coins. To share his good fortune, he tossed XXV of his coins into the crowd.

How many people watched the races? _____

How many chariots were in the race? _____

How much money was given to the winner? _____

How many coins did the winner throw to the crowd? _____

Name _____

Counting and Order

All numbers are made up of the **digits**
0, 1, 2, 3, 4, 5, 6, 7, 8, and 9. When you count
numbers, you name the numbers in order.

The numbers 13, 14, 15, 16, 17, 18, and 19 are
in order. 14 comes before ____ , 18 comes
after ____ , and 16 is between ____ and ____ .

Ordinal numbers show the position of things in order.

Spot is _____ and Pal is _____ .

Look at some other ordinal numbers.

10th	22nd	68th	101st	463rd
tenth	twenty-second	sixty-eighth	one-hundred first	four hundred sixty-third

Getting Started

Write the number that comes after.

1. 46, ____   2. 72, ____   3. 187, ____   4. 463, ____   5. 869, ____

Write the number that comes before.

6. ____ , 27   7. ____ , 44   8. ____ , 271   9. ____ , 493   10. ____ , 978

Complete each series.

11. 31, ____ , 33, ____ , ____ , ____ , ____ , 38

12. 457, ____ , 455, ____ , ____ , 452, ____

Write the ordinal number that comes after.

13. thirty-second, _____   14. two hundred fourteenth, _____

15. sixty-first, _____   16. five hundred twenty-second, _____

Practice

Write the number that comes after.

1. 27, _____   2. 35, _____   3. 41, _____   4. 69, _____   5. 83, _____

6. 139, _____   7. 356, _____   8. 279, _____   9. 822, _____   10. 747, _____

Write the number that comes before.

11. _____ , 31   12. _____ , 25   13. _____ , 49   14. _____ , 93   15. _____ , 100

16. _____ , 262 17. _____ , 191 18. _____ , 534 19. _____ , 980 20. _____ , 771

Complete each sequence.

21. 70, _____, _____, _____, _____, _____   22. _____, 48, _____, _____, 51, _____

23. _____, _____, 89, 90, _____, 92   24. 267, _____, _____, 264, _____, _____

25. 655, _____, _____, 652, _____, _____   26. 999, _____, _____, _____, 1,003, _____

Write the ordinal number that comes after.

27. seventh, _____   28. fourteenth, _____

29. ninety-second, _____

30. two hundred fiftieth, _____

[Now Try This!]

In a sequence, the numbers follow a particular pattern.
Complete each number sequence.

1. 2, 4, _____ , _____ , 10, 12   2. 10, _____ , _____ , 25, 30, 35

3. 15, 12, 9, 6, _____ , _____   4. 100, 98, _____ , 94, 92, _____

5. 1, 2, 4, 7, 11, _____   6. 20, _____ , 34, _____ , 48, _____ , _____

Name _____

It's Algebra!

Comparing and Ordering Numbers

Anna and Steve are earning exercise merit badges by riding their bicycles. Who rode more miles?

We want to know which person rode farther.

Anna rode _____ miles.

Steve rode _____ miles.

We need to compare _____ and _____.

Start with the digits on the left.	Look at the next number.
Anna 351	Anna 351
Steve 316	Steve 316
Anna and Steve have the same number of hundreds.	Anna has more tens than Steve.

We write 351 > 316 and say 351 is _____ than 316.

We write 316 < 351 and say 316 is _____ than 351.

_____ rode more miles.

Getting Started

Compare. Write < or > in the circle.

1. 582 ◯ 536   2. 118 ◯ 116   3. 504 ◯ 540

Write the numbers in order from least to greatest.

4. 651, 647, 663   5. 492, 490, 497   6. 650, 649, 651

_____ , _____ , _____   _____ , _____ , _____   _____ , _____ , _____

Circle the greatest number in each group.

7. 363, 481, 294, 421   8. 752, 749, 767, 755   9. 304, 310, 309, 315

Practice

Compare these numbers. Write < or > in the circle.

1. 9 ◯ 11
2. 36 ◯ 29
3. 127 ◯ 138

4. 139 ◯ 136
5. 257 ◯ 243
6. 512 ◯ 675

7. 405 ◯ 403
8. 826 ◯ 806
9. 715 ◯ 725

10. 888 ◯ 999
11. 480 ◯ 481
12. 517 ◯ 516

13. 255 ◯ 156
14. 319 ◯ 320
15. 157 ◯ 148

Write the numbers in order from least to greatest.

16. 27, 19, 30

____ , ____ , ____

17. 82, 90, 86

____ , ____ , ____

18. 125, 135, 115

____ , ____ , ____

19. 512, 510, 514

____ , ____ , ____

20. 327, 347, 337

____ , ____ , ____

21. 926, 916, 925

____ , ____ , ____

22. 731, 729, 730

____ , ____ , ____

23. 887, 885, 883

____ , ____ , ____

24. 625, 725, 825

____ , ____ , ____

25. 421, 429, 412

____ , ____ , ____

Circle the greatest number in each group.

26. 245, 376, 151, 236
27. 356, 421, 351, 450
28. 605, 603, 608, 600

29. 961, 851, 947, 875
30. 400, 425, 475, 500
31. 871, 878, 787, 788

32. 520, 525, 530, 535
33. 747, 737, 777, 757
34. 256, 265, 656, 566

35. 180, 185, 183, 188
36. 321, 371, 301, 312
37. 499, 409, 419, 439

Lesson 2-11 • Comparing and Ordering Numbers

Name _____

Problem Solving: Make a List

Jeryl is a cashier in a store. He needs to give a customer 50¢ change. Show five different ways he can do this without using any pennies.

 SEE

We know Jeryl needs to make change for _____.

We are looking for _____ different ways to make

_____.

 PLAN

We can make an organized list. We can start with 2 quarters and exchange coins until we have five different ways to make 50¢.

 DO

Fill in the list with the number of coins that make 50¢.

Quarters	Dimes	Nickels	Total Amount
2	0	0	50¢
	2	1	
0		0	50¢
0	4		
0		4	

⭐ **CHECK**

We can check by adding the amount of money in each row.

25¢	25¢	10¢	10¢	10¢
+ 25¢	10¢	10¢	10¢	10¢
		10¢		10¢
	+ 5¢	+ 10¢	10¢	5¢
			5¢	5¢
			+ ___	+ ___

Apply

Make an organized list to help you solve each problem.

1. How many different 3-digit numbers can you make using the digits 1, 2, and 3?

2. How many different 4-digit numbers can you write using the digits 4, 5, 6, and 7?

3. List all the addition number sentences in which the sum of two numbers is 10. You may use a number more than once.

4. There were 9 people at the party and each shook hands with the other. How many handshakes were there?

5. The planet Logo has 2-legged and 3-legged creatures. If in one day you count 25 legs passing by, how many of each creature did you see?

6. Jeans come in blue, black, and brown. The three sizes are small, medium, and large. How many different types of jeans can shoppers buy?

7. What if the digits in Exercise 2 were changed to 2, 4, 6, and 8. How many different 4-digit numbers could you write?

8. There was a collection of bicycles and tricycles on the playground. One day there was a total of 25 wheels. How many bicycles and tricycles were there?

9. How many different ways can you make change for a dollar without using any pennies? Also, do not use any coins more than 4 times in any group.

10. List four ways Jessica can make change for $1.51 using only coins.

Write each number.

1. 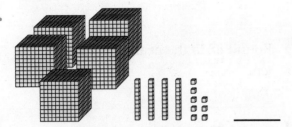 _____

2.  _____

3. six hundred fifty-five _____

4. seventy-eight _____

5. four hundred nine _____

6. two thousand one _____

Compare. Write < or > in the circle.

7. 65 ◯ 56

8. 129 ◯ 205

9. 634 ◯ 624

10. 435 ◯ 453

Round each number or amount of money to the nearest ten.

11. 84¢ _____

12. 59 _____

13. 43 _____

14. 25¢ _____

Round each number or amount of money to the nearest hundred or dollar.

15. 451 _____

16. 828 _____

17. $6.07 _____

18. 215 _____

Write the place value of the 2 in each number.

19. 672,591 _____

20. 375,028 _____

21. 236,480 _____

22. 826,695 _____

Complete each sequence.

23. 32, _____ , _____ , _____ , _____ , 42

24. 105, _____ , _____ , 90, _____ , _____

25. _____ , 12, _____ , _____ , 21, _____

26. _____ , _____ , _____ , 70, _____ , 80

Circle the letter of the correct answer.

1. $9 + 8$
   - a. 16
   - b. 17
   - c. 18
   - d. NG

2. $13 - 7$
   - a. 9
   - b. 8
   - c. 7
   - d. NG

3. $15 - 9$
   - a. 8
   - b. 7
   - c. 6
   - d. NG

4. 36 ◯ 34
   - a. >
   - b. <

5. 448 ◯ 484
   - a. >
   - b. <

6. 761 ◯ 763
   - a. >
   - b. <

7. Round 52¢ to the nearest ten cents.
   - a. 50¢
   - b. 60¢

8. Round 87 to the nearest ten.
   - a. 80
   - b. 90

9. Round 35¢ to the nearest ten cents.
   - a. 30¢
   - b. 40¢

10. Round 435 to the nearest hundred.
    - a. 400
    - b. 500

11. Round $6.25 to the nearest dollar.
    - a. $6.00
    - b. $7.00

12. Round 809 to the nearest hundred.
    - a. 800
    - b. 900

13. What is the value of the 8 in 786,326?
    - a. ten thousands
    - b. hundreds
    - c. ones
    - d. NG

14. What is the value of the 8 in 420,851?
    - a. thousands
    - b. hundreds
    - c. tens
    - d. NG

15. In the problem $74 - 29 = 45$, what is the 29 called?
    - a. difference
    - b. subtrahend
    - c. minuend
    - d. NG

☐ score

Addition

Adding 2-Digit Numbers, Regrouping Ones

Chen's score for the first 9 holes of miniature golf is 37. His score is 26 for the last nine holes. What is his final score?

We want to find Chen's total score.

Chen's two scores are _____ and _____.

To find the total, we add _____ and _____.

Add the ones.	Regroup.	Add the tens.
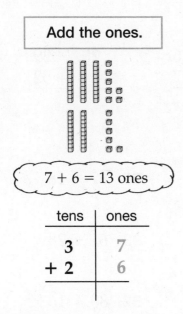	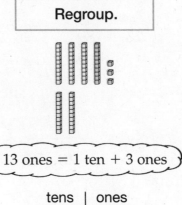	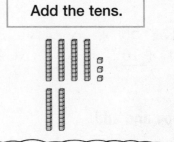
$7 + 6 = 13$ ones	13 ones = 1 ten + 3 ones	$1 + 3 + 2$ tens = 6 tens

tens	ones		tens	ones		tens	ones
3	7		¹3	7		¹3	7
+ 2	6		+ 2	6		+ 2	6
				3		6	3

Chen's final score is _____.

Getting Started

Add.

1. 45
    + 19

2. 53
    + 14

3. 28
    + 63

4. 82
    + 15

Copy and add.

5. 57 + 23   6. 76 + 20   7. 67 + 28   8. 39 + 46

Practice

Add.

1. 25
  + 49

2. 37
  + 56

3. 48
  + 21

4. 19
  + 63

5. 66
  + 14

6. 28
  + 29

7. 44
  + 18

8. 85
  + 14

9. 14
  + 31

10. 83
  + 9

11. 26
  + 12

12. 76
  + 15

13. 28
  + 37

14. 21
  + 49

15. 67
  + 30

16. 9
  + 46

17. 43
  + 42

18. 37
  + 19

19. 72
  + 18

20. 36
  + 25

21. 58
  + 16

22. 38
  + 42

23. 89
  + 9

24. 16
  + 77

25. 39
  + 52

Copy and add.

26. 48 + 16

27. 9 + 36

28. 74 + 13

29. 67 + 18

30. 76 + 15

31. 55 + 15

32. 57 + 38

33. 61 + 28

34. 14 + 48

35. 75 + 17

36. 11 + 29

37. 80 + 16

38. 52 + 19

39. 38 + 39

40. 26 + 48

41. 87 + 9

Problem Solving

Solve each problem.

42. Bob has saved $46 for a bike from money he earned washing cars. He needs $39 more. How much does the bike cost?

43. Mr. Ling's food stand sold 58 hot dogs on a sunny day. The next day it rained and he sold only 37. How many hot dogs did Mr. Ling sell both days?

42 forty-two

Lesson 3-1 • Adding 2-Digit Numbers, Regrouping Ones

Copyright © Savvas Learning Company LLC. All Rights Reserved.

Adding 2-Digit Numbers, Two Regroupings

A Pony Express rider often had to do double duty. How far did a rider travel if he rode west from Kansas City to the second relay station?

We want the total distance from Kansas City to the second relay station. The distance from Kansas City to the first relay station was _____ miles. From there to the second relay station was _____ miles.

To find the total distance, we add _____ and _____.

Add the ones. Regroup if necessary.	Add the tens.	Regroup.

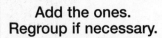

$3 + 9 = 1$ ten $+ 2$ ones

tens	ones
1	
9	3
+ 8	9
	2

$1 + 9 + 8 = 18$ tens

tens	ones
1	
9	3
+ 8	9
	2

18 tens $= 1$ hundred $+ 8$ tens

hundreds	tens	ones
	1	1
	9	3
+	8	9
1	8	2

A rider traveled _____ miles.

Getting Started

Add.

1.	2.	3.	4.
67	49	82	91
+ 71	+ 87	+ 59	+ 88

Copy and add.

5. $66 + 87$ 6. $53 + 97$ 7. $79 + 60$ 8. $59 + 86$

Add.

1. $\begin{array}{r} 97 \\ + 48 \\ \hline \end{array}$	2. $\begin{array}{r} 67 \\ + 75 \\ \hline \end{array}$	3. $\begin{array}{r} 38 \\ + 29 \\ \hline \end{array}$	4. $\begin{array}{r} 77 \\ + 63 \\ \hline \end{array}$	5. $\begin{array}{r} 57 \\ + 82 \\ \hline \end{array}$
6. $\begin{array}{r} 68 \\ + 59 \\ \hline \end{array}$	7. $\begin{array}{r} 26 \\ + 91 \\ \hline \end{array}$	8. $\begin{array}{r} 82 \\ + 89 \\ \hline \end{array}$	9. $\begin{array}{r} 73 \\ + 65 \\ \hline \end{array}$	10. $\begin{array}{r} 47 \\ + 86 \\ \hline \end{array}$
11. $\begin{array}{r} 33 \\ + 90 \\ \hline \end{array}$	12. $\begin{array}{r} 9 \\ + 96 \\ \hline \end{array}$	13. $\begin{array}{r} 28 \\ + 57 \\ \hline \end{array}$	14. $\begin{array}{r} 49 \\ + 99 \\ \hline \end{array}$	15. $\begin{array}{r} 53 \\ + 78 \\ \hline \end{array}$
16. $\begin{array}{r} 68 \\ + 54 \\ \hline \end{array}$	17. $\begin{array}{r} 37 \\ + 88 \\ \hline \end{array}$	18. $\begin{array}{r} 58 \\ + 8 \\ \hline \end{array}$	19. $\begin{array}{r} 47 \\ + 73 \\ \hline \end{array}$	20. $\begin{array}{r} 67 \\ + 82 \\ \hline \end{array}$

Copy and add.

21. 78 + 36	22. 23 + 98	23. 54 + 89	24. 33 + 75
25. 86 + 49	26. 63 + 65	27. 55 + 47	28. 84 + 97
29. 76 + 86	30. 52 + 68	31. 79 + 86	32. 57 + 94

[Now Try This!]

In a magic square, every row, column, and diagonal has the same sum. Complete these squares using the digits 0 through 9. Do not use the same digit twice in the same square.

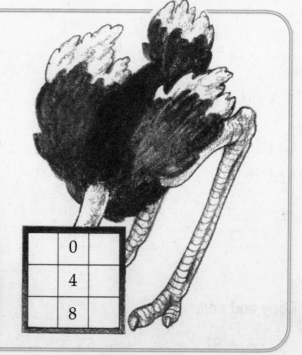

Adding 3-Digit Numbers, One Regrouping

What is the entire length of Route 44
through Oklahoma and Missouri?

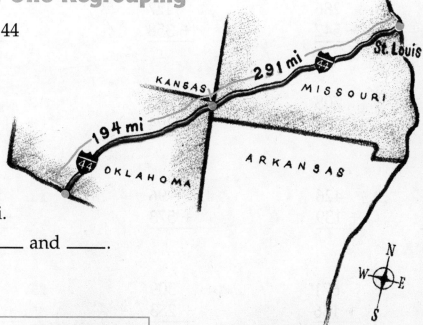

We must find the total length
of Route 44 in both states.

Route 44 is ____ miles long
in Oklahoma.

It is ____ miles long in Missouri.

To get the total miles, we add ____ and ____.

Add the ones. Regroup if needed.	Add the tens. Regroup if needed.	Add the hundreds.
194 + 291 _____ 5	¹ 194 + 291 _____ 85	¹ 194 + 291 _____ 485

Route 44 is _____ miles long through Oklahoma and Missouri.

Getting Started _____

Add.

1.	326 + 455	2.	675 + 183	3.	517 + 284
4.	222 + 108	5.	263 + 362	6.	449 + 311

Copy and add.

7. 359 + 138   8. 196 + 353   9. 428 + 139

10. 518 + 237   11. 295 + 643   12. 348 + 536

Add.

1. 286
    + 542

2. 427
    + 358

3. 615
    + 239

4. 362
    + 218

5. 708
    + 209

6. 523
    + 294

7. 819
    + 175

8. 273
    + 571

9. 426
    + 139

10. 96
    + 573

11. 377
    + 615

12. 517
    + 242

13. 671
    + 186

14. 309
    + 283

15. 558
    + 170

16. 253
    + 638

17. 583
    + 236

18. 154
    + 683

19. 210
    + 596

20. 781
    + 196

Copy and add.

21. 436 + 281

22. 509 + 186

23. 391 + 196

24. 321 + 144

25. 783 + 195

26. 565 + 283

27. 373 + 445

28. 308 + 154

29. 119 + 453

30. 256 + 728

31. 649 + 280

32. 709 + 127

Problem Solving

Solve each problem.

33. Mr. Jimenez drove 384 miles on his delivery route on Monday. On Tuesday he drove 243 miles. How many miles did he drive both days?

34. Daryle collected 129 pounds of old newspapers for the paper drive. Ronald collected 119 pounds. How many pounds of paper did the boys collect?

Lesson 3-3 • Adding 3-Digit Numbers, One Regrouping

Adding 3-Digit Numbers, Two Regroupings

Mike was in training for the school swim meet. How many laps did he complete on the first two days?

DAYS	LAPS
Monday	155
Tuesday	175
Wednesday	140
Thursday	165
Friday	130

We want to know the total number of laps Mike swam on Monday and Tuesday.

Mike swam ____ laps on Monday.

He swam ____ laps on Tuesday.

To get the total we add ____ and ____.

Add the ones. Regroup if needed.	Add the tens. Regroup if needed.	Add the hundreds.
$\overset{1}{15}5$ $+175$ $\overline{0}$	$\overset{11}{15}5$ $+175$ $\overline{30}$	$\overset{1}{155}$ $+175$ $\overline{330}$

Mike swam ____ laps on the first two days.

Getting Started

Add.

1. 628
   + 196

2. 427
   + 196

3. 243
   + 277

4. 311
   + 175

5. 259
   + 442

6. 155
   + 166

Copy and add.

7. 285 + 476

8. 297 + 684

9. 363 + 458

10. 463 + 289

11. 615 + 296

12. 375 + 235

Practice

Add.

1. 583
    + 279

2. 285
    + 391

3. 673
    + 182

4. 296
    + 648

5. 783
    + 139

6. 306
    + 147

7. 295
    + 476

8. 409
    + 391

Copy and add.

9. 459 + 473

10. 116 + 293

11. 346 + 485

12. 196 + 547

13. 754 + 196

14. 236 + 129

15. 509 + 366

16. 658 + 276

Problem Solving

Solve each problem.

17. On Monday 278 cartons of milk were served in the lunchroom. On Tuesday 349 cartons were served. How many cartons were served both days?

18. Mrs. Allen is tiling in her house. She used 458 tiles in the kitchen and 396 tiles in the hall. How many tiles did Mrs. Allen use?

(Now Try This!)

Answer _____

Lesson 3-4 • Adding 3-Digit Numbers, Two Regroupings

Adding 4-Digit Numbers

Washington High School presented an outdoor band concert. How many people attended both nights?

Concert
Attendance

Friday   1,452
Saturday 1,868

We must find the total attendance.

Concert attendance was _____ for Friday.

Attendance for Saturday was _____.

To get the total, we add _____ and _____.

Add the ones. Regroup if needed.	Add the tens. Regroup if needed.	Add the hundreds. Regroup if needed.	Add the thousands.
$\overset{1}{1},452$ $+\ 1,868$ 0	$\overset{11}{1},452$ $+\ 1,868$ 20	$\overset{1\ 1}{1},452$ $+\ 1,868$ 320	$\overset{1}{1},452$ $+\ 1,868$ 3,320

The total concert attendance was _____.

Getting Started _____

Add.

1. 5,136
   + 1,597

2. 4,878
   + 2,364

3. 2,819
   + 1,504

Copy and add.

4. 1,847 + 7,697

5. 1,996 + 4,283

6. 2,487 + 7,368

7. 7,621 + 1,596

8. 2,965 + 5,859

9. 3,428 + 2,596

Practice

Add.

1. 3,256
   + 1,684

2. 2,965
   + 4,309

3. 7,059
   + 1,827

4. 4,372
   + 1,891

5. 6,387
   + 1,953

6. 5,806
   + 2,759

7. 1,678
   + 7,593

8. 3,424
   + 2,386

9. 5,874
   + 3,685

10. 3,651
    + 3,324

11. 6,437
    + 2,974

12. 2,864
    + 4,928

13. 1,396
    + 1,569

14. 2,573
    + 6,558

15. 1,987
    + 4,837

16. 2,465
    + 4,776

Copy and add.

17. 3,826 + 1,947
18. 6,035 + 1,968
19. 2,456 + 6,817
20. 1,509 + 7,624

Now Try This!

Fill in the missing digits in Exercises 1 through 4.
Each time you find a missing digit, write it on a blank line in Row 1.
In Row 2, decode the digits in Row 1 to discover a secret message.

1. 2 , 4 7 3
   + 1 , ☐ 6 ☐
   ───────────
    4 , 0 4 1

2. 3 , 5 7 2
   + 5 , ☐ 4 9
   ───────────
    9 , 2 ☐ 1

3. 2 , 4 6 7
   + ☐ , 3 ☐ 9
   ───────────
    9 , ☐ 6 ☐

4. 5 , ☐ 6 8
   + ☐ , 8 ☐ 7
   ───────────
   10 , 0 0 ☐

Code	
1 T	6 O
2 G	7 N
3 A	8 I
4 H	9 D
5 M	

Row 1

___ ___   ___ ___ ___ ___   ___ ___ ___

Row 2

___ ___ ,   ___ ___ ___ ___   ___ ___ ___

Name _____

Column Addition

On his first trip to the new world,
Columbus landed at San Salvador.
He explored the area for 95 days.
How long was he gone from Spain?

We want to find the total number of days
Columbus was away from Spain.

It took _____ days for Columbus to reach San Salvador.

He spent _____ days exploring.

His return trip took _____ days.

To find the total number of days,

we add _____ and _____ and _____.

Add the ones. Regroup if needed.	Add the tens.
$\overset{1}{7}1$	$\overset{1}{7}1$
$9\,5$	$9\,5$
$+\ 58$	$+\ 58$
4	224

Columbus was away from Spain for _____ days.

Getting Started

Add.

1.	4,926	2.	3,516	3.	6,213	4.	376
	3,151		297		1,276		1,939
	+ 2,138		+ 385		480		68
					+ 1,124		+ 5,432

Copy and add.

5. 2,176 + 159 + 3,641

6. 2,136 + 25 + 951 + 3,237

Practice

Add.

1.	4,396 2,374 + 653	2.	7,286 459 + 1,621	3.	1,096 1,374 + 2,915	4.	96 475 + 3,826

5.	1,524 2,361 + 4,184	6.	1,830 916 + 1,385	7.	148 696 + 4,832	8.	2,261 4,186 + 2,083

9.	2,748 3,956 + 1,285	10.	8,654 1,298 + 845	11.	2,295 1,876 + 1,381	12.	1,003 1,659 + 3,288

13.	4,862 937 85 + 1,629	14.	3,926 2,738 4,456 + 963	15.	2,391 1,586 2,428 + 1,860	16.	985 1,821 764 + 2,476

Copy and add.

17. 96 + 128 + 376 + 1,532

18. 3,219 + 126 + 4,173 + 83

19. 2,033 + 178 + 332

20. 5,611 + 44 + 3,123 + 4,111

21. 3,257 + 2,816 + 1,821 + 1,036

22. 8,223 + 32 + 439 + 925

Problem Solving

Use the chart to solve each problem.

23. How much does Mr. Ryan spend on rent and food?

24. How much does Mr. Ryan spend on rent, auto, and other expenses?

Mr. Ryan's Budget	
Food	$456
Auto	$358
Rent	$839
Other	$510

Lesson 3-6 • Column Addition

Name _____

Adding Money

Rachel was chosen to play on the third-grade baseball team. She must earn the money to buy her equipment. How much will she need to buy the glove and ball?

We want to know the cost of both the glove and the ball.

The glove costs _____.

The baseball costs _____.

To find the total cost, we add _____ and _____.

REMEMBER Line up the dollars and cents. Don't forget the dollar sign.

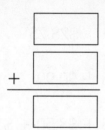

Rachel must earn _____.

Getting Started

Add.

1.	$36.25	2.	$27.79	3.	$25.65	4.	$67.45
	+ 5.36		+ 8.62		11.36		14.75
					+ 6.50		+ 9.55

Copy and add.

5. $11.53 + $7.65

6. $32.36 + $29.63 + $12.08

Practice

Add.

1.	$5.25 + 1.36	**2.**	$3.85 + 5.75	**3.**	$9.72 + 4.53	**4.**	$5.37 + 8.94

5.	$23.40 + 6.56	**6.**	$ 8.96 + 37.43	**7.**	$51.43 + 12.48	**8.**	$43.58 + 29.29

9.	$3.86 5.48 + 7.56	**10.**	$25.16 2.46 + 1.59	**11.**	$73.28 19.15 + 3.50	**12.**	$ 7.80 19.25 + 0.35

13.	$12.48 26.85 + 39.95	**14.**	$71.50 9.65 + 4.36	**15.**	$11.09 14.51 + 22.66	**16.**	$78.51 12.85 + 9.56

Copy and add.

17. $8.75 + $6.38 + $4.56

18. $11.75 + $0.59 + $28.75

19. $83.61 + $25.76

20. $57.98 + $2.36 + $0.99

21. $35.25 + $16.37 + $29.15 + $8.76

22. $23.45 + $1.75 + $8.50 + $17.25

23. $19.42 + $43.89

24. $36.22 + $0.55 + $21.17

Problem Solving

Solve each problem.

25. What is the cost of a hat and a coat?

26. What is the cost of a book, a pen, and a watch?

Estimating Sums

Yoko wants to practice for soccer tryouts. She wants to buy a soccer ball and kneepads. Yoko has saved $25. Does she have enough money to buy the soccer ball and the kneepads?

Soccer Equipment	
Soccer ball	$19.99
Soccer shoes	$22.50
Kneepads	$ 6.85
Socks	$ 3.57

We need to estimate the cost of a soccer ball and kneepads.

The soccer ball costs _____ and the kneepads cost _____.

To estimate the total cost, we round each amount and add.

$19.99   rounds to → $20.00
$6.85   rounds to → + 7.00

Compare _____ and $25.00. _____ > $25.00

Yoko _____ enough money to buy the soccer ball and the kneepads.

Getting Started

Round to the nearest ten to estimate each sum.

1.   86
   + 34

2.   44
   + 53

3.   86
   + 97

4.   53
   + 85

Round to the nearest hundred to estimate each sum.

5.   367
   + 186

6.   851
   + 365

7.   456
     238
   + 940

Round to the nearest dollar to estimate each sum.

8. $9.65
   + 3.85

9. $37.45
   + 16.40

10. $16.57
      23.21
    + 52.75

Practice

Round to the nearest ten to estimate each sum.

1. 83
    + 66

2. 74
    + 29

3. 67
    + 88

4. 75
    + 98

5. 19
    38
    + 26

6. 48
    72
    + 65

7. 31
    47
    + 59

8. 83
    39
    + 78

Round to the nearest hundred to estimate each sum.

9. 263
    + 129

10. 357
    + 463

11. 273
    + 189

12. 675
    286
    + 391

13. 426
    538
    + 780

14. 621
    845
    + 396

Round to the nearest dollar to estimate each sum.

15. $8.36
    + 4.56

16. $74.56
    + 8.19

17. $37.51
    + 22.38

18. $4.75
    5.36
    + 8.79

19. $16.58
    7.95
    + 11.36

20. $23.48
    21.30
    + 37.89

Problem Solving

Circle the best estimate.

21. Betty kicked the soccer ball 18 feet. Then Alice kicked the ball another 12 feet. About how many feet was the ball kicked?

    60 feet   50 feet   30 feet

22. Samson scored 24 points. Derek scored 32 points. About how many points did they score altogether?

    190 points   70 points   50 points

Problem Solving: Use an Exact Answer or an Estimate

The students in the third and fourth grades of District 21 want to attend a play together at the Academy of Music. The theater has 1,500 seats. Does the theater have enough seats for both grades to attend the play on the same day?

Students in District 21	
Third grade	748
Fourth grade	675

⭐ SEE

The Academy of Music has _____ seats.

The third grade has _____ students.

The fourth grade has _____ students.

⭐ PLAN

We do not need an **exact answer**. We just want to know if both grades can attend the play on the same day. We need to **estimate** the total number of students in both grades.

Then, we need to **compare** the estimate to _____ to make sure there are enough seats in the theater. Make sure the estimate is enough.

⭐ DO

To estimate the total number of students, we can use **front-end estimation**. We add the **front digits** and write zeros for the other digits.

```
  748
+ 675
─────
1,300
```

The estimated number of students in the third and fourth

grades is _____.   _____ < 1,500

Both grades can attend the play on the same day.

⭐ CHECK

Find the actual total number of students in both grades. Compare that number to 1,500 to make sure the estimate is less than the number of seats.

748 + 675 = _____.   _____ < 1,500

Apply

Tell if you need an exact answer or an estimate. Solve each problem. Use front-end estimation to make sure the estimate is enough. Check when needed.

Basketball Equipment	
Basketball	$15.77
Sneakers	$25.99
Socks	$ 2.55
Kneepads	$ 7.29
Wristbands	$ 1.59

1. Burt has a $20 bill. Does he have enough money to buy a basketball and socks?

2. Jake buys a basketball, sneakers, and socks. How much money does Jake need to give the cashier?

3. Megan wants to buy 3 pairs of socks and 2 pairs of wristbands. About how much money does Megan need?

4. Juan has two $10 bills. Does he have enough money to buy a basketball, kneepads, and a pair of wristbands?

5. About how much money is needed to buy one of every item on the list of equipment?

6. Juan thinks he needs about $35 to buy a basketball, sneakers, and socks. Is he correct?

7. Kareem's mom wants to give him enough money to buy one of each item on the list. How much money should she give him?

8. Laura wants to know if $15 is enough money to buy 4 pairs of wristbands and 1 pair of kneepads.

Add.

1.   57
    + 38

2.   34
    + 23

3.   48
    + 37

4.   62
    + 29

5.   236
    + 175

6.   392
    + 568

7.   485
    + 296

8.   609
    + 257

9.   3,248
    + 1,568

10.   7,586
    + 1,798

11.   5,263
    + 1,079

12.   2,179
    + 6,391

13.   875
    1,321
    +   68

14.   5,729
    175
    +   315

15. $26.41
    37.85
    + 26.91

16. $38.21
    16.58
    + 24.17

Round to the nearest ten to estimate each sum.

17.   23
    + 47

18.   39
    + 45

19.   22
    + 28

20.   41
    + 37

Round to the nearest hundred to estimate each sum.

21.   237
    + 189

22.   575
    + 386

23.   453
    + 387

Round to the nearest dollar to estimate each sum.

24. $9.27
    + 8.57

25. $12.75
    +   4.36

26. $26.38
    + 32.45

27. $7.75
    + 4.60

28. $15.95
    +   8.10

29. $73.29
    + 12.50

Circle the letter of the correct answer.

1 6 + 7
- a. 12
- b. 13
- c. 14
- d. NG

2 15 − 7
- a. 7
- b. 8
- c. 9
- d. NG

3 367 ◯ 358
- a. >
- b. <

4 Round 749 to the nearest hundred.
- a. 700
- b. 800

5 What is the value of the 3 in 357?
- a. ones
- b. tens
- c. hundreds
- d. NG

6 What is the value of the 7 in 372,980?
- a. hundreds
- b. thousands
- c. ten thousands
- d. NG

7 Which digit is out of place in the series: 3, 4, 5, 2, 6, 7?
- a. 6
- b. 5
- c. 3
- d. NG

8
```
  136
+ 249
```
- a. 375
- b. 387
- c. 485
- d. NG

9
```
  357
+ 288
```
- a. 545
- b. 635
- c. 645
- d. NG

10
```
  3,256
+ 1,847
```
- a. 4,103
- b. 5,093
- c. 5,103
- d. NG

11
```
  $27.45
+  10.68
```
- a. $37.03
- b. $38.13
- c. $48.13
- d. NG

12
```
  1,496
    275
+ 3,857
```
- a. 5,628
- b. 5,629
- c. 6,628
- d. NG

13 Round to the nearest ten to estimate the sum.
```
  43
+ 36
```
- a. 70
- b. 80
- c. 90
- d. NG

☐ score

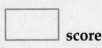

STOP

Subtraction

Regrouping Tens for Ones

How many tens rods and ones units will Rodd have if he regroups 1 tens rod for 10 ones units?

We want to regroup _____ ten as _____ ones.

Rodd has _____ tens and _____ ones.

tens	ones
3	4

We regroup _____ ten as _____ ones.

tens	ones
₂ 3̸	¹⁴ 4̸

After regrouping, Rodd has _____ tens and _____ ones.

Getting Started

Regroup 1 ten for 10 ones. Record the number of tens and ones.

1. 64 = _____ tens _____ ones

2. 48 = _____ tens _____ ones

3. 91 = _____ tens _____ ones

4. 32 = _____ tens _____ ones

5. 64 = _____ tens _____ ones

6. 99 = _____ tens _____ ones

7.
tens	ones
5	3

8.
tens	ones
7	5

9.
tens	ones
2	4

10.
tens	ones
8	1

Practice

Regroup 1 ten for 10 ones. Record the number of tens and ones.

1. 78 = _____ tens _____ ones

2. 58 = _____ tens _____ ones

3. 43 = _____ tens _____ ones

4. 94 = _____ tens _____ ones

5. 46 = _____ tens _____ ones

6. 29 = _____ ten _____ ones

7. 37 = _____ tens _____ ones

8. 82 = _____ tens _____ ones

9. 21 = _____ ten _____ ones

10. 66 = _____ tens _____ ones

11.	tens	ones
	6	3

12.	tens	ones
	7	7

13.	tens	ones
	7	1

14.	tens	ones
	3	4

15.	tens	ones
	5	5

16.	tens	ones
	4	7

17.	tens	ones
	2	8

18.	tens	ones
	5	6

19.	tens	ones
	6	4

20.	tens	ones
	3	3

21.	tens	ones
	9	7

22.	tens	ones
	8	1

23.	tens	ones
	7	2

24.	tens	ones
	4	5

25.	tens	ones
	6	0

26.	tens	ones
	6	5

27.	tens	ones
	2	7

28.	tens	ones
	9	6

Lesson 4-1 • Regrouping Tens for Ones

Subtracting 2-Digit Numbers, One Regrouping

Miss Valdez's class is selling magazines to raise money for a class trip. How many magazines did the class have left to sell on Wednesday? We want to find how many magazines Miss Valdez's class had left to sell on Wednesday.

Day	Start	Sold	Left
Monday	96	18	78
Tuesday	78	15	63
Wednesday	63	25	
Thursday		19	
Friday		8	

The class started with ____ magazines on Wednesday.

They sold ____ by the end of the day.

To get the number left, we subtract ____

from ____.

Subtract the ones. Regroup if needed.	Regroup a ten for ones.	Subtract the ones.	Subtract the tens.

tens	ones
6	3
− 2	5

tens	ones
5̶6̶	1̶3̶
− 2	5

tens	ones
5̶6̶	1̶3̶
− 2	5
	8

tens	ones
5̶6̶	1̶3̶
− 2	5
3	8

Miss Valdez's class had ____ magazines left by the end of Wednesday.

Getting Started

Subtract. Regroup a ten if needed.

1. 73
   − 29

2. 72
   − 64

3. 51
   − 37

4. 26
   − 18

Copy and subtract.

5. 75 − 48

6. 38 − 16

7. 55 − 49

8. 48 − 29

Practice

Subtract.

1. 81
    − 32

2. 33
    − 25

3. 51
    − 29

4. 63
    − 27

5. 88
    − 43

6. 82
    − 9

7. 45
    − 29

8. 38
    − 29

9. 90
    − 13

10. 49
    − 19

11. 73
    − 28

12. 72
    − 35

13. 40
    − 20

14. 81
    − 67

15. 97
    − 93

16. 81
    − 37

17. 38
    − 16

18. 91
    − 36

19. 75
    − 58

20. 66
    − 39

21. 29
    − 15

22. 46
    − 37

23. 63
    − 28

24. 35
    − 12

25. 80
    − 59

Copy and subtract.

26. 62 − 21

27. 86 − 28

28. 71 − 67

29. 92 − 27

30. 80 − 21

31. 38 − 7

32. 46 − 28

33. 53 − 47

34. 72 − 58

35. 47 − 23

36. 66 − 27

37. 91 − 63

38. 44 − 17

39. 70 − 46

40. 55 − 15

41. 22 − 9

Problem Solving

Solve each problem.

42. Danielle packed 63 first-aid kits for a service project. Pat packed 47. How many more kits did Danielle pack than Pat?

43. Trish earned $60 walking dogs for her neighbors. She spent $47 on school clothes. How much money does she have left?

Subtracting 3-Digit Numbers, One Regrouping

Amtrak trains connect major cities in the United States. How many more trains travel the route between New York and Washington, D.C., than the Los Angeles to San Diego route?

We want to know the difference between the number of trains.

Two-Way Amtrak Routes	
Route	Monthly Trains
New York City—Washington, D.C.	952
Philadelphia—Harrisburg	593
New York City—Philadelphia	419
New Haven—Springfield	400
Boston—Washington, D.C.	377
Los Angeles—San Diego	362

In one month, _____ trains travel between New York and Washington, D.C.

During the same time period, _____ trains travel between Los Angeles and San Diego. To find how many more trains travel one route than the other, we subtract _____ from _____.

Subtract the ones. Regroup if needed.	Subtract the tens. Regroup if needed.	Subtract the hundreds.
95 −36	952 −362 90	952 − 62 90

In one month, _____ more trains travel the New York to Washington, D.C. route, than between Los Angeles and San Diego.

Getting Started

Subtract.

1. 376
− 149

2. 827
− 356

3. 627
− 253

4. 968
− 794

Copy and subtract.

5. 473 − 151

6. 727 − 18

7. 947 − 156

8. 685 − 237

9. 590 − 163

10. 635 − 281

11. 656 − 212

12. 984 − 645

Practice

Subtract.

1. 436
    − 118

2. 596
    − 358

3. 729
    − 258

4. 651
    − 519

5. 813
    − 290

6. 753
    − 281

7. 381
    − 19

8. 816
    − 132

9. 459
    − 183

10. 915
    − 283

11. 685
    − 527

12. 728
    − 235

13. 185
    − 16

14. 883
    − 628

15. 520
    − 370

16. 327
    − 75

17. 927
    − 861

18. 182
    − 9

19. 761
    − 528

20. 627
    − 190

Copy and subtract.

21. 821 − 318

22. 583 − 238

23. 816 − 753

24. 793 − 424

25. 429 − 150

26. 456 − 275

27. 691 − 385

28. 556 − 237

29. 752 − 28

30. 464 − 392

31. 823 − 560

32. 972 − 754

33. 537 − 228

34. 925 − 809

35. 737 − 281

36. 864 − 646

Problem Solving

Solve each problem.

37. Miss Shaw flew 391 miles crop dusting on Friday. On Saturday, she flew 186 miles. How much farther did Miss Shaw fly on Friday?

38. On opening day, 783 people visited the science museum. On the same day, 417 people went to the aquarium. How many more people visited the museum?

Subtracting 3-Digit Numbers, Two Regroupings

The Great Lakes form the largest body of fresh water in the world. How much longer is Lake Superior than Lake Ontario?

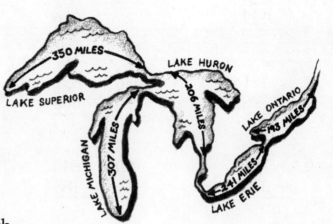

We need to find how much longer Lake Superior is than Lake Ontario.

Lake Superior is _____ miles long.

Lake Ontario is only _____ miles in length.

To find the difference, we subtract _____ from _____.

Subtract the ones. Regroup if needed.	Subtract the tens. Regroup if needed.	Subtract the hundreds.
$\begin{array}{r} {\scriptstyle 4\ 10} \\ 3\cancel{5}\cancel{0} \\ -193 \\ \hline 7 \end{array}$	$\begin{array}{r} {\scriptstyle 2\ 14} \\ 3\cancel{5}\cancel{0} \\ -193 \\ \hline 57 \end{array}$	$\begin{array}{r} {\scriptstyle 2} \\ 3\cancel{5}0 \\ -193 \\ \hline 157 \end{array}$

Lake Superior is _____ miles longer than Lake Ontario.

Getting Started

Subtract.

1.	536	2.	743	3.	637	4.	850
	− 257		− 468		− 258		− 572

Copy and subtract.

5. 917 − 429   6. 385 − 296   7. 625 − 177   8. 972 − 784

9. 731 − 559   10. 858 − 379   11. 558 − 144   12. 678 − 499

Practice

Subtract.

1.   628
    −139
	2. 535
	    −286
		3. 815
		    −426
			4. 773
			    − 396

5.   351
    − 96
	6. 832
	    − 686
		7. 925
		    − 387
			8. 136
			    − 88

9.   714
    − 329
	10. 646
	    − 188
		11. 423
		    − 175
			12. 821
			    − 256

13.   912
    − 87
	14. 630
	    − 258
		15. 815
		    − 379
			16. 462
			    − 185

Copy and subtract.

17. 372 − 96

18. 920 − 387

19. 731 − 285

20. 967 − 789

21. 582 − 369

22. 421 − 259

23. 163 − 78

24. 758 − 579

25. 612 − 224

26. 851 − 273

27. 426 − 387

28. 634 − 556

29. 274 − 198

30. 519 − 258

31. 231 − 138

32. 876 − 488

33. 516 − 278

34. 823 − 258

35. 315 − 98

36. 532 − 355

Problem Solving

Solve each problem.

37. The Washington Monument is 169 meters tall. The Great Pyramid is 32 meters shorter than the Washington Monument. How tall is the Great Pyramid?

38. The Sears Tower is 443 meters tall. The Eiffel Tower is 322 meters tall. How much taller is the Sears Tower?

Zeros in Subtraction

The states of North and South Carolina both are bounded on the east by the Atlantic Ocean. How much longer is North Carolina's coastline than South Carolina's?

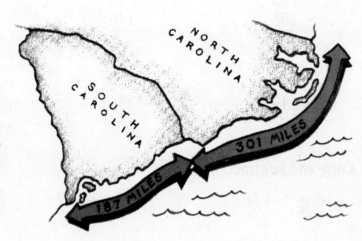

We are looking for how much longer North Carolina's coast is than South Carolina's.

The North Carolina coast is _____ miles long.

South Carolina's coast is _____ miles long.

To find the difference, we subtract _____ from _____.

Subtract the ones. Regroup if needed.	Subtract the tens. Regroup if needed.	Subtract the hundreds.
$\begin{array}{r} \overset{9}{\cancel{2}\,\overset{10}{\cancel{0}}\,\overset{11}{\cancel{1}}} \\[-2pt] 3\,0\,1 \\ -\,1\,8\,7 \\ \hline 4 \end{array}$	$\begin{array}{r} \overset{9}{\cancel{2}\,\overset{10}{\cancel{0}}} \\[-2pt] 3\,0\,1 \\ -\,1\,8\,7 \\ \hline 1\,4 \end{array}$	$\begin{array}{r} \overset{2}{\cancel{3}}\,0\,1 \\ -\,1\,8\,7 \\ \hline 1\,1\,4 \end{array}$

North Carolina has _____ more miles of coastline than South Carolina.

Getting Started

Subtract.

1. 603
    − 258

2. 700
    − 217

3. 201
    − 83

4. 909
    − 435

5. 509
    − 318

6. 903
    − 605

7. 820
    − 299

8. 405
    − 376

Copy and subtract.

9. 804 − 685   10. 200 − 198   11. 303 − 172   12. 610 − 88

Practice

Subtract.

1. 705
    − 158

2. 302
    − 146

3. 606
    − 351

4. 500
    − 396

5. 903
    − 649

6. 802
    − 356

7. 405
    − 138

8. 603
    − 427

Copy and subtract.

9. 502 − 376

10. 903 − 658

11. 801 − 433

12. 202 − 193

13. 700 − 95

14. 307 − 140

15. 607 − 409

16. 600 − 87

Problem Solving

Solve each problem.

17. Mr. Lewin bought a stereo for $503. He made a down payment of $218. How much does Mr. Lewin still owe on the stereo?

18. It is 405 miles from Jim's home to his uncle's farm. It is 167 miles farther to his grandfather's. How far does Jim live from his grandfather?

(Now Try This!)

Make two number cubes. Number the first cube with the numbers 1 through 6, and the second cube with the numbers 4 through 9. Roll the cubes and add the two numbers displayed. This sum is called an event.

What is the lowest possible sum you can get? ____

What is the greatest possible sum? ____

Make a chart of all the sums possible from rolling the cubes. Roll them 25 times. Record each event by making a tally mark next to the correct sum on the chart.

Lesson 4-5 • Zeros in Subtraction

Subtracting 4-Digit Numbers

Many major cities in the United States have beautiful parks. How much larger is Pelham Bay Park than Lincoln Park?

We want to find how much larger Pelham Bay Park is than Lincoln Park.

Pelham Bay Park covers _____ acres.

Lincoln Park takes up _____ acres.

We can compare their sizes by using subtraction.

To find the difference, we subtract _____ from _____.

Subtract the ones. Regroup if needed.	Subtract the tens. Regroup if needed.	Subtract the hundreds. Regroup if needed.	Subtract the. thousands.
2,117 − 1,185 _____ 2	2,1̸17 − 1,185 _____ 932	2,1̸17 − 1,185 _____ 932	2,117 − 1,185 _____ 932

Pelham Bay Park is _____ acres larger than Lincoln Park.

Getting Started

Subtract.

1. 5,438
    − 2,684

2. 8,843
    − 4,578

3. 9,214
    − 3,587

4. 3,276
    − 1,485

5. 7,534
    − 6,657

6. 8,264
    − 1,865

Copy and subtract.

7. 4,213 − 967

8. 5,915 − 5,386

9. 4,655 − 2,849

Practice

Subtract.

1. 6,825
   − 1,384

2. 4,326
   − 1,598

3. 8,754
   −   139

4. 2,391
   − 1,836

5. 3,791
   − 2,118

6. 9,213
   − 3,654

7. 5,186
   − 1,392

8. 4,528
   − 4,236

9. 8,286
   − 6,395

10. 7,526
    − 3,867

11. 9,215
    − 1,863

12. 1,265
    −   848

Copy and subtract.

13. 8,275 − 826

14. 3,216 − 2,148

15. 7,217 − 4,328

16. 4,376 − 1,111

17. 6,370 − 2,342

18. 5,888 − 1,189

19. 9,235 − 6,562

20. 8,256 − 98

21. 4,324 − 2,875

22. 3,516 − 3,047

23. 7,911 − 4,555

24. 5,923 − 3,010

25. 7,296 − 3,468

26. 5,608 − 1,909

27. 9,275 − 8,588

Problem Solving

Use the chart to solve each problem.

28. How much deeper is the Indian Ocean than the Arctic Ocean?

29. How much deeper is the Atlantic Ocean than the Arctic Ocean?

Ocean	Depth
Arctic	5,625 meters
Atlantic	9,219 meters
Indian	7,455 meters

Name _____

Subtracting Money

Paula was given $20 for her birthday. She plans to use the money to buy a computer game. How much change will she receive?

We want to see how much change Paula will receive.

She has _____ to spend.

The computer game costs _____.

To find how much money is left,

we subtract _____ from _____.

Subtract the ones. Regroup if needed.	Complete the subtraction.	Check by adding.
$$\begin{array}{r} \overset{9}{\overset{1\;\;\overset{9}{10}\;\;\overset{9}{10}\;\;10}{\$2\cancel{0}.\cancel{0}\cancel{0}}} \\ -\ 17.59 \\ \hline 1 \end{array}$$	$$\begin{array}{r} \overset{9}{\overset{1\;\;\overset{9}{10}\;\;\overset{9}{10}\;\;10}{\$2\cancel{0}.\cancel{0}\cancel{0}}} \\ -\ 17.59 \\ \hline \$\ 2.41 \end{array}$$	$$\begin{array}{r} \$\ 2.41 \\ +\ 17.59 \\ \hline \$20.00 \end{array}$$

Paula will receive _____ in change.

Getting Started

Subtract.

1. $8.05
   − 3.86

2. $6.00
   − 4.75

3. $87.00
   − 19.39

4. $27.15
   − 9.38

5. $36.21
   − 21.56

6. $10.00
   − 3.50

Copy and subtract.

7. $25.15 − $13.89

8. $75.00 − $29.79

9. $86.30 − $29.55

Practice

Subtract.

1. $9.00
   − 2.37

2. $7.56
   − 0.29

3. $8.50
   − 2.78

4. $18.39
   − 6.87

5. $37.68
   − 9.89

6. $52.00
   − 8.63

7. $39.24
   − 15.96

8. $42.36
   − 29.84

9. $85.35
   − 19.19

Copy and subtract.

10. $84.60 − $29.39

11. $36.43 − $19.26

12. $93.24 − $57.85

13. $67.23 − $28.25

14. $72.00 − $29.09

15. $96.29 − $27.58

Problem Solving

Solve each problem.

16. Devin bought a sweatshirt for $14.56 and a jacket for $29.85. How much more did Devin spend on the jacket?

17. Natalie has saved $20 to buy CDs. She chooses one CD for $7.53 and another for $8.79. How much money does Natalie have left?

Now Try This!

In each problem the sum is not correct. Find the correct sum and write it on the blank below each problem. Then find the addend that was left out and circle it.

1. $2.13
   1.75
   5.23
   + 3.40
   ─────
   $10.76

2. $3.02
   1.38
   4.27
   + 2.33
   ─────
   $ 6.73

3. $1.79
   2.83
   0.85
   + 1.23
   ─────
   $4.91

_____   _____   _____

Estimating Differences

The goals of the Apollo space project were to orbit the Moon and land a man on it. About how many more orbits around the Moon did Apollo–*Saturn 18* make than Apollo–*Saturn 17*?

Apollo Orbits	
Apollo–*Saturn 17*	75 orbits
Apollo–*Saturn 18*	136 orbits

We do not need an exact number. We need to estimate the difference between the number of orbits.

Apollo–Saturn 18 made _____ orbits.

Apollo–Saturn 17 made _____ orbits.

To estimate the difference, we round each number to the nearest ten and subtract.

$$136 \xrightarrow{\text{rounds to}} 140$$
$$75 \xrightarrow{\text{rounds to}} -\ 80$$

Apollo–Saturn 18 made about _____ more orbits than Apollo–Saturn 17.

Getting Started

Round to the nearest ten and estimate each difference.

1.	78	2.	53	3.	41	4.	85
	− 36		− 27		− 19		− 44

Round to the nearest hundred and estimate each difference.

5.	768	6.	478	7.	750
	− 245		− 112		− 325

Round to the nearest dollar and estimate each difference.

8.	$26.45	9.	$56.48	10.	$84.57
	− 13.21		− 23.75		− 51.85

Practice _____

Round to the nearest ten and estimate each difference.

1. 59
    − 26

2. 78
    − 24

3. 92
    − 56

4. 57
    − 23

5. 73
    − 52

6. 87
    − 38

7. 42
    − 29

8. 62
    − 19

Round to the nearest hundred and estimate each difference.

9. 376
    − 126

10. 875
    − 350

11. 625
    − 516

12. 646
    − 429

13. 556
    − 210

14. 889
    − 846

15. 775
    − 121

16. 909
    − 119

17. 529
    − 383

Round to the nearest dollar and estimate each difference.

18. $9.89
    − 6.15

19. $42.57
    − 8.75

20. $36.25
    − 15.18

21. $74.39
    − 55.45

22. $86.28
    − 39.85

23. $65.00
    − 21.38

24. $10.81
    − 9.40

25. $87.25
    − 62.00

26. $72.42
    − 11.27

Lesson 4-8 • Estimating Differences

Name _____

Problem Solving: Write a Number Sentence

Mr. Carter traveled 2,224 miles from Salt Lake City to New York City on a business trip. He stopped in Chicago along the way. How many miles did he travel from Chicago to New York City?

 SEE

Mr. Carter traveled _____ miles from Salt Lake City to New York City.

It is _____ miles from Salt Lake City to Chicago.

We want to find out how many miles it is from

_____ to New York City.

Chicago

1,403 miles

New York City

Salt Lake City

 PLAN

We subtract the number of miles from _____ to Chicago from the total number of miles traveled.

We can write a number sentence to show this.

We can use a ☐ to represent what we want to find.

2,224 miles − 1,403 miles = ☐

⭐ **DO**

2,224 − 1,403 = ☐

_____ = ☐

Mr. Carter traveled _____ miles from Chicago to New York.

⭐ **CHECK**

Add to check your answer.

1,403
+ 821
_____

Apply

Write a number sentence. Then solve.

1. A one-way trip from Los Angeles to Albuquerque through Flagstaff is 810 miles. It is 329 miles from Flagstaff to Albuquerque. How many miles is it from Los Angeles to Flagstaff?

2. It is 460 miles from Calgary to Regina. The distance from Calgary through Regina to Winnepeg is 816 miles. What is the distance from Regina to Winnepeg?

3. Gary lives in San Francisco. He traveled 2,197 miles one way to visit friends in Dallas and Atlanta. It is 792 miles from Dallas to Atlanta. How many miles did he travel from San Francisco to Dallas?

4. Mrs. Kelly traveled 2,197 miles going from San Francisco to New York through Detroit. It is 640 miles from Detroit to New York. What is the distance from San Francisco to Detroit?

5. The distance from Detroit to San Francisco is 1,557. The distance from San Francisco to Dallas is 1,405. How many more miles is it from Detroit to San Francisco than from San Francisco to Dallas?

6. It is 2,197 miles one way from New York to San Francisco through Dallas. How many miles is it round trip from San Francisco to New York through Dallas?

7. The distance from El Paso to San Antonio is 556 miles and then from San Antonio to Houston is 198 miles. The distance from El Paso to Austin is 628 miles and from Austin to Houston it is 166 miles. Which is the shorter route from El Paso to Houston? What is the difference in mileage?

Lesson 4-9 • Problem Solving: Write a Number Sentence

Calculator Codes

A calculator has a screen and a keyboard. The keyboard has an **on/off key**. The keyboard also has **number keys**, **operation keys**, and **special keys**. When any of these keys are pressed, an **entry** is made in the calculator.

Number Keys	Operation Keys	Special Keys

Turn your calculator on. A zero should appear on the screen. [0]

Getting Started

A calculator code tells you in what order to press the keys on the calculator.

Follow each code below and show each result.

1. [1] [7] [7] [+] [6] [4] [=] [   ]

2. [3] [8] [5] [−] [4] [9] [=] [   ]

We use a short cut to show calculator numbers.

We write [8][7] as 87 and [1][7][3] as 173.

Show the result of each code.

3. 87 [+] 173 [=] [   ]   4. 282 [−] 73 [=] [   ]

The [C] key clears the calculator. You must start the problem from the beginning.

The [CE] key cancels only the last number entered. The calculator will still remember earlier entries.

Show the result of each code.

5. 515 [+] 816 [C] = [   ]   6. 713 [+] 214 [CE] 16 [=] [   ]

Practice _____

Enter each code. Show the results.

1. 535 ⊞ 88 ⊟ ▭

2. 244 ⊞ 79 ⊟ ▭

3. 106 ⊟ 15 ⊟ ▭

4. 325 ⊟ 37 ⊟ ▭

5. 764 ⊞ 9 ⊞ 23 ⊟ ▭

6. 463 ⊞ 68 ⊞ 189 ⊟ ▭

7. 387 ⊟ 79 ⊟ 36 ⊟ ▭

8. 894 ⊟ 56 ⊟ 79 ⊟ ▭

9. 239 CE 26 ⊞ 142 ⊟ ▭

10. 647 CE 487 ⊟ 239 ⊟ ▭

11. 914 ⊞ 139 ⊞ 64 C ▭

12. 129 ⊟ 64 ⊟ 34 ⊟ ▭

Use your calculator to find each sum or difference.

13.   439
     + 225
     ─────

14.   236
     + 795
     ─────

15.   979
     + 858
     ─────

16.   761
       835
     + 679
     ─────

17.   116
       734
     + 910
     ─────

18.   207
       711
     + 938
     ─────

19.   296
     − 156
     ─────

20.   921
     − 365
     ─────

21.   986
     − 750
     ─────

22. 139 + 985 = _____

23. 256 + 483 + 796 = _____

24. 346 + 958 + 231 = _____

25. 435 + 871 + 905 = _____

26. 812 − 794 = _____

27. 750 − 185 = _____

Find the sum or difference of each pair of number neighbors.
Write the answer in the box below each pair.

28. ▭ 846 ▭ + 636

29. ▭ 402 ▭ − 309

▭

▭

Name _____

Subtract.

1.	96	2.	85	3.	73	4.	52
	− 23		− 21		− 28		− 19

5.	526	6.	826	7.	621	8.	924
	− 315		− 419		− 274		− 657

9.	509	10.	804	11.	700	12.	905
	− 108		− 329		− 251		− 268

13.	6,725	14.	7,215	15.	3,321	16.	9,510
	− 1,319		− 3,852		− 1,876		− 3,854

Round to the nearest ten and estimate each difference.

17.	58	18.	71	19.	45	20.	83
	− 26		− 37		− 25		− 19

Round to the nearest hundred and estimate each difference.

21.	523	22.	750	23.	949
	− 296		− 385		− 527

Round to the nearest dollar and estimate each difference.

24.	$27.38	25.	$38.87	26.	$57.85
	− 9.75		− 21.50		− 29.35

Circle the letter of the correct answer.

1 739 ◯ 736

    a. >
    b. <

2 Round 652 to the nearest hundred.

    a. 500
    b. 600
    c. NG

3 What is the value of the 6 in 326,489?

    a. tens
    b. thousands
    c. ten thousands
    d. NG

4
$$\begin{array}{r} 76 \\ + 18 \\ \hline \end{array}$$

    a. 914
    b. 94
    c. 84
    d. NG

5
$$\begin{array}{r} 256 \\ + 385 \\ \hline \end{array}$$

    a. 741
    b. 531
    c. 641
    d. NG

6
$$\begin{array}{r} \$82.96 \\ + 15.89 \\ \hline \end{array}$$

    a. $98.84
    b. $98.86
    c. $97.85
    d. NG

7
$$\begin{array}{r} 3,250 \\ 786 \\ + 75 \\ \hline \end{array}$$

    a. 4,101
    b. 4,011
    c. 4,111
    d. NG

8 Round each number to the nearest hundred and add.
$$\begin{array}{r} 428 \\ + 367 \\ \hline \end{array}$$

    a. 800
    b. 700
    c. 600
    d. NG

9 In the problem $87 + 65 = 152$, what is the 152 called?

    a. difference
    b. addend
    c. sum
    d. NG

10
$$\begin{array}{r} 723 \\ - 187 \\ \hline \end{array}$$

    a. 664
    b. 646
    c. 636
    d. NG

11
$$\begin{array}{r} 903 \\ - 254 \\ \hline \end{array}$$

    a. 751
    b. 649
    c. 559
    d. NG

12
$$\begin{array}{r} \$27.38 \\ - 18.87 \\ \hline \end{array}$$

    a. $18.41
    b. $8.41
    c. $11.51
    d. NG

13 Round each number to the nearest ten and subtract.
$$\begin{array}{r} 86 \\ - 27 \\ \hline \end{array}$$

    a. 60
    b. 70
    c. 50
    d. NG

◻ **score**

STOP

Time and Customary Measurement

Time to the Half-Hour and Quarter-Hour

Janet will eat dinner in a half-hour.
Show on the clocks what time that will be.

We want to show what time it will be in a half-hour.

Now, the time is _____.

One half-hour and _____ minutes are the same.

Janet will eat at _____. We read this as **seven thirty**.

Study the clock times.

 8:00    8:15    8:30    8:45

eight o'clock   **eight fifteen**   **eight thirty**   **eight forty-five**

Getting Started

Write the time as you would see it on a digital clock.

1.
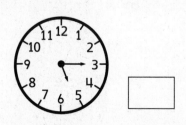

Write the time as you would say it.

2.

_____

Practice

Write each time as you would see it on a digital clock.

1.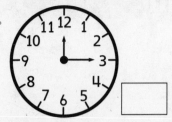

2.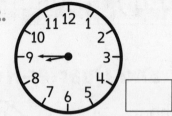

3.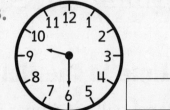

4.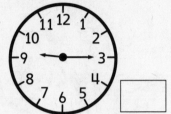

5.

6.

Write each time as you would say it.

7.

_____

8.

_____

9.

_____

10.

_____

11.

_____

12.

_____

Problem Solving

Circle the most sensible time for each.

13. eating lunch

8:15 A.M.   12:30 P.M.

10:00 A.M.   6:45 P.M.

14. getting up to go to school

1:30 A.M.   12:45 A.M.

6:45 P.M.   7:00 A.M.

Lesson 5-1 • Time to the Half-Hour and Quarter-Hour

Name _____

Name _____

Time to One Minute

It takes Manuel 20 minutes to walk home from soccer practice. Show on the clocks what time Manuel will arrive home.

We want to know what time Manuel will get home. He leaves practice at _____.

It takes him _____ minutes to walk home. It takes 5 minutes for the minute hand to move from one number to the next.

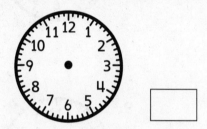

Manuel will get home at _____. We read and write

this as _____ or **twenty-five minutes to five**.

Study the clock times.

9:03

three minutes after nine

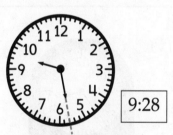

9:28

nine twenty-eight

9:47

nine forty-seven or thirteen minutes to ten

Getting Started

For Exercises 1 and 2, write the time as you would see it on a digital clock.

Write the time as you would say it.

1.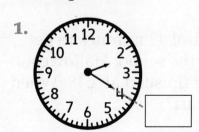

2.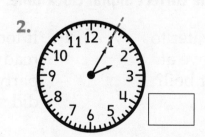

3.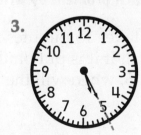

Practice

Write the time as you would see it on a digital clock.

1.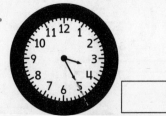

2.

3.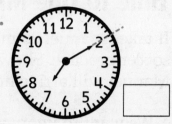

4.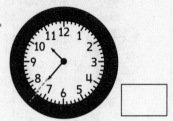

5.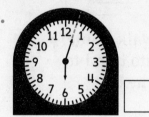

6.

Write the time as you would say it.

7.

8.

9.

10.

11.

12.

Problem Solving

Solve each problem by writing the correct digital clock time.

13. It takes 15 minutes for water to boil. If it is put on the stove at 4:25, when will the water boil?

14. It took Carol 42 minutes to get ready for the school Halloween party. She finished at 2:48. When did she start?

Lesson 5-2 • Time to One Minute

Name _____

Elapsed Time

Maria started to practice the piano at 10:30 A.M. She finished at 11:45 A.M. How long did she practice the piano?

We want to find out how much time **elapsed** or

passed from _____ to _____.

To find the elapsed time, we count on from _____.

Start time: _____ A.M.

Count the hours.

1 hour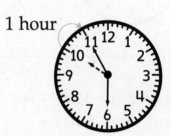

There is ____ hour(s) from 10:30 to 11:30.

Count the minutes.

End time: 11:45 A.M.

There are ____ minutes from 11:30 to 11:45.

Maria practiced the piano for _____.

5 minutes

Getting Started

Write each elapsed time.

1.

_____

2. Start time: 1:30 P.M.
   End time: 6:00 P.M. _____

3. Start time: 6:35 P.M.
   End time: 9:00 P.M. _____

Practice

Write each elapsed time.

1.

_____

2.

_____

3.

_____

4.

_____

5. Start time: 12:00 P.M
   End time: 4:10 P.M.

   _____

6. Start time: 7:25 P.M.
   End time: 12 A.M.

   _____

7. Start time: 4:55 P.M.
   End time: 6:15 P.M.

   _____

8. Start time: 10:00 P.M.
   End time: 11:55 P.M.

   _____

Problem Solving

Solve each problem.

9. Soccer practice started at 4:40 P.M. and ended at 6:00 P.M. How long was soccer practice?

10. Lenny got on the bus at 7:45 A.M. He arrived at school at 8:10 A.M. How long was the bus ride?

11. The field trip to the museum started at 9:00 A.M. and ended at noon. How long was the field trip?

12. A concert lasted from 8:30 P.M. to 9:20 P.M. How long did it last? Did it last more or less than an hour?

Lesson 5-3 • Elapsed Time

Using a Calendar

A **calendar** is a table that shows **days, weeks,** and **months** of the **year**. Look at the calendar month below. Each column of boxes with a number shows a date under a day of the week.

1 week = 7 days	
1 year = 12 months	
1 year = 52 weeks	
1 year = 365 days	
1 leap year = 366 days	
1 decade = 10 years	
1 century = 100 years	

When is the third-grade's class trip?

November 2005

Sun	Mon	Tues	Wed	Th	Fri	Sat
		1	2 class play	3	4 Report Cards	5
6 Laura's birthday	7	8	9	10	11 Veterans Day	12
13	14	15 Wayne's birthday	16	17 class trip	18	19 Levon's birthday
20	21 PTA bake sale	22	23	24 Thanksgiving -No school	25 Holiday No school	26
27	28	29	30 Art project due			

We know that the class trip is on _____.

We can write the date of the class trip using only numbers:

We write the number of the month, ____, the day, ____, and the last two digits of the year, ____.

The date of the class trip is _____.

Getting Started

Answer the questions about November. Write the date two ways for Exercises 1 and 2.

1. When is the bake sale? _____

2. When are report cards given out? _____

3. What is happening on 11/11/05? _____

Practice

Use the calendar to answer each question.

January 2006

Sun	Mon	Tues	Wed	Th	Fri	Sat
1 New Year's Day	2 Holiday- No school	3	4 Start science project	5	6	7
8	9 Maria's birthday	10	11 Math Club 3:30	12	13	14
15	16 MLK Jr.'s birthday (observed)	17	18 Class trip to museum	19	20 Science project due	21 Jason's birthday
22	23	24 4:00 Choral practice	25	26	27	28
29 Juan's birthday	30	31				

1. When is the class trip? Write the date two ways.

   _____

2. What is the date of the second Thursday? Write the date two ways.

   _____

3. Why is the third Friday an important day for the class?

   _____

4. Which Saturday is Jason's birthday?

   _____

5. What is the date after 1/31/06? Write the date two ways.

   _____

6. What is your date of birth? Write the date two ways.

   _____

❲ Now Try This! ❳

Sometimes dates must be written a certain way on forms. Write each date.

1. Today's date (mm/dd/yy)

   _____

2. Date of Birth or D.O.B (mm/dd/yy)

   _____

Lesson 5-4 • Using a Calendar

Measuring to the Nearest Quarter- and Half-Inch

Jared and Nina are measuring the length of a pencil.
Jared wants to find the length to the nearest half-inch.
Nina wants to find the length to the nearest quarter-inch.

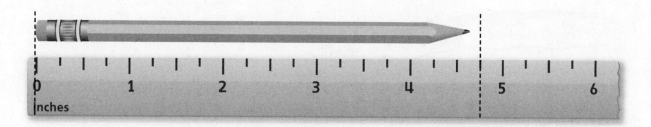

Jared's measurement of the pencil to

the nearest half-inch is _____ inches.

Nina's measurement of the pencil to

the nearest quarter-inch is _____ inches.

Getting Started _____

Measure the length of each item to the nearest half-inch.

1. 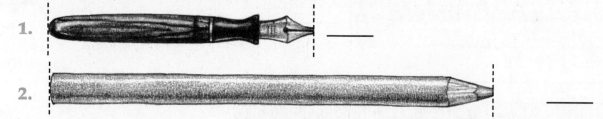 _____

2. _____

Measure the length of each item to the nearest quarter-inch.

3. 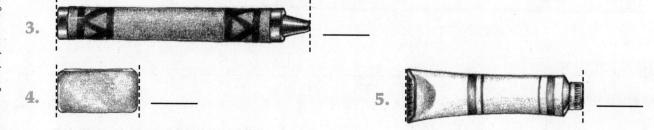 _____

4. _____

5. _____

Practice

Measure the length of each item to the nearest half-inch.

1. 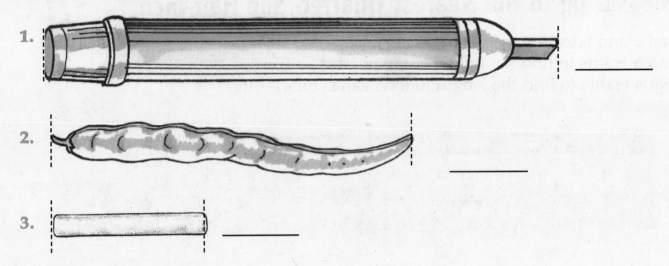 _____

2. _____

3. _____

Measure the length of each item to the nearest quarter-inch.

4. 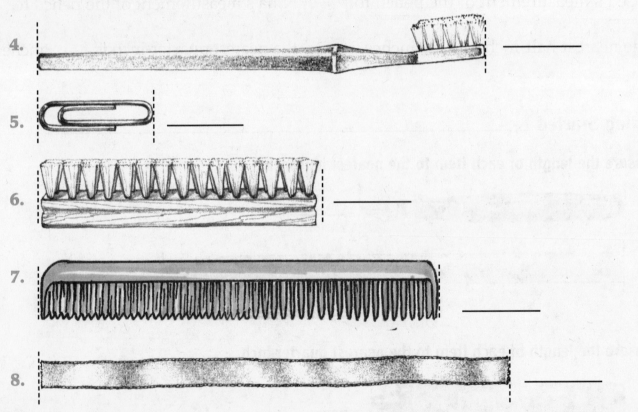 _____

5. _____

6. _____

7. _____

8. _____

Problem Solving

Solve each problem.

9. Yoko made a paper chain that was 145 inches long. Liz made one 96 inches long. If they joined them together, how long would the chain be?

10. Sherry bought 108 inches of ribbon to use on a school project. She only needed 79 inches for the project. How many inches of ribbon were left over?

Lesson 5-5 • Measuring to the Nearest Quarter- and Half-Inch

Inches, Feet, Yards, and Miles

Bert is measuring the flagpole at the center of Birch Park playground. Would you guess it to be about 30 feet, 30 yards, or 30 miles high?

We want to know if the flagpole measures 30 feet, 30 yards, or 30 miles.

We know:

1 foot = 12 inches   **1 yard = 3 feet**   **1 mile = 5,280 feet**

1 ft = _____ in.   **1 yd = _____ ft**   **1 mi = _____ ft**

                            1 yd = _____ in.   **1 mi = _____ yd**

The flagpole is probably about 30 _____ high.

Getting Started

Choose inches, feet, yards, or miles to measure each.

1. height of a house _____

2. width of a desk _____

3. height of a tall building _____

4. length of a paper clip _____

5. length of a freight train _____

6. length of your foot _____

7. length of a soccer field _____

8. distance to the moon _____

Circle the better estimate.

9. basketball player's height

    2 ft   2 yd

10. length of the Mississippi River

    2,300 ft   2,300 mi

11. width of a book

    11 ft   11 in.

12. length of a football field

    100 yd   100 ft

Practice

Choose inches, feet, yards, or miles to measure each.

1. length of an Olympic swimming pool
   _____

2. length of your fingernail
   _____

3. distance from Houston to New Orleans
   _____

4. distance from home plate to first base
   _____

5. width of your classroom
   _____

6. length of a pencil
   _____

7. length of a book
   _____

8. distance around a track
   _____

Circle the better estimate.

9. width of your foot
   4 ft   4 in.

10. the height of a mountain
    6 ft   2 mi

11. distance traveled by a well-hit baseball
    300 in.   300 ft

12. distance traveled on a bicycle in one hour
    15 yd   15 mi

13. height of a tree
    10 mi   10 yd

14. size of your waist
    23 in.   23 ft

Write the equivalent for each unit.

15. 12 in. = _____ ft

16. 24 in. = _____ ft

17. 3 ft = _____ yd

18. 6 ft = _____ yd

19. 1 yd = _____ in.

20. 2 yd = _____ in.

21. 5,280 ft = _____ mi

22. 10,560 ft = _____ mi

23. 1,760 yd = _____ mi

24. 3,520 yd = _____ mi

Name _____

Perimeter

The Lin family is fencing in their backyard. How many feet of fencing will they need to buy?

We need to find the total distance around the backyard.

The four sides of the back yard measure ____ feet, ____ feet, ____ feet and ____ feet. The distance around a figure is called the **perimeter.**

To find the perimeter, we add all the sides.

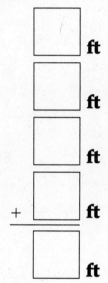

ft

ft

ft

+ ☐ ft

The perimeter is ____ feet.

☐ ft

The Lins must buy ____ feet of fencing.

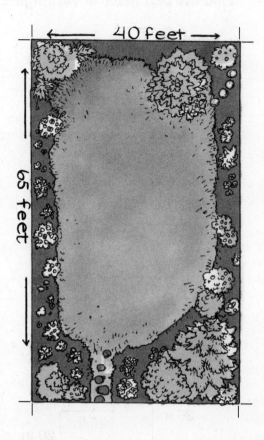

40 feet

65 feet

Getting Started

Find the perimeter of each figure.

1.
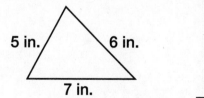

5 in.   6 in.

7 in.

_____

2.
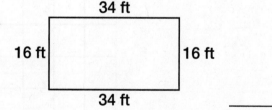

34 ft

16 ft   16 ft

34 ft

_____

3.
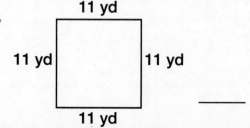

11 yd

11 yd   11 yd

11 yd

_____

4.
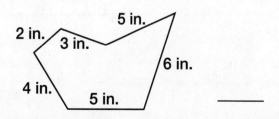

5 in.

2 in.   3 in.

6 in.

4 in.   5 in.

_____

Practice

Find the perimeter of each figure.

1.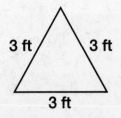

_____

2.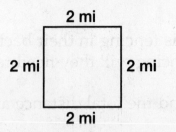

_____

3.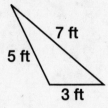

_____

4.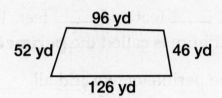

_____

5.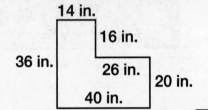

_____

6.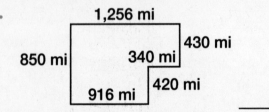

_____

(Now Try This!)

There are three paths from A to B. Count the edges of the blocks along each path to discover an interesting fact.

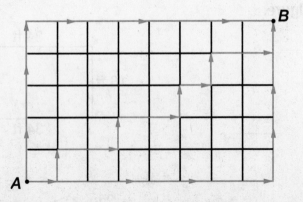

Name _____

Cups, Pints, Quarts, and Gallons

Miss Herrara needs to fill her lawn mower
with gas. Will she buy 5 gallons, 5 quarts,
or 5 pints of gas?

We want to know if Miss Herrara buys
gallons, quarts, or pints of gas.

We know:

1 gallon = 4 quarts   **1 quart = 2 pints**   **1 pint = 2 cups**

    1 gal = _____ qt   **1 qt = _____ pt**   **1 pt = _____ c**

Miss Herrara will probably buy 5 _____ of fuel.

Getting Started

Circle the better estimate.

1.

   1 gallon   1 quart

2.

   1 quart   1 gallon

3.

   2 pints   2 gallons

4.

   2 cups   2 pints

5.

   1 pint   1 gallon

6.

   2 pints   2 gallons

Practice

Circle the better estimate.

1.
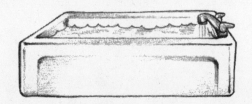

22 quarts   22 gallons

2.
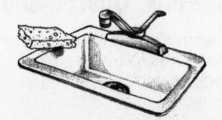

20 pints   20 quarts

3.

6 gallons   6 quarts

4.

1 pint   1 gallon

5.

2 cups   2 quarts

6.

1 quart   1 pint

7.

16 pints   16 gallons

8.

20 quarts   20 gallons

Write the equivalent for each unit.

9. 4 quarts = ___ gallon   10. 2 pints = ___ quart   11. 2 cups = ___ pint

12. 8 quarts = ___ gallons   13. 4 pints = ___ quarts   14. 4 cups = ___ pints

15. 16 quarts = ___ gallons   16. 8 pints = ___ quarts   17. 8 cups = ___ pints

Lesson 5-8 • Cups, Pints, Quarts, and Gallons

Ounces and Pounds

Laura's puppy made his first trip to the veterinarian to get a checkup. Did the puppy weigh about 5 ounces or 5 pounds?

We want to know if the puppy's weight will be in ounces or pounds.

We know:

1 pound = 16 ounces

1 lb = _____ oz

The puppy weighs about 5 _____.

Getting Started

Choose ounces or pounds to measure the weight of each.

1.

_____

2.

_____

3.

_____

4.

_____

Circle the better estimate.

5.

50 oz   50 lb

6.

10 oz   10 lb

Practice

Choose ounces or pounds to measure the weight of each.

1.

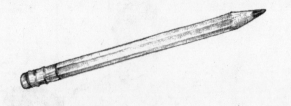

_____

2.

_____

3.

_____

4.

_____

5.

_____

6.

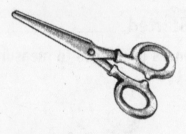

_____

Circle the better estimate.

7.

7 oz   7 lb

8.

14 oz   14 lb

9.

25 oz   25 lb

10.

18 oz   18 lb

The Fahrenheit Scale

A **Fahrenheit** thermometer measures temperature in **degrees** Fahrenheit. To read the temperature, look at the top of the shaded column. Count the marks to find the number of degrees.

At what temperature does water freeze

The shaded column ends between _____ and _____.

It is one tick mark above _____. Each tick mark

stands for _____. The temperature is _____.

We write _____ F.

Water freezes at _____ degrees Fahrenheit.

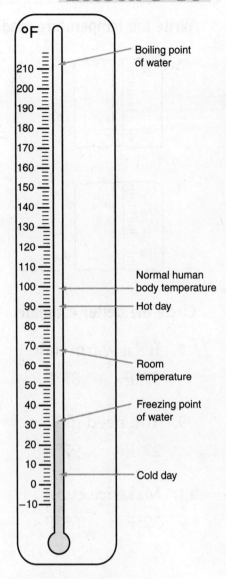

°F
Boiling point of water
Normal human body temperature
Hot day
Room temperature
Freezing point of water
Cold day

Getting Started

Write the temperature reading for each Fahrenheit thermometer.

1.
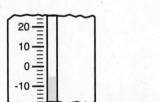
_____

2.
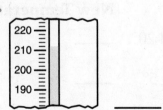
_____

3.
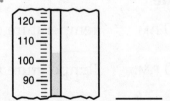
_____

Circle the better estimate.

4. It is a cold day.

   20°F   50°F

5. The water is boiling.

   200°F   212°F

6. You're feeling well.

   98°F   103°F

Practice

Write the temperature reading for each Fahrenheit thermometer.

1. [thermometer: 10, 0, -10, -20] _____

2. [thermometer: 110, 100, 90, 80] _____

3. [thermometer: 90, 80, 70, 60] _____

4. [thermometer: 10, 0, -10, -20] _____

5. [thermometer: 210, 200, 190, 180] _____

6. [thermometer: 70, 60, 50, 40] _____

Circle the better estimate.

7. It's a warm day.

   37°F   87°F

8. The tea water is hot.

   80°F   180°F

9. You need gloves.

   27°F   97°F

10. You have a fever.

    47°F   101°F

11. Make ice cubes.

    32°F   65°F

12. Go on a picnic.

    30°F   75°F

Now Try This!

The temperature at 1:00 P.M. was 47°F. Write each new temperature.

Time		New Temperature
2:00 P.M.	Temperature dropped 20°.	_____
3:00 P.M.	Temperature went up 5°.	_____
4:00 P.M.	Temperature fell 30°.	_____
5:00 P.M.	Temperature dropped 2°.	_____
6:00 P.M.	Temperature rose 5°.	_____

Name _____

Problem Solving: Work Backward

Kara wants to see a movie that starts at 7:15 P.M. It will take her 30 minutes to eat dinner and 20 minutes to get to the theater. Kara wants to arrive at the theater 15 minutes early. What time should Kara start to get ready?

★ SEE

The movie starts at _____ It will take her _____ minutes

to eat dinner and _____ minutes to get to the theater. Kara

wants to arrive at the theater _____ minutes early.

We need to find out what time Kara should start to get ready.

★ PLAN

We can **work backward** from the time the movie starts.

We can use a demonstration clock and move the minute hand back

_____ minutes to 6:45. Then, we can move the hand back another

_____ minutes to 6:25. Next, we can move the minute hand back

_____ minutes to find the time Kara should start to get ready.

★ DO

Kara should start to get ready at _____ P.M.

★ CHECK

We can check our answer by moving the minute hand ahead for each length of time starting at 6:10 P.M.

Apply

Work backward to solve each problem.

**Problem-Solving Strategy:
Using the Four-Step Plan**

★ SEE What do you need to find?

★ PLAN What do you need to do?

★ DO Follow the plan.

★ CHECK Does your answer make sense?

1. Ms. Raymond's class is making a quilt. She gave Janice, Gayle, Jeryl, Jamie, and Errol each a yard of striped fabric. Gayle discovered that the fabric did not match with what she had already chosen. Jeryl and Jamie decided that they wanted different fabric. Ms. Raymond now had 5 yards of the striped fabric left. How many yards of the striped fabric did Ms. Raymond start with?

2. Gabe was in charge of pouring the lemonade into cups at the class picnic. At one table, 8 students wanted lemonade. At another table, 10 students asked for lemonade. Luckily, two students changed their minds. Gabe had no more lemonade left in the container. How many cups of lemonade were in the container? What was the size of the container?

3. Lynn baked a cake and served it for dinner at 6:00 P.M. It took her 15 minutes to mix the batter. It took her 1 hour to bake the cake. The cake had to cool for 30 minutes before serving it. When did she start to prepare the cake?

4. It takes Cindy 35 minutes to get to soccer practice. It will take her 45 minutes to do her homework and 25 minutes to eat dinner. Soccer practice begins at 5:30 P.M. What time does Cindy need to begin getting ready?

5. Kurt cuts 3 inches off a board to make a shelf. Then he cuts the rest of the board into 3 equal pieces. Each piece is 7 inches long. How many feet long was the original board?

6. Larry cut a piece of wire into two equal pieces. Then he cut 4 inches off one of the pieces that is now 10 inches long. How long was the original piece of wire?

Name _____

Write each time as you would see it on a digital clock.

1.  ☐

2. 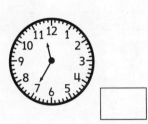 ☐

3. 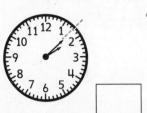 ☐

4. 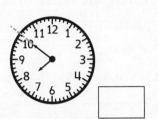 ☐

Circle the better estimate.

5. distance a car drives in one hour

55 feet   55 miles

6. height of a puppy

15 inches   15 feet

Find the perimeter of each figure.

7.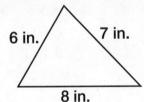

6 in.   7 in.

8 in.   _____

8.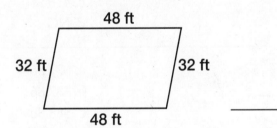

48 ft

32 ft   32 ft

48 ft   _____

Circle the better estimate.

9.

2 ounces   2 quarts

10.

26°F   66°F

Circle the letter of the correct answer.

1   432 ◯ 562

     a. <
     b. >

2 Round 741 to the nearest hundred.

     a. 700
     b. 800
     c. NG

3 What is the value of the 2 in 231,470?

     a. tens
     b. thousands
     c. ten thousands
     d. NG

4   249
  + 167

     a. 316
     b. 406
     c. 416
     d. NG

5 $38.27
  + 49.59

     a. $77.86
     b. $87.86
     c. $88.86
     d. NG

6   4,739
    2,156
  +   847

     a. 7,642
     b. 7,752
     c. 7,842
     d. NG

7 Round to the nearest hundred to estimate the sum.

    526
  + 295

     a. 700
     b. 800
     c. 600
     d. NG

8   634
  − 259

     a. 425
     b. 385
     c. 325
     d. NG

9   805
  − 328

     a. 523
     b. 427
     c. 477
     d. NG

10 $64.26
  − 12.87

     a. $52.61
     b. $51.39
     c. $52.39
     d. NG

11 Round to the nearest ten to estimate the difference.

    79
  − 24

     a. 40
     b. 50
     c. 60
     d. NG

12 Round to the nearest hundred to estimate the difference.

    725
  − 278

     a. 400
     b. 500
     c. 300
     d. NG

13

     a. 8:15
     b. 3:09
     c. 3:42
     d. NG

 score

STOP

Name _____

Metric Measurement

Measuring to the Nearest Centimeter and Decimeter

A centimeter is a unit of length in the metric system. We can measure the length of objects using a **centimeter ruler.**

What is the length of the crayon to the nearest centimeter?

REMEMBER When the end of an object falls halfway between two centimeters, round to the greater centimeter.

The crayon is about _____ centimeters long.

We can write _____ cm.

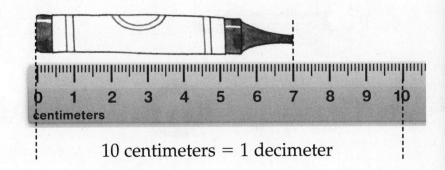

10 centimeters = 1 decimeter

A **decimeter** is another unit of measure in the metric system. There are 10 centimeters in 1 decimeter.

Getting Started

Estimate each length. Then measure to the nearest centimeter.

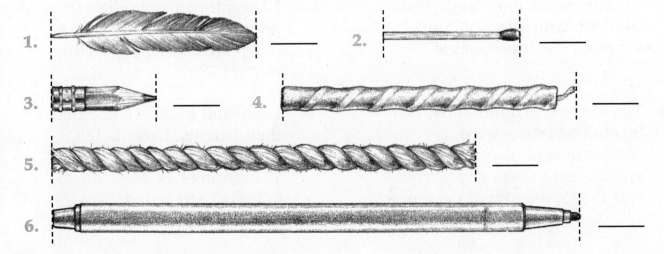

1. _____   2. _____

3. _____   4. _____

5. _____

6. _____

Practice

Estimate each length. Then measure to the nearest centimeter.

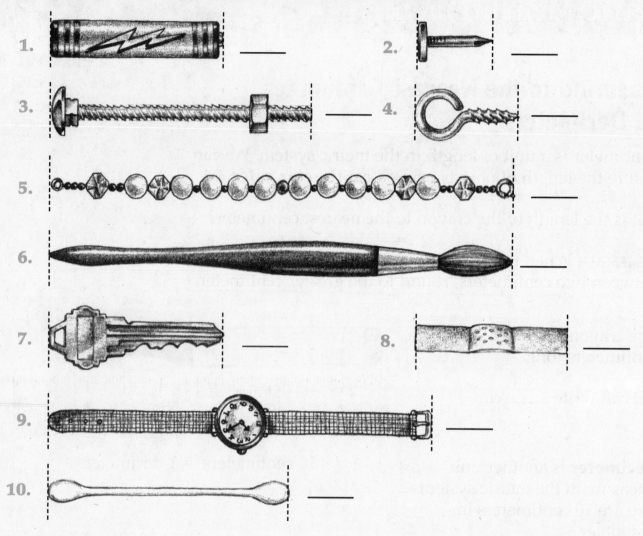

1. _____

2. _____

3. _____

4. _____

5. _____

6. _____

7. _____

8. _____

9. _____

10. _____

Problem Solving

Solve each problem.

11. Angelina's mother had 63 centimeters of sausage. She used 47 centimeters of it for supper. How much was left?

12. Julie's bullfrog jumped 127 centimeters. Willie's frog jumped 88 centimeters. How much farther did Julie's frog jump?

13. The sections of a mural painted by student artists were 65 centimeters, 82 centimeters, and 56 centimeters wide. What was the total width of the mural?

14. Larry and his dad compared their heights. Larry is 125 centimeters tall. His father is 172 centimeters. How much taller is Larry's dad?

Lesson 6-1 • Measuring to the Nearest Centimeter and Decimeter

Meters and Kilometers

To keep animals away from the corn, Mrs. Lawrence wants to put a fence around the whole cornfield. How much fencing will she need?

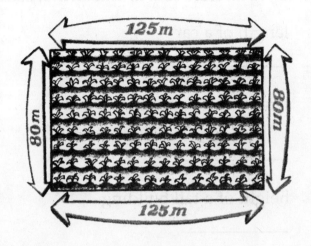

We want to find the perimeter, or total distance, around the field.

We know:

1 meter = 100 centimeters   **1 kilometer = 1,000 meters**

   1 m = _____ cm   **1 km = _____ m**

The sides of the cornfield measure _____ meters,

_____ meters, _____ meters, and _____ meters.

To find the perimeter, we add all the sides.

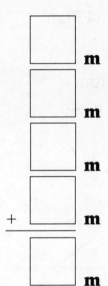

Mrs. Lawrence needs _____ meters of fencing.

Getting Started

Would you measure each in centimeters, meters, or kilometers?

1. height of a house

   _____

2. length of a river

   _____

Circle the better estimate.

3. width of a book

   22 cm   22 m

Find the perimeter.

4.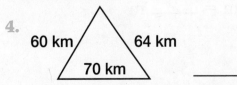

                     _____

Practice

Would you measure each in centimeters, meters, or kilometers?

1. length of a car

   _____

2. distance to the moon

   _____

3. length of a paper clip

   _____

4. distance you can run in 15 seconds

   _____

5. height of a tall building

   _____

6. length of your arm

   _____

Circle the better estimate.

7. your height

   138 cm   138 m

8. distance run in 30 minutes

   8 m   8 km

9. home run at Yankee Stadium

   98 cm   98 m

10. distance around the world at the equator

    40,000 m   40,000 km

Find the perimeter.

11.

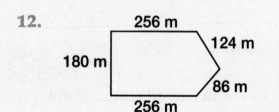

30 m   50 m   40 m

_____

12.

256 m   124 m   180 m   86 m   256 m

_____

Write the equivalent for each unit.

13. 1 m = _____ cm

14. 5 m = _____ cm

15. 12 m = _____ cm

16. 1 km = _____ m

17. 5 km = _____ m

18. 12 km = _____ m

Milliliters and Liters

Jerry is making breakfast for his mother on Mother's Day. Will the bottle he is filling hold about 1 milliliter or 1 liter of orange juice?

We know:

1 liter = 1,000 milliliters

$1\ L = \underline{\hspace{1cm}}\ mL$

Liters and milliliters are measures of **volume.**

Volume is the amount of space inside something.

   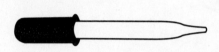

It takes about 4 glasses to fill one liter bottle.

It takes an eyedropper to measure about one milliliter.

The volume of the juice bottle is about 1 _____.

Getting Started

Would you measure the volume of these in milliliters or liters?

1.

_____

2.

_____

3.

_____

4.

_____

Practice

Would you measure the volume of these in milliliters or liters?

1.

_____

2.

_____

3.

_____

4.

_____

5.

_____

6.

_____

7.

_____

8.

_____

Now Try This!

Circle the best estimate.

cup of hot chocolate	2,100 mL	210 mL	21 mL
beach pail	1,500 mL	150 mL	15 mL
bottle of eyedrops	2,500 mL	250 mL	25 mL
aquarium	10,000 mL	1,000 mL	100 mL
bathroom sink	3,000 mL	300 mL	30 mL
bathtub	50,000 mL	5,000 mL	500 mL

Lesson 6-3 • Milliliters and Liters

Grams and Kilograms

Matthew and his brother are unpacking the groceries. Does the bag of flour weigh about 2 grams or 2 kilograms?

We know:

1 kilogram = 1,000 grams

1 kg = _____ g

A paper clip weighs about 1 gram.

A large book weighs about 1 kilogram.

The bag of flour weighs about 2 _____.

Getting Started

Would you weigh each in grams or kilograms?

1.

   _____

2.

   _____

3.

   _____

4.

   _____

5.

   _____

6.

   _____

Practice _____

Would you weigh each in grams or kilograms?

1.

_____

2.

_____

3.

_____

4.

_____

5.

_____

6.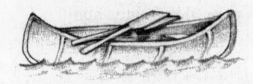

_____

(Now Try This!)

How much do you weigh on Earth? _____ pounds

Will you weigh the same on the Moon? _____

As you travel out into space, your weight decreases but your mass stays the same. The amount of matter in something is its **mass**.

Grams and _____ are units of mass.

What is the mass of 2 large books
on Earth?

_____

What is the mass of 2 large books
on the Moon?

_____

Circle the best estimate.

dollar bill	1,000 g	100 g	1 g
apple	1,600 g	160 g	6 g
a brick	1,000 g	100 g	1 g

Lesson 6-4 • Grams and Kilograms

The Celsius Scale

The first warm days of spring make the flowers bloom. Read the Celsius thermometer to see what the temperature might be on such a day.

A **Celsius** thermometer measures temperature in degrees Celsius. To read the temperature, look at the top of the shaded column. Count the marks to find the number of degrees.

The shaded column ends between _____ and _____.

It is one tick mark above _____. Each tick mark

stands for _____. The temperature is _____.

We write _____.

The temperature on a warm spring day might be

_____ degrees Celsius.

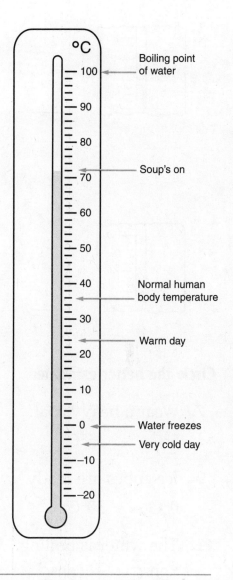

Getting Started

Write each Celsius temperature shown.

1. 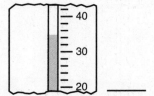 _____

2. 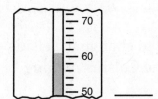 _____

3. 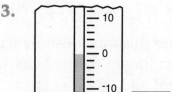 _____

Circle the better estimate.

4. Brrr, it's cold outside.

   0°C   20°C

5. I like my soup hot.

   30°C   70°C

6. It's a hot day.

   20°C   30°C

Practice

Write each Celsius temperature shown.

1. 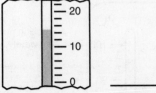 _____

2. 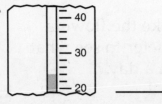 _____

3. 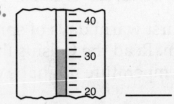 _____

4. 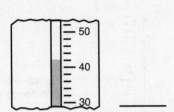 _____

5. 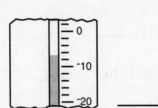 _____

6. 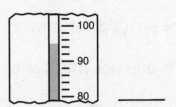 _____

Circle the better estimate.

7. Wear a heavy coat.
   5°C   35°C

8. The cocoa is hot.
   35°C   75°C

9. Ice cubes are ready.
   0°C   50°C

10. Turn on the air conditioner.
    10°C   38°C

11. The water is boiling.
    ⁻20°C   100°C

12. My body's temperature is normal.
    37°C   70°C

[Now Try This!]

Use this quick-estimate method to change a Celsius reading to Fahrenheit: double the Celsius reading and add 30°.

Change each reading.

1. 20°C is about _____ °F

2. 60°C is about _____ °F

3. 14°C is about _____ °F

4. 35°C is about _____ °F

5. 0°C is about _____ °F

6. 100°C is about _____ °F

7. 25°C is about _____ °F

8. 5°C is about _____ °F

9. 89°C is about _____ °F

Lesson 6-5 • The Celsius Scale

Name _____

Problem Solving: Solve Multi-Step Problems

It's Algebra!

The third-grade class at the Main Street School is collecting pennies for a math project. They need a total of 1,000 pennies. How many more pennies do they need to collect?

Day of the Week	Pennies Collected
Monday	137
Tuesday	201
Wednesday	356

⭐ **SEE**

We want to know how many more pennies the third grade needs to collect.

On Monday, ＿＿ pennies were collected.

On Tuesday, ＿＿ pennies were collected.

On Wednesday, ＿＿ pennies were collected.

⭐ **PLAN**

We can add the number of pennies collected each

day. Then, we can subtract that total from ＿＿＿.

⭐ **DO**

Add.   Subtract.

  137   1,000
  201   − 694
+ 356

The third grade needs to collect ＿＿ more pennies.

⭐ **CHECK**

We can check the subtraction by adding.

    694
 + ＿＿＿

Practice

Solve each problem.

1. Rich had $10.00. He spent $4.75 on a birthday present and $2.50 on ice cream. How much does he have left?

2. The school has 2,000 tickets to sell. If 1,248 were sold over the weekend and 409 were sold on Monday, how many still need to be sold?

3. Sara bought a ball for $1.59. She wants to buy a baseball hat for $4.99 and a bat for $3.49. If Sara has $10, can she buy all three items?

4. Potatoes in the grocery store sell for $1.39 a pound. The potatoes dug at the truck farm sell for $0.68 a pound. How much did Carrie's mother save by buying two pounds of potatoes at the truck farm?

5. Mr. Lance had to pay $2.75 to get into the zoo. His son had to pay only $1.45. How much change did he get from his $10 bill?

6. Sam ordered 140 baseball cards through the mail. If 74 arrived yesterday and 33 arrived today, how many still have to come?

7. Chuck, Rob, and Sal have babysitting jobs. In one week Chuck earned $10.50, while Rob earned $13.75, and Sal earned $11.25. If they combine their money, will they be able to buy a computer game that costs $40?

8. One-hundred fifty potatoes were ready to harvest. Carrie dug 38 potatoes. Her sister dug 21 and her mother dug 45. How many potatoes did they harvest altogether? How many potatoes were left to harvest?

Lesson 6-6 • Problem Solving: Solve Multi-Step Problems

Measure each to the nearest centimeter.

1.  ___

2.  ___

3.  ___

Would you measure each in centimeters, meters, or kilometers?

4. length of a paper clip

_____

5. distance traveled by a car in one day

_____

Find the perimeter of each.

6.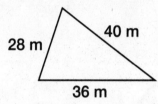

28 m   40 m

36 m   _____

7.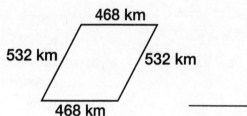

468 km

532 km   532 km

468 km   _____

Circle the unit you would use to measure each item.

8.

9.

10.

mL   L   mL   L   g   kg

Write the temperature reading for each Celsius thermometer.

11.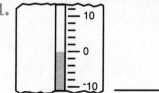

10
0
-10   _____

12.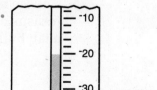

-10
-20
-30   _____

13.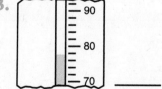

90
80
70   _____

Circle the letter of the correct answer.

1 778 ◯ 709
     a. >
     b. <

2 What is the value of the 5 in 390,516?
     a. tens
     b. thousands
     c. hundred thousands
     d. NG

3
```
  684
+ 926
```
     a. 1,510
     b. 1,600
     c. 1,610
     d. NG

4
```
  $28.36
+  51.47
```
     a. $79.73
     b. $79.83
     c. $80.83
     d. NG

5
```
  6,254
  1,862
+   485
```
     a. 8,601
     b. 8,691
     c. 8,701
     d. NG

6 Round to the nearest hundred to estimate the sum.
```
  624
+ 256
```
     a. 800
     b. 900
     c. 1,000
     d. NG

7
```
  836
- 259
```
     a. 557
     b. 623
     c. 667
     d. NG

8
```
  605
- 296
```
     a. 209
     b. 309
     c. 491
     d. NG

9
```
  $82.46
-  27.38
```
     a. $45.08
     b. $55.08
     c. $65.12
     d. NG

10 Round to the nearest hundred to estimate the difference.
```
  896
- 359
```
     a. 500
     b. 600
     c. 700
     d. NG

11

     a. 6:08
     b. 6:38
     c. 7:30
     d. NG

12 Find the perimeter.

156 in. △ 156 in.
200 in.
     a. 312 in.
     b. 502 in.
     c. 512 in.
     d. NG

13 Choose the best unit for measuring the height of a tall building.
     a. centimeters
     b. meters
     c. kilometers
     d. NG

☐ **score**

Multiplication Facts Through Five

Understanding Multiplication

There is a Collector's Fair at the playground this Saturday. Silvia plans to show her penny collection. How many coins will she have in her display?

We want to find how many coins are in Silvia's display.

There are _____ rows of pennies.

There are _____ pennies in each row.

We can add the number of coins in each row.

4 + 4 + 4 + 4 + 4 = _____

We can multiply the number of rows by the number of coins in each.

5 groups of 4 = _____

$\qquad$ **5 fours = _____** $\qquad$ 4

$\quad$ **5 × 4 = _____** $\qquad$ ×5

$\quad\uparrow\qquad\quad\uparrow\qquad\quad\uparrow$

factor $\quad$ factor $\quad$ product

We can add the number of coins in each column.

5 + 5 + 5 + 5 = _____

We can multiply the number of columns by the number of coins in each.

4 groups of 5 = _____

$\qquad$ **4 fives = _____** $\qquad$ 5

$\quad$ **4 × 5 = _____** $\qquad$ ×4

$\quad\uparrow\qquad\quad\uparrow\qquad\quad\uparrow$

factor $\quad$ factor $\quad$ product

There are _____ pennies in Silvia's display.

Getting Started

Use both addition and multiplication to show how many coins are in each picture.

1.

$\quad$ 3 $\quad$ 2 × 3 = _____
$\quad$ +3 $\quad$ 3 × 2 = _____

2.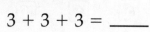

$\quad$ 3 + 3 + 3 = _____
$\quad$ 3 × 3 = _____

Practice

Use both addition and multiplication to show how many buttons are in each picture.

1.

$$4 + 4 = \underline{\quad}$$

$$2 \times 4 = \underline{\quad}$$

$$4 \times 2 = \underline{\quad}$$

2.

$$3 + 3 + 3 + 3 + 3 = \underline{\quad}$$

$$5 \times 3 = \underline{\quad}$$

$$3 \times 5 = \underline{\quad}$$

3.

$$3 + 3 + 3 + 3 + 3 + 3 + 3 = \underline{\quad}$$

$$7 \times 3 = \underline{\quad}$$

$$3 \times 7 = \underline{\quad}$$

4.

$$\begin{array}{r} 7 \\ 7 \\ 7 \\ + 7 \\ \hline \end{array}$$

$$4 \times 7 = \underline{\quad}$$

$$7 \times 4 = \underline{\quad}$$

5.

$$\begin{array}{r} 3 \\ 3 \\ 3 \\ 3 \\ 3 \\ + 3 \\ \hline \end{array}$$

$$6 \times 3 = \underline{\quad}$$

$$3 \times 6 = \underline{\quad}$$

6.

$$\begin{array}{r} 4 \\ 4 \\ 4 \\ + 4 \\ \hline \end{array}$$

$$4 \times 4 = \underline{\quad}$$

Lesson 7-1 • Understanding Multiplication

Name _____

Multiplying, the Factor 2

Sun Li is helping her mother pack eggs in cartons. How many eggs does she pack into each carton?

The carton has 6 groups of _____ eggs each.

We can add. **2 + 2 + 2 + 2 + 2 + 2 = _____**

We can also multiply.

$6 \times 2 = $ _____ $\begin{array}{r} 2 \\ \times\, 6 \\ \hline \end{array}$

We can also think of it as 2 groups of _____ eggs each.

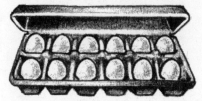

$2 \times 6 = $ _____ $\begin{array}{r} 6 \\ \times\, 2 \\ \hline \end{array}$

Sun Li packs _____ eggs into each carton.

Getting Started

Use both addition and multiplication to show how many eggs are in each picture.

1.

$2 + 2 + 2 = $ _____

$3 \times 2 = $ _____

$2 \times 3 = $ _____

2.

$2 + 2 + 2 + 2 + 2 = $ _____

$5 \times 2 = $ _____

$2 \times 5 = $ _____

Multiply.

3. $7 \times 2 = $ _____

4. $2 \times 6 = $ _____

5. $\begin{array}{r} 4 \\ \times\, 2 \\ \hline \end{array}$

6. $\begin{array}{r} 2 \\ \times\, 2 \\ \hline \end{array}$

Practice

Use both addition and multiplication to show how many are in each picture.

1.

$2 + 2 + 2 + 2 + 2 + 2 + 2 + 2 + 2 =$ ____

$9 \times 2 =$ ____

$2 \times 9 =$ ____

2.

$2 + 2 + 2 + 2 =$ ____

$4 \times 2 =$ ____

$2 \times 4 =$ ____

3.

$2 + 2 + 2 + 2 + 2 + 2 =$ ____

$6 \times 2 =$ ____

$2 \times 6 =$ ____

4.

$2 + 2 + 2 + 2 + 2 + 2 + 2 =$ ____

$7 \times 2 =$ ____

$2 \times 7 =$ ____

Multiply.

5. $\begin{array}{r} 3 \\ \times\, 2 \\ \hline \end{array}$
6. $\begin{array}{r} 2 \\ \times\, 2 \\ \hline \end{array}$
7. $\begin{array}{r} 2 \\ \times\, 4 \\ \hline \end{array}$
8. $\begin{array}{r} 5 \\ \times\, 2 \\ \hline \end{array}$
9. $\begin{array}{r} 6 \\ \times\, 2 \\ \hline \end{array}$
10. $\begin{array}{r} 2 \\ \times\, 7 \\ \hline \end{array}$

11. $\begin{array}{r} 6 \\ \times\, 2 \\ \hline \end{array}$
12. $\begin{array}{r} 2 \\ \times\, 8 \\ \hline \end{array}$
13. $\begin{array}{r} 9 \\ \times\, 2 \\ \hline \end{array}$
14. $\begin{array}{r} 2 \\ \times\, 6 \\ \hline \end{array}$
15. $\begin{array}{r} 2 \\ \times\, 3 \\ \hline \end{array}$
16. $\begin{array}{r} 4 \\ \times\, 2 \\ \hline \end{array}$

17. $2 \times 9 =$ ____
18. $3 \times 2 =$ ____
19. $5 \times 2 =$ ____

20. $2 \times 6 =$ ____
21. $8 \times 2 =$ ____
22. $2 \times 4 =$ ____

Problem Solving

Solve each problem.

23. Kim has 2 trays of ice cubes. Each tray makes 8 cubes. How many cubes does Kim have?

24. Guido bought 6 sacks of fish hooks. Each sack held 2 fish hooks. How many fish hooks did Guido have?

Lesson 7-2 • Multiplying, the Factor 2

Multiplying, the Factor 3

Karen's grandmother puts a star on the chart every time Karen finishes a new book. How many books has she read?

We need to know how many stars are on Karen's chart.

There are ____ rows of stars.

There are ____ stars in each row.

We can add. $4 + 4 + 4 =$ ____

We can also multiply.

$3 \times 4 =$ ____ $\begin{array}{r} 4 \\ \times 3 \\ \hline \end{array}$

We can also think of it as 4 groups of ____ stars each.

$4 \times 3 =$ ____ $\begin{array}{r} 3 \\ \times 4 \\ \hline \end{array}$

Karen has read ____ new books.

Getting Started

Use both addition and multiplication to show how many are in the picture.

1.

   $3 + 3 + 3 + 3 + 3 =$ ____

   $5 \times 3 =$ ____

   $3 \times 5 =$ ____

Multiply.

2. $\begin{array}{r} 3 \\ \times 3 \\ \hline \end{array}$

3. $\begin{array}{r} 3 \\ \times 8 \\ \hline \end{array}$

4. $3 \times 6 =$ ____

5. $9 \times 3 =$ ____

Practice

Use both addition and multiplication to show how many are in each picture.

1.

$3 + 3 + 3 + 3 + 3 + 3 + 3 + 3 + 3 = $ _____

$9 \times 3 = $ _____

$3 \times 9 = $ _____

2.

$3 + 3 + 3 = $ _____

$3 \times 3 = $ _____

Multiply.

3.	4.	5.	6.	7.	8.
$\begin{array}{r} 3 \\ \times\, 4 \\ \hline \end{array}$	$\begin{array}{r} 5 \\ \times\, 3 \\ \hline \end{array}$	$\begin{array}{r} 3 \\ \times\, 2 \\ \hline \end{array}$	$\begin{array}{r} 3 \\ \times\, 6 \\ \hline \end{array}$	$\begin{array}{r} 2 \\ \times\, 5 \\ \hline \end{array}$	$\begin{array}{r} 4 \\ \times\, 3 \\ \hline \end{array}$

9.	10.	11.	12.	13.	14.
$\begin{array}{r} 2 \\ \times\, 3 \\ \hline \end{array}$	$\begin{array}{r} 2 \\ \times\, 8 \\ \hline \end{array}$	$\begin{array}{r} 6 \\ \times\, 3 \\ \hline \end{array}$	$\begin{array}{r} 7 \\ \times\, 2 \\ \hline \end{array}$	$\begin{array}{r} 3 \\ \times\, 8 \\ \hline \end{array}$	$\begin{array}{r} 4 \\ \times\, 2 \\ \hline \end{array}$

15.	16.	17.	18.	19.	20.
$\begin{array}{r} 9 \\ \times\, 2 \\ \hline \end{array}$	$\begin{array}{r} 3 \\ \times\, 5 \\ \hline \end{array}$	$\begin{array}{r} 8 \\ \times\, 2 \\ \hline \end{array}$	$\begin{array}{r} 8 \\ \times\, 3 \\ \hline \end{array}$	$\begin{array}{r} 3 \\ \times\, 7 \\ \hline \end{array}$	$\begin{array}{r} 5 \\ \times\, 2 \\ \hline \end{array}$

21. $9 \times 3 = $ _____   22. $3 \times 7 = $ _____   23. $4 \times 3 = $ _____

24. $3 \times 8 = $ _____   25. $2 \times 6 = $ _____   26. $3 \times 9 = $ _____

27. $5 \times 2 = $ _____   28. $6 \times 3 = $ _____   29. $3 \times 5 = $ _____

Problem Solving

Solve each problem.

30. Tennis cans hold 3 tennis balls each. How many tennis balls are in 6 cans?

31. Pencils are sold in packages of 8. Dan bought 3 packages. How many pencils did Dan buy?

Multiplying, the Factor 4

Mrs. Franklin put tomato plants in her garden so she can make tomato juice in the fall. How many plants is she growing?

We want to know the total number of tomato plants in the garden.

The garden has ____ rows of plants.

There are ____ plants across in each row.

We can add. **4 + 4 + 4 + 4 + 4 + 4 + 4 + 4 = ____**

We can also multiply.

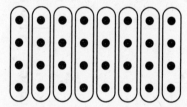

$8 \times 4 =$ ____
$$\begin{array}{r} 4 \\ \times\,8 \\ \hline \end{array}$$

We can also think of it as 4 groups of ____ plants each.

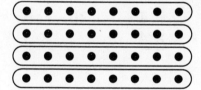

$4 \times 8 =$ ____
$$\begin{array}{r} 8 \\ \times\,4 \\ \hline \end{array}$$

Mrs. Franklin has ____ tomato plants in her garden.

Getting Started

Use both addition and multiplication to show how many are in the picture.

1.

$4 + 4 + 4 + 4 + 4 + 4 =$ ____

$6 \times 4 =$ ____

$4 \times 6 =$ ____

Multiply.

2. $\begin{array}{r} 5 \\ \times\,4 \\ \hline \end{array}$ 3. $\begin{array}{r} 3 \\ \times\,4 \\ \hline \end{array}$ 4. $4 \times 4 =$ ____   5. $4 \times 2 =$ ____

Practice

Use both addition and multiplication to show how many are in each picture.

1.

$4 + 4 + 4 + 4 + 4 + 4 =$ _____

$6 \times 4 =$ _____

$4 \times 6 =$ _____

2.

$4 + 4 + 4 + 4 + 4 =$ _____

$5 \times 4 =$ _____

$4 \times 5 =$ _____

Multiply.

3. 3
    $\times 4$

4. 5
    $\times 4$

5. 3
    $\times 2$

6. 2
    $\times 9$

7. 8
    $\times 3$

8. 2
    $\times 7$

9. 4
    $\times 6$

10. 7
    $\times 4$

11. 3
    $\times 7$

12. 4
    $\times 2$

13. 9
    $\times 4$

14. 9
    $\times 3$

15. 8
    $\times 2$

16. 6
    $\times 4$

17. 7
    $\times 2$

18. 2
    $\times 3$

19. 4
    $\times 4$

20. 6
    $\times 3$

21. $6 \times 4 =$ _____

22. $3 \times 4 =$ _____

23. $9 \times 4 =$ _____

24. $4 \times 8 =$ _____

25. $3 \times 9 =$ _____

26. $2 \times 8 =$ _____

Problem Solving

Solve each problem.

27. There are 4 tables in the room. There are 6 children at each table. How many children are there?

28. Mrs. Golic bought 4 toys for $8 apiece. How much did the toys cost Mrs. Golic?

Multiplying, the Factor 5

Five students in Ms. Teller's class are working together on a science project. Each student has collected 5 sand dollars. How many sand dollars do they have?

We need to find the total number of sand dollars collected.

We can see there are ____ rows of sand dollars.

Each row has ____ sand dollars.

We can add. **5 + 5 + 5 + 5 + 5 = ____**

We can also multiply.

$$5 \times 5 = \underline{\quad} \qquad \begin{array}{r} 5 \\ \times\, 5 \\ \hline \end{array}$$

The students have collected ____ sand dollars.

Getting Started

Use both addition and multiplication to show how many are in the picture.

1.

$5 + 5 + 5 + 5 = \underline{\quad}$

$4 \times 5 = \underline{\quad}$

$5 \times 4 = \underline{\quad}$

Multiply.

2. $\begin{array}{r} 3 \\ \times\, 5 \\ \hline \end{array}$

3. $\begin{array}{r} 8 \\ \times\, 5 \\ \hline \end{array}$

4. $5 \times 6 = \underline{\quad}$

5. $9 \times 5 = \underline{\quad}$

Practice

Use both addition and multiplication to show how many are in each picture.

1.

$5 + 5 + 5 + 5 + 5 + 5 + 5 = $ ____

$7 \times 5 = $ ____

$5 \times 7 = $ ____

2.

$5 + 5 + 5 + 5 + 5 + 5 = $ ____

$6 \times 5 = $ ____

$5 \times 6 = $ ____

Multiply.

3. $\begin{array}{r} 6 \\ \times 5 \\ \hline \end{array}$
4. $\begin{array}{r} 4 \\ \times 3 \\ \hline \end{array}$
5. $\begin{array}{r} 3 \\ \times 5 \\ \hline \end{array}$
6. $\begin{array}{r} 5 \\ \times 7 \\ \hline \end{array}$
7. $\begin{array}{r} 8 \\ \times 5 \\ \hline \end{array}$
8. $\begin{array}{r} 9 \\ \times 4 \\ \hline \end{array}$
9. $\begin{array}{r} 4 \\ \times 8 \\ \hline \end{array}$

10. $\begin{array}{r} 7 \\ \times 3 \\ \hline \end{array}$
11. $\begin{array}{r} 4 \\ \times 5 \\ \hline \end{array}$
12. $\begin{array}{r} 5 \\ \times 9 \\ \hline \end{array}$
13. $\begin{array}{r} 5 \\ \times 5 \\ \hline \end{array}$
14. $\begin{array}{r} 2 \\ \times 5 \\ \hline \end{array}$
15. $\begin{array}{r} 6 \\ \times 4 \\ \hline \end{array}$
16. $\begin{array}{r} 5 \\ \times 2 \\ \hline \end{array}$

17. $5 \times 3 = $ ____
18. $6 \times 5 = $ ____
19. $5 \times 7 = $ ____
20. $5 \times 9 = $ ____

Now Try This!

A multiple of 5 is a number that has 5 as one of its factors. For example, 35 is a multiple of 5 because 5 times 7 is 35. When we count by fives, like 5, 10, 15, 20, we are naming some more multiples of five. Circle the numbers that are multiples of five. Then write a rule to use for deciding if a number is a multiple of five.

5,673	4,220	7,110	3,245	23,320	4,373	77,770
35,556	55,551	47,315	2,222	40,000	21,502	1,115

Rule: _____

Lesson 7-5 • Multiplying, the Factor 5

Multiplying, the Factors 1 and 0

Ahmed is scooping ice cream into cones. How
many scoops of ice cream are in the cones in
the green stand? How many scoops of ice
cream are in the cones in the gray stand?

We want to know how many scoops of ice
cream each stand has.

In the green stand, we see _____ cones with _____
scoop of ice cream each.

In the gray stand, we see _____ cones with _____
scoops each.

To find the total number of scoops of ice cream in the

green stand, we multiply _____ by _____.

To find the total number of scoops of ice cream in the

gray stand, we multiply _____ by _____.

4 cones with 1 scoop each   **4 cones with 0 scoops each**

   $4 \times 1 =$ _____ $4 \times 0 =$ _____

   $1 \times 4 =$ _____ $0 \times 4 =$ _____

The green stand has _____ scoops of ice cream.

The gray stand has _____ scoops of ice cream.

Getting Started

Multiply.

1. $\begin{array}{r}1\\ \times\,0\\ \hline\end{array}$	2. $\begin{array}{r}0\\ \times\,9\\ \hline\end{array}$	3. $\begin{array}{r}3\\ \times\,1\\ \hline\end{array}$	4. $\begin{array}{r}3\\ \times\,3\\ \hline\end{array}$	5. $\begin{array}{r}1\\ \times\,5\\ \hline\end{array}$	6. $\begin{array}{r}0\\ \times\,0\\ \hline\end{array}$

7. $8 \times 1 =$ _____   8. $0 \times 3 =$ _____   9. $5 \times 2 =$ _____   10. $1 \times 6 =$ _____

Practice

Multiply.

1. $\begin{array}{r} 6 \\ \times\,0 \\ \hline \end{array}$ 2. $\begin{array}{r} 5 \\ \times\,9 \\ \hline \end{array}$ 3. $\begin{array}{r} 3 \\ \times\,7 \\ \hline \end{array}$ 4. $\begin{array}{r} 1 \\ \times\,7 \\ \hline \end{array}$ 5. $\begin{array}{r} 8 \\ \times\,4 \\ \hline \end{array}$ 6. $\begin{array}{r} 0 \\ \times\,7 \\ \hline \end{array}$ 7. $\begin{array}{r} 1 \\ \times\,1 \\ \hline \end{array}$

8. $\begin{array}{r} 7 \\ \times\,4 \\ \hline \end{array}$ 9. $\begin{array}{r} 2 \\ \times\,0 \\ \hline \end{array}$ 10. $\begin{array}{r} 6 \\ \times\,5 \\ \hline \end{array}$ 11. $\begin{array}{r} 4 \\ \times\,9 \\ \hline \end{array}$ 12. $\begin{array}{r} 3 \\ \times\,2 \\ \hline \end{array}$ 13. $\begin{array}{r} 0 \\ \times\,1 \\ \hline \end{array}$ 14. $\begin{array}{r} 9 \\ \times\,1 \\ \hline \end{array}$

15. $4 \times 5 =$ _____   16. $0 \times 8 =$ _____   17. $3 \times 1 =$ _____   18. $5 \times 0 =$ _____

19. $6 \times 2 =$ _____   20. $1 \times 8 =$ _____   21. $9 \times 0 =$ _____   22. $4 \times 3 =$ _____

23. $5 \times 5 =$ _____   24. $4 \times 1 =$ _____   25. $8 \times 3 =$ _____   26. $0 \times 6 =$ _____

Problem Solving

Solve each problem.

27. If 8 students each have 1 pencil, how many pencils do they have all together?

28. A box of pencils costs $1. How much do 9 boxes cost?

Now Try This!

It's Algebra!

Do the work inside the parentheses first.
Then circle yes or no to answer the question.

1. $5 + (4 \times 0) =$ _____
   $(5 + 4) \times 0 =$ _____
   Does $5 + (4 \times 0) = (5 + 4) \times 0$?
   yes   or   no

2. $(3 \times 1) \times 5 =$ _____
   $3 \times (1 \times 5) =$ _____
   Does $(3 \times 1) \times 5 = 3 \times (1 \times 5)$?
   yes   or   no

3. $4 \times (0 + 1) =$ _____
   $4 \times (1 + 0) =$ _____
   Does $4 \times (0 + 1) = 4 \times (1 + 0)$?
   yes   or   no

4. $2 \times (5 - 0) =$ _____
   $(2 \times 5) - 0 =$ _____
   Does $2 \times (5 - 0) = (2 \times 5) - 0$?
   yes   or   no

Name _____

Multiplication Facts and Mixed Skills

Multiply.

1. $\begin{array}{r} 3 \\ \times 9 \\ \hline \end{array}$	2. $\begin{array}{r} 9 \\ \times 0 \\ \hline \end{array}$	3. $\begin{array}{r} 3 \\ \times 7 \\ \hline \end{array}$	4. $\begin{array}{r} 2 \\ \times 8 \\ \hline \end{array}$	5. $\begin{array}{r} 2 \\ \times 9 \\ \hline \end{array}$	6. $\begin{array}{r} 1 \\ \times 6 \\ \hline \end{array}$	7. $\begin{array}{r} 5 \\ \times 6 \\ \hline \end{array}$
8. $\begin{array}{r} 0 \\ \times 6 \\ \hline \end{array}$	9. $\begin{array}{r} 2 \\ \times 2 \\ \hline \end{array}$	10. $\begin{array}{r} 4 \\ \times 6 \\ \hline \end{array}$	11. $\begin{array}{r} 9 \\ \times 2 \\ \hline \end{array}$	12. $\begin{array}{r} 3 \\ \times 0 \\ \hline \end{array}$	13. $\begin{array}{r} 4 \\ \times 8 \\ \hline \end{array}$	14. $\begin{array}{r} 4 \\ \times 4 \\ \hline \end{array}$
15. $\begin{array}{r} 9 \\ \times 3 \\ \hline \end{array}$	16. $\begin{array}{r} 3 \\ \times 3 \\ \hline \end{array}$	17. $\begin{array}{r} 6 \\ \times 1 \\ \hline \end{array}$	18. $\begin{array}{r} 8 \\ \times 0 \\ \hline \end{array}$	19. $\begin{array}{r} 7 \\ \times 4 \\ \hline \end{array}$	20. $\begin{array}{r} 2 \\ \times 7 \\ \hline \end{array}$	21. $\begin{array}{r} 4 \\ \times 2 \\ \hline \end{array}$
22. $\begin{array}{r} 8 \\ \times 4 \\ \hline \end{array}$	23. $\begin{array}{r} 0 \\ \times 8 \\ \hline \end{array}$	24. $\begin{array}{r} 1 \\ \times 2 \\ \hline \end{array}$	25. $\begin{array}{r} 4 \\ \times 7 \\ \hline \end{array}$	26. $\begin{array}{r} 6 \\ \times 5 \\ \hline \end{array}$	27. $\begin{array}{r} 5 \\ \times 8 \\ \hline \end{array}$	28. $\begin{array}{r} 4 \\ \times 0 \\ \hline \end{array}$
29. $\begin{array}{r} 4 \\ \times 5 \\ \hline \end{array}$	30. $\begin{array}{r} 0 \\ \times 7 \\ \hline \end{array}$	31. $\begin{array}{r} 9 \\ \times 5 \\ \hline \end{array}$	32. $\begin{array}{r} 1 \\ \times 7 \\ \hline \end{array}$	33. $\begin{array}{r} 5 \\ \times 3 \\ \hline \end{array}$	34. $\begin{array}{r} 4 \\ \times 1 \\ \hline \end{array}$	35. $\begin{array}{r} 6 \\ \times 0 \\ \hline \end{array}$
36. $\begin{array}{r} 5 \\ \times 1 \\ \hline \end{array}$	37. $\begin{array}{r} 6 \\ \times 4 \\ \hline \end{array}$	38. $\begin{array}{r} 8 \\ \times 2 \\ \hline \end{array}$	39. $\begin{array}{r} 7 \\ \times 3 \\ \hline \end{array}$	40. $\begin{array}{r} 1 \\ \times 1 \\ \hline \end{array}$	41. $\begin{array}{r} 0 \\ \times 5 \\ \hline \end{array}$	42. $\begin{array}{r} 5 \\ \times 5 \\ \hline \end{array}$

43. $9 \times 1 =$ _____   44. $0 \times 5 =$ _____   45. $1 \times 9 =$ _____   46. $3 \times 7 =$ _____

47. $8 \times 3 =$ _____   48. $9 \times 5 =$ _____   49. $6 \times 4 =$ _____   50. $7 \times 5 =$ _____

51. $0 \times 0 =$ _____   52. $2 \times 6 =$ _____   53. $4 \times 3 =$ _____   54. $5 \times 0 =$ _____

55. $5 \times 5 =$ _____   56. $4 \times 6 =$ _____   57. $2 \times 7 =$ _____   58. $9 \times 4 =$ _____

59. $3 \times 9 =$ _____   60. $2 \times 8 =$ _____   61. $4 \times 7 =$ _____   62. $8 \times 0 =$ _____

63. $8 \times$ ___ $= 32$ 64. $6 \times$ ___ $= 54$ 65. ___ $\times 5 = 40$ 66. $7 \times$ ___ $= 14$

67. $5 \times$ ___ $= 35$ 68. $3 \times$ ___ $= 15$ 69. $2 \times$ ___ $= 18$ 70. $4 \times$ ___ $= 16$

Practice

Write the answer for each.

1. 3×5 2. $6 + 7$ 3. 1×8 4. 4×7 5. $8 + 2$ 6. 8×2 7. $11 - 4$

8. $6 + 9$ 9. 2×3 10. $18 - 9$ 11. 2×0 12. $4 + 3$ 13. $5 + 8$ 14. 5×9

15. 2×1 16. 1×4 17. 7×0 18. $17 - 8$ 19. 6×3 20. 5×1 21. 0×4

22. $7 + 5$ 23. 2×5 24. $9 + 6$ 25. 0×1 26. 7×5 27. $4 - 0$ 28. $8 + 5$

29. 4×4 30. $12 - 6$ 31. 8×5 32. 9×4 33. $0 + 7$ 34. 3×6 35. $9 - 1$

36. $8 + 8$ 37. 3×2 38. 7×1 39. $8 - 8$ 40. 2×6 41. $7 + 9$ 42. $4 - 3$

43. 7×3 44. $6 + 4$ 45. 1×3 46. $15 - 8$ 47. 1×5 48. 9×5 49. $14 - 6$

50. 4×3 51. $11 - 5$ 52. $9 + 9$ 53. 3×1 54. 4×9 55. $10 - 7$ 56. 8×1

57. $15 - 7$ 58. 3×6 59. 4×1 60. $7 + 6$ 61. $8 + 9$ 62. 3×4 63. $3 + 4$

64. $1 + 0$ 65. $16 - 9$ 66. 5×4 67. $2 + 3$ 68. 6×5 69. $9 - 6$ 70. $8 + 7$

Lesson 7-7 • Multiplication Facts and Mixed Skills

Name _____

Problem Solving: Look for a Pattern

Janet finished writing a number pattern as homework for math class. Her paper fell on the kitchen floor and her dog walked across the paper with muddy paws. Now, some of the numbers are covered with mud! What numbers are covered with mud?

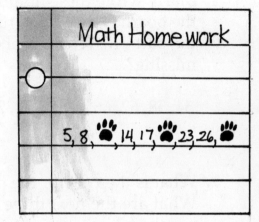

⭐ **SEE**

We know that the pattern looks like this

5, 8, 🐾, 14, 17, 🐾, 23, 26, 🐾 .

We want to find the numbers that come after

_____ , _____ , and _____.

⭐ **PLAN**

We can find out how Janet decided what number to use. We can look for a **pattern**.

⭐ **DO**

To get from 5 to 8, Janet _____.

To get from 14 to 17, she _____ , and to get from

23 to 26, she also _____.

The rule is to _____.

5,   8,   _____ ,   14,   17,   _____ ,   23,   26,   _____
      ↑   ↑   ↑   ↑   ↑   ↑   ↑   ↑
   add 3 add 3   add 3 add 3 add 3   add 3 add 3

⭐ **CHECK**

We can check by **adding 3** to each number.

5	8	11	14	17	20	23	26
+ 3	+ 3	+ 3	+ 3	+ 3	+ 3	+ 3	+ 3

We can also check by **subtracting 3** from each number.

29	26	23	20	17	14	11	8
− 3	− 3	− 3	− 3	− 3	− 3	− 3	− 3

Apply

Solve each problem.

1. Marty wrote these numbers on the board. What is the rule for the pattern? What number is missing?

   54, 58, 62, 66, _____ , 74, 78, 82

2. What is the rule for the pattern? What are the next three numbers?

   60, 65, 70, 75, _____ , _____ , _____

3. Complete Ben's pattern. Write the rule for the pattern

   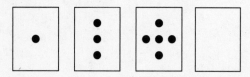

4. Continue the pattern.

   ★★◇★★◇★★◇★ _____

   _____ _____ _____

5. Jason wrote these numbers on a card. What is the rule for the pattern? What are the next three numbers?

   100, 150, 200, 250, _____ ,

   _____ , _____

6. Continue the pattern.

   ○■○○■■○○○■■■

   _____ _____ _____ _____ _____ _____

   _____ _____ _____

7. Elena dropped some globs of ink on this number pattern. What is the rule for the pattern? What numbers are under the globs of ink?

   1, 5, 9, ⬛ , 17, ⬛ , 25

8. Yoko wrote these numbers in her math notebook. Describe the rule for this pattern. What numbers are missing?

   40, 35, _____ , 25, 20, _____ ,

   _____ , 5, 0

Multiply.

1. $\begin{array}{r}7\\ \times 3\end{array}$ $\begin{array}{r}1\\ \times 3\end{array}$ $\begin{array}{r}1\\ \times 5\end{array}$ $\begin{array}{r}5\\ \times 8\end{array}$ $\begin{array}{r}4\\ \times 3\end{array}$ $\begin{array}{r}6\\ \times 0\end{array}$ $\begin{array}{r}3\\ \times 1\end{array}$ $\begin{array}{r}4\\ \times 9\end{array}$ $\begin{array}{r}8\\ \times 1\end{array}$

2. $\begin{array}{r}4\\ \times 5\end{array}$ $\begin{array}{r}0\\ \times 7\end{array}$ $\begin{array}{r}9\\ \times 5\end{array}$ $\begin{array}{r}1\\ \times 7\end{array}$ $\begin{array}{r}5\\ \times 3\end{array}$ $\begin{array}{r}4\\ \times 1\end{array}$ $\begin{array}{r}3\\ \times 6\end{array}$ $\begin{array}{r}1\\ \times 9\end{array}$ $\begin{array}{r}5\\ \times 0\end{array}$

3. $\begin{array}{r}3\\ \times 9\end{array}$ $\begin{array}{r}9\\ \times 0\end{array}$ $\begin{array}{r}3\\ \times 7\end{array}$ $\begin{array}{r}2\\ \times 8\end{array}$ $\begin{array}{r}2\\ \times 9\end{array}$ $\begin{array}{r}1\\ \times 6\end{array}$ $\begin{array}{r}5\\ \times 6\end{array}$ $\begin{array}{r}0\\ \times 6\end{array}$ $\begin{array}{r}2\\ \times 2\end{array}$

4. $\begin{array}{r}9\\ \times 2\end{array}$ $\begin{array}{r}3\\ \times 0\end{array}$ $\begin{array}{r}4\\ \times 8\end{array}$ $\begin{array}{r}0\\ \times 3\end{array}$ $\begin{array}{r}9\\ \times 3\end{array}$ $\begin{array}{r}3\\ \times 3\end{array}$ $\begin{array}{r}6\\ \times 1\end{array}$ $\begin{array}{r}8\\ \times 0\end{array}$ $\begin{array}{r}7\\ \times 4\end{array}$

5. $\begin{array}{r}4\\ \times 2\end{array}$ $\begin{array}{r}8\\ \times 4\end{array}$ $\begin{array}{r}7\\ \times 0\end{array}$ $\begin{array}{r}4\\ \times 4\end{array}$ $\begin{array}{r}6\\ \times 5\end{array}$ $\begin{array}{r}8\\ \times 5\end{array}$ $\begin{array}{r}4\\ \times 0\end{array}$ $\begin{array}{r}2\\ \times 6\end{array}$ $\begin{array}{r}0\\ \times 2\end{array}$

6. $\begin{array}{r}3\\ \times 8\end{array}$ $\begin{array}{r}6\\ \times 4\end{array}$ $\begin{array}{r}5\\ \times 9\end{array}$ $\begin{array}{r}1\\ \times 0\end{array}$ $\begin{array}{r}8\\ \times 3\end{array}$ $\begin{array}{r}0\\ \times 0\end{array}$ $\begin{array}{r}5\\ \times 2\end{array}$ $\begin{array}{r}5\\ \times 5\end{array}$ $\begin{array}{r}6\\ \times 2\end{array}$

7. $7 \times 2 =$ ___ $3 \times 4 =$ ___ $5 \times 4 =$ ___ $0 \times 5 =$ ___

8. $7 \times 0 =$ ___ $8 \times 2 =$ ___ $2 \times 3 =$ ___ $2 \times 0 =$ ___

9. $1 \times 7 =$ ___ $4 \times 1 =$ ___ $5 \times 2 =$ ___ $5 \times 7 =$ ___

10. In the problem $5 \times 3 = 15$,

the 5 is called a _____,

the 3 is called a _____,

and the 15 is called a _____.

CUMULATIVE ASSESSMENT

Circle the letter of the correct answer.

1 527 ◯ 636

    a. >
    b. <

2 What is the value of the 9 in 439,206?

    a. ones
    b. thousands
    c. ten thousands
    d. NG

3
$$\begin{array}{r} 592 \\ +\ 837 \\ \hline \end{array}$$

    a. 1,329
    b. 1,429
    c. 1,439
    d. NG

4
$$\begin{array}{r} \$36.26 \\ +\ \ \ 7.97 \\ \hline \end{array}$$

    a. $43.13
    b. $44.13
    c. $44.23
    d. NG

5
$$\begin{array}{r} 979 \\ 6,450 \\ +\ \ 926 \\ \hline \end{array}$$

    a. 7,354
    b. 8,255
    c. 8,354
    d. NG

6 Round to the nearest hundred to estimate the sum.
$$\begin{array}{r} 583 \\ +\ 268 \\ \hline \end{array}$$

    a. 700
    b. 800
    c. 900
    d. NG

7
$$\begin{array}{r} 802 \\ -\ 157 \\ \hline \end{array}$$

    a. 545
    b. 645
    c. 755
    d. NG

8
$$\begin{array}{r} \$78.56 \\ -\ 37.88 \\ \hline \end{array}$$

    a. $30.68
    b. $40.68
    c. $41.32
    d. NG

9 Round to the nearest hundred to estimate the difference.
$$\begin{array}{r} 723 \\ -\ 475 \\ \hline \end{array}$$

    a. 200
    b. 300
    c. 400
    d. NG

10

    a. 6:00
    b. 6:30
    c. 12:30
    d. NG

11 Find the perimeter.

65 cm
57 cm   57 cm
65 cm

    a. 114 cm
    b. 112 cm
    c. 130 cm
    d. NG

12 Choose the best estimate for the height of an adult.

    a. 2 cm
    b. 2 m
    c. 2 km

13 Choose the better estimate for the weight of a paper clip.

    a. 1 g
    b. 1 kg

☐ **score**

STOP

Multiplication Facts Through Nine

Reviewing Multiplication

Trudy helps her father take inventory in his hardware store every year. The first year she counted each object. Now she has learned a faster way to take inventory. Help Trudy count the number of boxes.

Trudy wants to know the total number of boxes.

She is counting _____ rows of boxes.

There are _____ boxes in each row.

Trudy can add the number of boxes.

6 + 6 + 6 + 6 + 6 = _____

But it would be faster to multiply.

5 × 6 = _____ $\begin{array}{r} 6 \\ \times 5 \\ \hline \end{array}$

Trudy can also think of it as 6 columns of _____ boxes each.

6 × 5 = _____ $\begin{array}{r} 5 \\ \times 6 \\ \hline \end{array}$

Trudy counts _____ boxes of light bulbs.

Getting Started

Use both addition and multiplication to show how many light bulbs are in the picture.

1.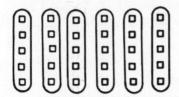

$4 + 4 + 4 + 4 + 4 + 4 + 4 =$ _____

$7 × 4 =$ _____

$4 × 7 =$ _____

Practice

Use both addition and multiplication to show how many objects are in each picture.

1.

$4 + 4 + 4 + 4 + 4 =$ _____

$5 \times 4 =$ _____

$4 \times 5 =$ _____

2.

$5 + 5 + 5 + 5 + 5 + 5 + 5 + 5 =$ _____

$8 \times 5 =$ _____

$5 \times 8 =$ _____

Multiply.

3.
$\begin{array}{r} 5 \\ \times\, 4 \\ \hline \end{array}$

4.
$\begin{array}{r} 8 \\ \times\, 5 \\ \hline \end{array}$

5.
$\begin{array}{r} 6 \\ \times\, 3 \\ \hline \end{array}$

6.
$\begin{array}{r} 0 \\ \times\, 7 \\ \hline \end{array}$

7.
$\begin{array}{r} 4 \\ \times\, 6 \\ \hline \end{array}$

8.
$\begin{array}{r} 8 \\ \times\, 1 \\ \hline \end{array}$

9.
$\begin{array}{r} 8 \\ \times\, 4 \\ \hline \end{array}$

10.
$\begin{array}{r} 6 \\ \times\, 5 \\ \hline \end{array}$

11.
$\begin{array}{r} 4 \\ \times\, 4 \\ \hline \end{array}$

12.
$\begin{array}{r} 3 \\ \times\, 0 \\ \hline \end{array}$

13.
$\begin{array}{r} 9 \\ \times\, 4 \\ \hline \end{array}$

14.
$\begin{array}{r} 3 \\ \times\, 8 \\ \hline \end{array}$

15.
$\begin{array}{r} 0 \\ \times\, 1 \\ \hline \end{array}$

16.
$\begin{array}{r} 5 \\ \times\, 5 \\ \hline \end{array}$

17. $7 \times 2 =$ _____

18. $3 \times 8 =$ _____

19. $5 \times 2 =$ _____

20. $1 \times 6 =$ _____

21. $6 \times 4 =$ _____

22. $3 \times 3 =$ _____

23. $8 \times 0 =$ _____

24. $7 \times 3 =$ _____

Problem Solving

Solve each problem.

25. Gina practices piano 2 hours a day, 3 days a week. How many hours does Gina practice each week?

26. A field goal is worth 3 points. Raul kicked 4 of them in one game. How many points did Raul score for his team?

Lesson 8-1 • Reviewing Multiplication

Name _____

Multiplying, the Factor 6

The Nature Club orders apples from the grocer for their spring hike. How many apples does the club order?

We want to know the total number of apples in the order.

The grocer puts _____ apples in each package.

He prepares _____ packages for the Nature Club.

We can add. **6 + 6 + 6 + 6 + 6 + 6 + 6 = _____**

We can also multiply.

$$7 \times 6 = \text{\underline{\hspace{1cm}}} \qquad \begin{array}{r} 6 \\ \times\ 7 \\ \hline \end{array}$$

We can also think of it as 6 groups of _____ apples each.

$$6 \times 7 = \text{\underline{\hspace{1cm}}} \qquad \begin{array}{r} 7 \\ \times\ 6 \\ \hline \end{array}$$

The Nature Club orders _____ apples.

Getting Started

Use both addition and multiplication to show how many oranges are in the picture.

1.

$$6 + 6 + 6 + 6 + 6 + 6 = \text{\underline{\hspace{1cm}}}$$

$$6 \times 6 = \text{\underline{\hspace{1cm}}}$$

Use both addition and multiplication to show how many pears are in the picture.

1.
$$6 + 6 + 6 + 6 + 6 + 6 + 6 + 6 + 6 = \underline{\quad}$$

$$9 \times 6 = \underline{\quad}$$

$$6 \times 9 = \underline{\quad}$$

Multiply.

2. $\begin{array}{r} 2 \\ \times 1 \\ \hline \end{array}$ 3. $\begin{array}{r} 2 \\ \times 3 \\ \hline \end{array}$ 4. $\begin{array}{r} 5 \\ \times 6 \\ \hline \end{array}$ 5. $\begin{array}{r} 3 \\ \times 5 \\ \hline \end{array}$ 6. $\begin{array}{r} 7 \\ \times 2 \\ \hline \end{array}$ 7. $\begin{array}{r} 4 \\ \times 7 \\ \hline \end{array}$ 8. $\begin{array}{r} 6 \\ \times 9 \\ \hline \end{array}$

9. $\begin{array}{r} 7 \\ \times 0 \\ \hline \end{array}$ 10. $\begin{array}{r} 5 \\ \times 8 \\ \hline \end{array}$ 11. $\begin{array}{r} 2 \\ \times 6 \\ \hline \end{array}$ 12. $\begin{array}{r} 4 \\ \times 4 \\ \hline \end{array}$ 13. $\begin{array}{r} 7 \\ \times 6 \\ \hline \end{array}$ 14. $\begin{array}{r} 1 \\ \times 3 \\ \hline \end{array}$ 15. $\begin{array}{r} 6 \\ \times 0 \\ \hline \end{array}$

16. $8 \times 6 = \underline{\quad}$ 17. $9 \times 5 = \underline{\quad}$ 18. $7 \times 4 = \underline{\quad}$ 19. $4 \times 6 = \underline{\quad}$

20. $6 \times 7 = \underline{\quad}$ 21. $8 \times 4 = \underline{\quad}$ 22. $3 \times 1 = \underline{\quad}$ 23. $2 \times 7 = \underline{\quad}$

24. $3 \times 3 = \underline{\quad}$ 25. $9 \times 6 = \underline{\quad}$ 26. $5 \times 7 = \underline{\quad}$ 27. $0 \times 5 = \underline{\quad}$

[Now Try This!]

It's Algebra!

One dozen is 12 or 6×2, so three dozen is $3 \times 6 \times 2$ or 18×2 or 36. Notice that when you multiply a number by 2, it is the same as doubling the number. You can think of 18×2 as $18 + 18$ or 36. Use this idea to find the missing numbers.

Seven dozen = $\underline{\quad} \times 6 \times 2 = \underline{\quad} \times 2 = \underline{\quad}$

Four dozen   = $\underline{\quad} \times 6 \times 2 = \underline{\quad} \times 2 = \underline{\quad}$

Six dozen   = $\underline{\quad} \times 6 \times 2 = \underline{\quad} \times 2 = \underline{\quad}$

Five dozen   = $\underline{\quad} \times 6 \times 2 = \underline{\quad} \times 2 = \underline{\quad}$

Multiplying, the Factor 7

Bananas grow best in a hot, damp climate. They grow in bunches at the end of long, tall stalks. How many bananas are there on this stalk?

We are looking for the total number of bananas on the stalk.

There are _____ bunches of bananas.

Each bunch has _____ bananas on it.

We can add. **7 + 7 + 7 + 7 + 7 + 7 + 7 + 7 = _____**

We can also multiply.

$$8 \times 7 = \underline{\hspace{1cm}} \qquad \begin{array}{r} 7 \\ \times\ 8 \\ \hline \end{array}$$

We can also think of it as 7 groups of _____ bananas each.

$$7 \times 8 = \underline{\hspace{1cm}} \qquad \begin{array}{r} 8 \\ \times\ 7 \\ \hline \end{array}$$

There are _____ bananas on the stalk.

Getting Started

Use both addition and multiplication to show how many bananas are in the picture.

1.

$7 + 7 + 7 + 7 + 7 + 7 + 7 = \underline{\hspace{1cm}}$

$7 \times 7 = \underline{\hspace{1cm}}$

Practice

Use addition and multiplication to show how many are in each picture.

1.

$7 + 7 + 7 + 7 =$ _____

$4 \times 7 =$ _____

$7 \times 4 =$ _____

2.

$7 + 7 + 7 + 7 + 7 =$ _____

$5 \times 7 =$ _____

$7 \times 5 =$ _____

Multiply.

3. $\begin{array}{r} 6 \\ \times 6 \\ \hline \end{array}$
4. $\begin{array}{r} 1 \\ \times 7 \\ \hline \end{array}$
5. $\begin{array}{r} 8 \\ \times 3 \\ \hline \end{array}$
6. $\begin{array}{r} 0 \\ \times 7 \\ \hline \end{array}$
7. $\begin{array}{r} 9 \\ \times 6 \\ \hline \end{array}$
8. $\begin{array}{r} 7 \\ \times 9 \\ \hline \end{array}$
9. $\begin{array}{r} 5 \\ \times 9 \\ \hline \end{array}$

10. $\begin{array}{r} 4 \\ \times 4 \\ \hline \end{array}$
11. $\begin{array}{r} 3 \\ \times 2 \\ \hline \end{array}$
12. $\begin{array}{r} 9 \\ \times 7 \\ \hline \end{array}$
13. $\begin{array}{r} 8 \\ \times 7 \\ \hline \end{array}$
14. $\begin{array}{r} 5 \\ \times 5 \\ \hline \end{array}$
15. $\begin{array}{r} 7 \\ \times 7 \\ \hline \end{array}$
16. $\begin{array}{r} 6 \\ \times 1 \\ \hline \end{array}$

17. $\begin{array}{r} 7 \\ \times 6 \\ \hline \end{array}$
18. $\begin{array}{r} 4 \\ \times 8 \\ \hline \end{array}$
19. $\begin{array}{r} 3 \\ \times 4 \\ \hline \end{array}$
20. $\begin{array}{r} 6 \\ \times 3 \\ \hline \end{array}$
21. $\begin{array}{r} 6 \\ \times 9 \\ \hline \end{array}$
22. $\begin{array}{r} 7 \\ \times 5 \\ \hline \end{array}$
23. $\begin{array}{r} 3 \\ \times 3 \\ \hline \end{array}$

24. $7 \times 8 =$ _____
25. $1 \times 8 =$ _____
26. $6 \times 8 =$ _____
27. $9 \times 4 =$ _____

28. $0 \times 0 =$ _____
29. $8 \times 6 =$ _____
30. $4 \times 6 =$ _____
31. $7 \times 3 =$ _____

Problem Solving

Solve each problem.

32. Rita bought 8 packages of cereal. Each package contained 7 ounces. How many ounces of cereal did Rita buy?

33. David ate 3 apricots with his lunch. He ate 4 more apricots for supper. How many apricots did David eat?

Lesson 8-3 • Multiplying, the Factor 7

Multiplying, the Factors 8 and 9

The boys and girls in the third grade like to play the game of Streets and Alleys. How many students are playing if there are 9 rows with 8 students in each row?

We want to know how many students are playing the game.

There are _____ rows of students.

There are _____ people in each row.

We can add. **8 + 8 + 8 + 8 + 8 + 8 + 8 + 8 + 8 = _____**

We can multiply.

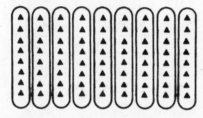

$9 \times 8 =$ _____
$$\begin{array}{r} 8 \\ \times\ 9 \\ \hline \end{array}$$

We can also think of this as 8 groups of _____ students each.

$8 \times 9 =$ _____
$$\begin{array}{r} 9 \\ \times\ 8 \\ \hline \end{array}$$

There are _____ students playing the game.

Getting Started

Use addition and multiplication to show how many are in the picture.

1.

$9 + 9 + 9 + 9 + 9 + 9 + 9 + 9 + 9 =$ _____

$9 \times 9 =$ _____

Practice

Use addition and multiplication to show how many are in the picture.

1. ⊚ ⊚ ⊚ ⊚ ⊚ ⊚ ⊚
⊚ ⊚ ⊚ ⊚ ⊚ ⊚ ⊚
⊚ ⊚ ⊚ ⊚ ⊚ ⊚ ⊚
⊚ ⊚ ⊚ ⊚ ⊚ ⊚ ⊚
⊚ ⊚ ⊚ ⊚ ⊚ ⊚ ⊚
⊚ ⊚ ⊚ ⊚ ⊚ ⊚ ⊚
⊚ ⊚ ⊚ ⊚ ⊚ ⊚ ⊚
⊚ ⊚ ⊚ ⊚ ⊚ ⊚ ⊚

$8 + 8 + 8 + 8 + 8 + 8 + 8 = $ ____

$7 \times 8 = $ ____

$8 \times 7 = $ ____

Multiply.

2.	6	3.	6	4.	0	5.	6	6.	9	7.	2	8.	1
	$\times 6$		$\times 9$		$\times 8$		$\times 8$		$\times 2$		$\times 8$		$\times 8$

9.	4	10.	6	11.	9	12.	8	13.	8	14.	9	15.	4
	$\times 4$		$\times 0$		$\times 7$		$\times 8$		$\times 9$		$\times 5$		$\times 9$

16. $7 \times 7 = $ ____   17. $9 \times 6 = $ ____   18. $5 \times 5 = $ ____   19. $1 \times 9 = $ ____

20. $7 \times 9 = $ ____   21. $5 \times 7 = $ ____   22. $8 \times 3 = $ ____   23. $7 \times 6 = $ ____

24. $3 \times 9 = $ ____   25. $8 \times 9 = $ ____   26. $6 \times 6 = $ ____   27. $4 \times 8 = $ ____

28. $7 \times 8 = $ ____   29. $0 \times 9 = $ ____   30. $9 \times 9 = $ ____   31. $7 \times 0 = $ ____

Problem Solving

Solve each problem.

32. Candles are sold 9 to a package. Tracy bought 6 packages. How many candles did she buy?

33. It takes 5 hours to roast a turkey. Mrs. Frank put the turkey in the oven at noon. At what time would the turkey be ready?

Basic Properties

It's Algebra!

There are some ideas that are important when we multiply.

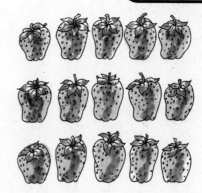

Order or Commutative Property

We can multiply in any order.

$$\begin{array}{c} 5 \\ \times\ 3 \\ \hline \end{array} \qquad \begin{array}{c} 3 \\ \times\ 5 \\ \hline \end{array}$$

$3 \times 5 =$ _____

$5 \times 3 =$ _____

Grouping or Associative Property

We can group any two factors.

$(4 \times 2) \times 3 =$? $\qquad$ $4 \times (2 \times 3) =$?

_____ $\times\ 3 =$ _____ $\qquad$ $4 \times$ _____ $=$ _____

Identity Property

Multiplying by 1 does not change the answer.

$3 \times 1 =$ _____ $\qquad$ $1 \times 3 =$ _____

Zero Property

Multiplying by 0 always results in 0.

$7 \times 0 =$ _____ $\qquad$ $0 \times 7 =$ _____

Getting Started

Multiply.

1. $\begin{array}{r} 0 \\ \times\ 0 \\ \hline \end{array}$ $\qquad$ 2. $\begin{array}{r} 6 \\ \times\ 4 \\ \hline \end{array}$ $\qquad$ 3. $\begin{array}{r} 4 \\ \times\ 6 \\ \hline \end{array}$ $\qquad$ 4. $\begin{array}{r} 3 \\ \times\ 1 \\ \hline \end{array}$

5. $5 \times 1 =$ _____ $\qquad$ 6. $7 \times 6 =$ _____ $\qquad$ 7. $6 \times 7 =$ _____ $\qquad$ 8. $0 \times 4 =$ _____

9. $(5 \times 1) \times 3 =$? $\qquad\qquad$ 10. $5 \times (1 \times 3) =$?

_____ $\times\ 3 =$ _____ $\qquad\qquad$ $5 \times$ _____ $=$ _____

11. $(5 \times 2) \times 2 =$? $\qquad\qquad$ 12. $5 \times (2 \times 2) =$?

_____ $\times\ 2 =$ _____ $\qquad\qquad$ $5 \times$ _____ $=$ _____

Practice

Multiply.

1. $\begin{array}{r} 6 \\ \times 0 \\ \hline \end{array}$
2. $\begin{array}{r} 1 \\ \times 9 \\ \hline \end{array}$
3. $\begin{array}{r} 8 \\ \times 7 \\ \hline \end{array}$
4. $\begin{array}{r} 4 \\ \times 1 \\ \hline \end{array}$
5. $\begin{array}{r} 3 \\ \times 9 \\ \hline \end{array}$
6. $\begin{array}{r} 9 \\ \times 3 \\ \hline \end{array}$
7. $\begin{array}{r} 0 \\ \times 4 \\ \hline \end{array}$

8. $\begin{array}{r} 8 \\ \times 8 \\ \hline \end{array}$
9. $\begin{array}{r} 5 \\ \times 1 \\ \hline \end{array}$
10. $\begin{array}{r} 1 \\ \times 8 \\ \hline \end{array}$
11. $\begin{array}{r} 8 \\ \times 1 \\ \hline \end{array}$
12. $\begin{array}{r} 9 \\ \times 6 \\ \hline \end{array}$
13. $\begin{array}{r} 5 \\ \times 7 \\ \hline \end{array}$
14. $\begin{array}{r} 7 \\ \times 5 \\ \hline \end{array}$

15. $4 \times 2 =$ _____
16. $0 \times 6 =$ _____
17. $8 \times 9 =$ _____
18. $3 \times 2 =$ _____

19. $0 \times 0 =$ _____
20. $4 \times 7 =$ _____
21. $6 \times 8 =$ _____
22. $7 \times 9 =$ _____

23. $(0 \times 3) \times 2 = ?$

    _____ $\times 2 =$ _____

24. $4 \times (1 \times 5) = ?$

    $4 \times$ _____ $=$ _____

25. $(2 \times 2) \times 3 = ?$

    _____ $\times 3 =$ _____

26. $(5 \times 1) \times 6 = ?$

    _____ $\times 6 =$ _____

27. $8 \times (3 \times 0) = ?$

    $8 \times$ _____ $=$ _____

28. $9 \times (1 \times 7) = ?$

    $9 \times$ _____ $=$ _____

Now Try This!

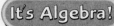

Circle the word or words that describe how the left side in each number sentence is different from the right side. Compute each side of the sentence.

1. $2 \times (1 \times 6) = (2 \times 1) \times 6$ order   grouping

    _____ $=$ _____

2. $3 \times (2 \times 0) = 0 \times (3 \times 2)$ order   grouping

    _____ $=$ _____

3. $(1 \times 4) \times (2 \times 3) = (3 \times 1) \times (2 \times 4)$ order   grouping

    _____ $=$ _____

Lesson 8-5 • Basic Properties

Name _____

Practicing Multiplication Facts

Multiply.

1. $\begin{array}{r}1\\\times3\end{array}$ $\begin{array}{r}2\\\times2\end{array}$ $\begin{array}{r}6\\\times3\end{array}$ $\begin{array}{r}7\\\times8\end{array}$ $\begin{array}{r}3\\\times5\end{array}$ $\begin{array}{r}3\\\times1\end{array}$ $\begin{array}{r}2\\\times0\end{array}$ $\begin{array}{r}4\\\times5\end{array}$ $\begin{array}{r}5\\\times3\end{array}$

2. $\begin{array}{r}9\\\times8\end{array}$ $\begin{array}{r}4\\\times2\end{array}$ $\begin{array}{r}6\\\times8\end{array}$ $\begin{array}{r}8\\\times5\end{array}$ $\begin{array}{r}3\\\times9\end{array}$ $\begin{array}{r}2\\\times6\end{array}$ $\begin{array}{r}9\\\times0\end{array}$ $\begin{array}{r}6\\\times0\end{array}$ $\begin{array}{r}3\\\times8\end{array}$

3. $\begin{array}{r}2\\\times5\end{array}$ $\begin{array}{r}0\\\times9\end{array}$ $\begin{array}{r}7\\\times5\end{array}$ $\begin{array}{r}8\\\times2\end{array}$ $\begin{array}{r}8\\\times8\end{array}$ $\begin{array}{r}7\\\times6\end{array}$ $\begin{array}{r}9\\\times5\end{array}$ $\begin{array}{r}6\\\times1\end{array}$ $\begin{array}{r}0\\\times2\end{array}$

4. $\begin{array}{r}1\\\times1\end{array}$ $\begin{array}{r}5\\\times5\end{array}$ $\begin{array}{r}4\\\times1\end{array}$ $\begin{array}{r}2\\\times8\end{array}$ $\begin{array}{r}4\\\times4\end{array}$ $\begin{array}{r}0\\\times0\end{array}$ $\begin{array}{r}7\\\times2\end{array}$ $\begin{array}{r}2\\\times4\end{array}$ $\begin{array}{r}3\\\times6\end{array}$

5. $\begin{array}{r}5\\\times9\end{array}$ $\begin{array}{r}0\\\times4\end{array}$ $\begin{array}{r}4\\\times7\end{array}$ $\begin{array}{r}1\\\times2\end{array}$ $\begin{array}{r}7\\\times3\end{array}$ $\begin{array}{r}1\\\times0\end{array}$ $\begin{array}{r}3\\\times3\end{array}$ $\begin{array}{r}6\\\times6\end{array}$ $\begin{array}{r}1\\\times6\end{array}$

6. $\begin{array}{r}7\\\times0\end{array}$ $\begin{array}{r}6\\\times9\end{array}$ $\begin{array}{r}0\\\times1\end{array}$ $\begin{array}{r}5\\\times8\end{array}$ $\begin{array}{r}7\\\times7\end{array}$ $\begin{array}{r}5\\\times6\end{array}$ $\begin{array}{r}9\\\times1\end{array}$ $\begin{array}{r}5\\\times1\end{array}$ $\begin{array}{r}4\\\times8\end{array}$

7. $\begin{array}{r}2\\\times9\end{array}$ $\begin{array}{r}0\\\times7\end{array}$ $\begin{array}{r}9\\\times3\end{array}$ $\begin{array}{r}5\\\times4\end{array}$ $\begin{array}{r}6\\\times2\end{array}$ $\begin{array}{r}9\\\times6\end{array}$ $\begin{array}{r}2\\\times3\end{array}$ $\begin{array}{r}7\\\times4\end{array}$ $\begin{array}{r}8\\\times4\end{array}$

8. $\begin{array}{r}6\\\times4\end{array}$ $\begin{array}{r}1\\\times4\end{array}$ $\begin{array}{r}8\\\times0\end{array}$ $\begin{array}{r}0\\\times8\end{array}$ $\begin{array}{r}4\\\times0\end{array}$ $\begin{array}{r}8\\\times3\end{array}$ $\begin{array}{r}9\\\times9\end{array}$ $\begin{array}{r}8\\\times1\end{array}$ $\begin{array}{r}3\\\times2\end{array}$

9. $\begin{array}{r}6\\\times5\end{array}$ $\begin{array}{r}5\\\times2\end{array}$ $\begin{array}{r}9\\\times7\end{array}$ $\begin{array}{r}4\\\times6\end{array}$ $\begin{array}{r}3\\\times0\end{array}$ $\begin{array}{r}1\\\times9\end{array}$ $\begin{array}{r}3\\\times7\end{array}$ $\begin{array}{r}3\\\times4\end{array}$ $\begin{array}{r}0\\\times5\end{array}$

10. $\begin{array}{r}8\\\times7\end{array}$ $\begin{array}{r}7\\\times1\end{array}$ $\begin{array}{r}4\\\times3\end{array}$ $\begin{array}{r}8\\\times9\end{array}$ $\begin{array}{r}0\\\times3\end{array}$ $\begin{array}{r}1\\\times8\end{array}$ $\begin{array}{r}8\\\times6\end{array}$ $\begin{array}{r}9\\\times2\end{array}$ $\begin{array}{r}1\\\times7\end{array}$

Practice

Complete each circle.

1.

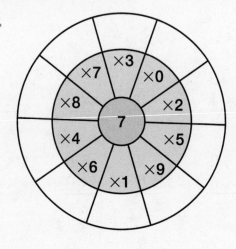

2.

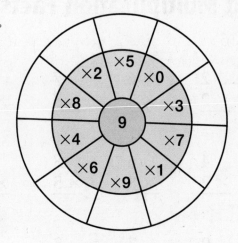

3.

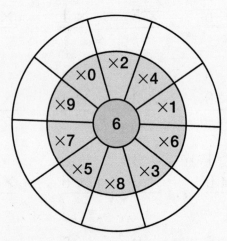

4.

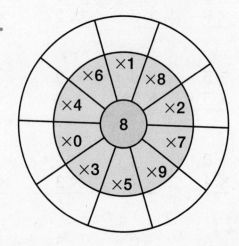

[Now Try This!]

These machines are programmed to multiply. Write the missing factors and products on the In and Out cards.

It's Algebra!

Lesson 8-6 • Practicing Multiplication Facts

Name _____

Problem Solving: Act It Out

Alia bought 36 square tiles to cover the rectangular floor of her bathroom. She used 9 tiles along the length of one wall. How many tiles wide is her bathroom?

⭐ SEE

Alia has _____ square tiles to cover her rectangular bathroom.

The bathroom is _____ tiles long.

⭐ PLAN

We can **act out** the problem by making a model with square tiles.

Make as many rows of 9 tiles as we can to find how many tiles wide Alia's bathroom is.

⭐ DO

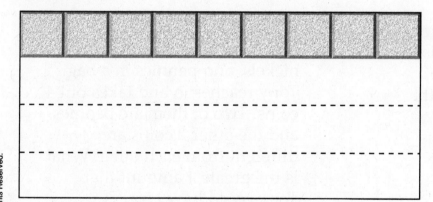

Alia's bathroom is _____ tiles wide

⭐ CHECK

Multiply the number of tiles in the length by the number of tiles in the width.

9 × _____ = _____

Apply

Act out each problem using people, name cards, or objects.

1. Ken, Linda, Maria, and Ryan are skiing down a hill. One boy is first and one boy is third. Maria is between Ken and Ryan. Ken is in front of Linda. In what order are they skiing down the hill?

2. The four students sitting in a row in a movie theater are Jake, Kayla, Megan, and Carlos. They are not sitting in that order. The girls are not sitting together but the boys are together. Kayla is sitting to the right of Carlos. Megan is sitting to the left of Jake. In what order are they sitting in the theater from left to right?

3. Amad planted some fruit trees in his yard. The apple tree is to the right of the garden. The plum tree is to the right of the apple tree and to the left of the cherry tree. Which tree is farthest from the garden?

4. Carlos put 37 CDs into boxes. Each box held 8 CDs. How many CDs were left over?

5. Anna, Cathy, Bruce, and Diego were walking in a single line to the lunchroom. One girl is first and the other girl is last. Bruce is walking after Diego. Diego is not walking after Anna. In what order are they walking to the lunchroom?

6. Four people meet at the park. Each person shakes the hand of the other. How many handshakes are there in all? Prove your answer.

7. There are quarters, dimes, nickels, and pennies in a bag. Tony reaches in and takes out 4 coins. Two of them are pennies, and the other 2 coins are different from each other. What is the greatest amount that Tony could have?

8. How many different ways can you make change for a dollar? Don't use any coin smaller than a nickel. Don't use any coin more than 4 times in any group.

Lesson 8-7 • Problem Solving: Act It Out

Multiply.

1. $\begin{array}{r} 9 \\ \times\, 9 \\ \hline \end{array}$
2. $\begin{array}{r} 8 \\ \times\, 7 \\ \hline \end{array}$
3. $\begin{array}{r} 5 \\ \times\, 5 \\ \hline \end{array}$
4. $\begin{array}{r} 7 \\ \times\, 9 \\ \hline \end{array}$
5. $\begin{array}{r} 7 \\ \times\, 6 \\ \hline \end{array}$
6. $\begin{array}{r} 6 \\ \times\, 9 \\ \hline \end{array}$
7. $\begin{array}{r} 9 \\ \times\, 5 \\ \hline \end{array}$

8. $\begin{array}{r} 8 \\ \times\, 5 \\ \hline \end{array}$
9. $\begin{array}{r} 5 \\ \times\, 7 \\ \hline \end{array}$
10. $\begin{array}{r} 7 \\ \times\, 8 \\ \hline \end{array}$
11. $\begin{array}{r} 7 \\ \times\, 7 \\ \hline \end{array}$
12. $\begin{array}{r} 7 \\ \times\, 9 \\ \hline \end{array}$
13. $\begin{array}{r} 9 \\ \times\, 6 \\ \hline \end{array}$
14. $\begin{array}{r} 8 \\ \times\, 9 \\ \hline \end{array}$

15. $\begin{array}{r} 9 \\ \times\, 8 \\ \hline \end{array}$
16. $\begin{array}{r} 6 \\ \times\, 8 \\ \hline \end{array}$
17. $\begin{array}{r} 8 \\ \times\, 6 \\ \hline \end{array}$
18. $\begin{array}{r} 8 \\ \times\, 8 \\ \hline \end{array}$
19. $\begin{array}{r} 6 \\ \times\, 6 \\ \hline \end{array}$
20. $\begin{array}{r} 8 \\ \times\, 9 \\ \hline \end{array}$
21. $\begin{array}{r} 6 \\ \times\, 5 \\ \hline \end{array}$

22. $7 \times 9 =$ _____
23. $7 \times 8 =$ _____
24. $6 \times 9 =$ _____
25. $6 \times 7 =$ _____

26. $9 \times 8 =$ _____
27. $6 \times 9 =$ _____
28. $6 \times 7 =$ _____
29. $7 \times 6 =$ _____

30. $7 \times 7 =$ _____
31. $8 \times 6 =$ _____
32. $8 \times 7 =$ _____
33. $9 \times 9 =$ _____

Solve each problem.

34. There are 6 rows of trees. Each row has 9 trees. How many trees are there?

35. Balloons are sold in packages of 8. Rhonda bought 7 packages. How many balloons did Rhonda buy?

36. Use the prices in the chart below to find the total cost of the order.

Sale	
Washers $1	
Hammers $9	
Screwdrivers $4	
Wrenches $3	
Pliers $7	

Order Form			
Number	Item	Cost	Total
5	Hammers		
4	Wrenches		
9	Pliers		
		Total Cost	

Circle the letter of the correct answer.

1   627 ◯ 623

     a. >
     b. <

2   What is the value of the 0 in 328,650?

     a. tens
     b. hundreds
     c. thousands
     d. NG

3 $28.37
    + 9.26

     a. $37.53
     b. $37.63
     c. $38.63
     d. NG

4   325
     87
   + 5,682

     a. 5,104
     b. 6,004
     c. 6,104
     d. NG

5   Round to the nearest hundred to estimate the sum.
     575
   + 385

     a. 900
     b. 800
     c. 700
     d. NG

6   703
   − 259

     a. 344
     b. 444
     c. 556
     d. NG

7 $39.26
   − 8.75

     a. $20.51
     b. $30.51
     c. $31.51
     d. NG

8   Round to the nearest hundred to estimate the difference.
     712
   − 379

     a. 300
     b. 400
     c. 500
     d. NG

9

     a. 7:15
     b. 8:15
     c. 3:40
     d. NG

10   Find the perimeter.

87 m   87 m
    125 m

     a. 174 m
     b. 212 m
     c. 299 m
     d. NG

11   Choose the better estimate of length.

     a. 6 ft
     b. 6 yd

12   Choose the better estimate of weight.

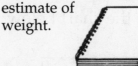

     a. 8 oz
     b. 8 lb

13

     a. $4 \times 5 = 20$
     b. $5 \times 5 = 25$
     c. $6 \times 5 = 30$
     d. NG

☐   score

Multiplication by 1-Digit Numbers

Multiplying by 10 and 100

Ted is getting ready for the Penny Toss game. How many pennies does he have stacked? How many pennies does he have in jars?

There are _____ stacks of 10 pennies each.

To find the total number of pennies in the stacks,

we multiply _____ by 10. _____ × 10 = _____

There are _____ pennies in stacks.

There are _____ jars with 100 pennies in each jar.

To find the total number of pennies in the jars,

we multiply _____ by 100. _____ × 100 = _____

There are _____ pennies in jars.

Look for a pattern in these multiplication problems.

5 × 1 = 5
5 × 10 = 50
5 × 100 = 500

Getting Started

Complete the pattern.

1. 8 × 1 = _____

   8 × 10 = _____

   8 × 100 = _____

2. 4 × 1 = _____

   4 × 10 = _____

   4 × 100 = _____

3. $5 × 1 = _____

   $5 × 10 = _____

   $5 × 100 = _____

Multiply.

4. 6 × 10 = _____

5. 4 × 10 = _____

6. $2 × 100 = _____

Practice

Complete each pattern.

1. $7 \times 1 =$ _____

   $7 \times 10 =$ _____

   $7 \times 100 =$ _____

2. $3 \times 1 =$ _____

   $3 \times 10 =$ _____

   $3 \times 100 =$ _____

3. $1 \times 1 =$ _____

   $1 \times 10 =$ _____

   $1 \times 100 =$ _____

4. $9 \times 1 =$ _____

   $9 \times 10 =$ _____

   $9 \times 100 =$ _____

5. $\$6 \times 1 =$ _____

   $\$6 \times 10 =$ _____

   $\$6 \times 100 =$ _____

6. $\$2 \times 1 =$ _____

   $\$2 \times 10 =$ _____

   $\$2 \times 100 =$ _____

Multiply.

7. $4 \times 10 =$ _____

8. $9 \times 100 =$ _____

9. $3 \times 1 =$ _____

10. $5 \times 100 =$ _____

11. $7 \times 100 =$ _____

12. $8 \times 10 =$ _____

13. $2 \times \$100 =$ _____

14. $3 \times 100 =$ _____

15. $8 \times 100 =$ _____

16. $1 \times 10 =$ _____

17. $5 \times 10 =$ _____

18. $5 \times 100 =$ _____

19. $4 \times \$10 =$ _____

20. $3 \times 10 =$ _____

21. $\$3 \times 100 =$ _____

Now Try This!

It's Algebra!

Think about each of these statements. All of these statements express the same idea.

$$4 \text{ oranges} + 6 \text{ oranges} = 10 \text{ oranges}$$
$$4 \text{ sixes} + 6 \text{ sixes} = 10 \text{ sixes}$$
$$(4 \times 6) + (6 \times 6) = 10 \times 6 = 60$$

Now use this idea to solve each problem.

$(2 \times 6) + (8 \times 6) =$ _____ $\times 6 =$ _____ $(3 \times 8) + (7 \times 8) =$ _____ $\times 8 =$ _____

$(5 \times 7) + (5 \times 7) =$ _____ $\times 7 =$ _____ $(6 \times 3) + (4 \times 3) =$ _____ $\times 3 =$ _____

$(1 \times 9) + (9 \times 9) =$ _____ $\times 9 =$ _____ $(4 \times 5) + (6 \times 5) =$ _____ $\times 5 =$ _____

Lesson 9-1 • Multiplying by 10 and 100

Multiplying Multiples of 10, 100, and 1,000

Mr. Wang cleaned out his garage and found some money hidden on a back shelf. How many pennies are in rolls? How many pennies are in bags?

To find the total number of pennies in

rolls, multiply _____ times 50. _____ × 50 = _____

To find the total number of pennies in bags,

multiply _____ times 500. _____ × 500 = _____

There are _____ pennies in rolls.

There are _____ pennies in bags.

Look for a pattern in these multiplication examples.

$$4 \times 5 = 20$$
$$4 \times 50 = 200$$
$$4 \times 500 = 2{,}000$$
$$4 \times 5{,}000 = 20{,}000$$

Getting Started

Use patterns to find each product.

1. $3 \times 2 =$ _____
   $3 \times 20 =$ _____
   $3 \times 200 =$ _____
   $3 \times 2{,}000 =$ _____

2. $7 \times \$6 =$ _____
   $7 \times \$60 =$ _____
   $7 \times \$600 =$ _____
   $7 \times \$6{,}000 =$ _____

3. $3 \times 5 =$ _____
   $3 \times 50 =$ _____
   $3 \times 500 =$ _____
   $3 \times 5{,}000 =$ _____

Multiply.

4. $4 \times 300 =$ _____

5. $9 \times \$20 =$ _____

6. $2 \times 4{,}000 =$ _____

Practice

Use patterns to find each product.

1. $8 \times 9 =$ _____

    $8 \times 90 =$ _____

    $8 \times 900 =$ _____

2. $2 \times \$5 =$ _____

    $2 \times \$50 =$ _____

    $2 \times \$500 =$ _____

3. $6 \times 8 =$ _____

    $6 \times 80 =$ _____

    $6 \times 800 =$ _____

4. $6 \times 4 =$ _____

    $6 \times 40 =$ _____

    $6 \times 400 =$ _____

    $6 \times 4,000 =$ _____

5. $5 \times 7 =$ _____

    $5 \times 70 =$ _____

    $5 \times 700 =$ _____

    $5 \times 7,000 =$ _____

6. $\$8 \times 7 =$ _____

    $\$8 \times 70 =$ _____

    $\$8 \times 700 =$ _____

    $\$8 \times 7,000 =$ _____

Multiply.

7. $5 \times 50 =$ _____

8. $2 \times 800 =$ _____

9. $7 \times 4,000 =$ _____

10. $3 \times 600 =$ _____

11. $9 \times 5,000 =$ _____

12. $0 \times 500 =$ _____

13. $6 \times 6,000 =$ _____

14. $\$3 \times 300 =$ _____

15. $4 \times 800 =$ _____

16. $\$3 \times 900 =$ _____

17. $9 \times 60 =$ _____

18. $3 \times 2,000 =$ _____

19. $\$4 \times 700 =$ _____

20. $9 \times 90 =$ _____

21. $5 \times 100 =$ _____

Problem Solving

Solve each problem.

22. Pencils are sold in packages of 20 each. The school store orders 9 packages. How many pencils does the store order?

23. A jet aircraft can travel 500 miles in an hour. How far can the jet travel in 3 hours?

24. Captain Barker flew 2,500 miles on Monday. She flew another 1,600 miles on Tuesday. How far did she fly both days?

25. A television set can be purchased for $200. How much do 7 sets cost?

Name _____

Multiplying by 1-Digit Factors, No Regrouping

Magda's dog eats one bag of dog food each week. How many ounces of dog food does her pet eat in 3 weeks?

We want the number of ounces of dog food eaten in ____ weeks.

Magda's dog eats ____ ounces of dog food in 1 week.

To find the total number of ounces, we multiply ____ by ____.

$3 \times 132 =$ ___	**Multiply ones.** 3×2 ones $= 6$ ones	**Multiply tens.** 3×3 tens $= 9$ tens	**Multiply hundreds.** 3×1 hundred $= 3$ hundreds

H	T	O
1	3	2
×		3

H	T	O
1	3	2
×		3
		6

H	T	O
1	3	2
×		3
	9	6

H	T	O
1	3	2
×		3
3	9	6

Magda's dog eats ____ ounces of dog food in 3 weeks.

Getting Started

Multiply.

1. 43
   × 2

2. 143
   × 2

3. 11
   × 8

4. 120
   × 4

Copy and multiply.

5. 3×21

6. 3×213

7. 1×48

8. 2×423

Practice

Multiply.

1. 32
   × 3

2. 124
   × 2

3. 242
   × 2

4. 41
   × 2

5. 112
   × 3

6. 310
   × 3

7. 121
   × 4

8. 33
   × 2

9. 131
   × 2

10. 313
    × 3

11. 142
    × 2

12. 212
    × 4

13. 121
    × 3

14. 333
    × 3

15. 414
    × 2

16. 31
    × 3

17. 444
    × 2

18. 536
    × 1

19. 344
    × 2

20. 212
    × 4

Copy and multiply.

21. 5×111

22. 1×987

23. 4×21

24. 3×223

25. 2×341

26. 3×33

27. 2×431

28. 1×892

29. 2×44

30. 3×232

31. 1×793

32. 2×143

Problem Solving

Solve each problem.

33. Martha has 3 sacks of marbles. Each sack contains 120 marbles. How many marbles does Martha have?

34. Lucia bought a clock for $29.36. She gave the clerk $30. How much change should Lucia get?

35. On Sunday, 2,456 people visited the art museum. We know 956 of the visitors were children. How many of the visitors were adults?

36. Sean ran 5 kilometers each day. How far did Sean run in 21 days?

Lesson 9-3 • Multiplying by 1-Digit Factors, No Regrouping

Understanding Multiplication by 1-Digit Factors

Jason collects stamps from foreign countries. He has filled 4 scrapbook pages with the same number of stamps. How many stamps has he collected?

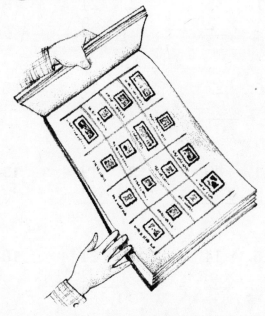

We want to find the number of stamps Jason has saved so far.

Each page contains _____ stamps.

Jason has filled _____ pages with stamps.

To find the total number of stamps,

we multiply _____ by _____.

4 × 16 = ☐	**Multiply ones.** **Regroup.** 4 × 6 ones = 24 ones 24 ones = 2 tens 4 ones	**Multiply tens.** **Regroup.** 4 × 1 ten = 4 tens 4 tens + 2 tens = 6 tens

```
  T | O              T | O              T | O
                       2                  2
  1 | 6              1 | 6              1 | 6
×   | 4            ×   | 4            ×   | 4
                       | 4              6 | 4
```

Jason has collected _____ stamps.

Getting Started

Multiply.

1. 25   2. 18   3. 32   4. 22
  × 3   × 4   × 3   × 5

Copy and multiply.

5. 19 × 4   6. 23 × 4   7. 14 × 6   8. 48 × 2

Practice

Multiply.

1.	35 × 2	2.	24 × 3	3.	16 × 5	4.	47 × 2	5.	33 × 3
6.	27 × 3	7.	19 × 4	8.	12 × 5	9.	26 × 3	10.	18 × 4
11.	49 × 1	12.	19 × 3	13.	13 × 4	14.	24 × 4	15.	37 × 2
16.	14 × 6	17.	24 × 2	18.	12 × 7	19.	38 × 2	20.	12 × 8

Copy and multiply.

21. 47×2 22. 36×2 23. 14×7 24. 16×3

25. 23×4 26. 17×4 27. 31×1 28. 11×5

29. 18×3 30. 12×6 31. 14×5 32. 42×2

[Now Try This!]

Study the following pattern.

$47 \times 2 = 40$ twos $+ 7$ twos $= 80 + 14 = 94$

Use the pattern to help you complete the rest of the multiplications.

1. $24 \times 3 = $ _____ threes $+$ _____ threes $= $ _____ $+$ _____ $= $ _____

2. $37 \times 2 = $ _____ twos $+$ _____ twos $= $ _____ $+$ _____ $= $ _____

3. $17 \times 4 = $ _____ fours $+$ _____ fours $= $ _____ $+$ _____ $= $ _____

4. $12 \times 7 = $ _____ sevens $+$ _____ sevens $= $ _____ $+$ _____ $= $ _____

Lesson 9-4 • Understanding Multiplication by 1-Digit Factors

Multiplying by 1-Digit Factors, One Regrouping

A railroad hired a crew of men to repair
its tracks. How many miles of track has the
crew repaired so far?

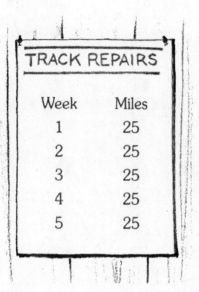

We want to find the total number of miles repaired.

The crew repaired _____ miles of track each week.

The men have worked for _____ weeks.

To find the total number of miles repaired,

we multiply _____ by _____.

Multiply the ones. Regroup if needed.	Multiply the tens. Add any extra tens.

$$\begin{array}{r} \overset{2}{2}5 \\ \times\ 5 \\ \hline 5 \end{array} \qquad \begin{array}{r} \overset{2}{2}5 \\ \times\ 5 \\ \hline 125 \end{array}$$

The crew has repaired _____ miles of track.

Getting Started

Multiply.

1. $\begin{array}{r} 37 \\ \times\ 3 \\ \hline \end{array}$
2. $\begin{array}{r} 48 \\ \times\ 4 \\ \hline \end{array}$
3. $\begin{array}{r} 29 \\ \times\ 6 \\ \hline \end{array}$
4. $\begin{array}{r} 82 \\ \times\ 7 \\ \hline \end{array}$

Copy and multiply.

5. 67×9
6. 73×3
7. 52×8
8. 9×81

Practice

Multiply.

1. 67
    × 4

2. 39
    × 6

3. 55
    × 7

4. 79
    × 2

5. 80
    × 8

6. 45
    × 7

7. 71
    × 8

8. 96
    × 7

9. 93
    × 2

10. 47
    × 3

11. 64
    × 9

12. 56
    × 4

13. 87
    × 8

14. 60
    × 6

15. 39
    × 7

16. 72
    × 3

17. 94
    × 9

18. 28
    × 6

19. 46
    × 8

20. 76
    × 5

21. 53
    × 7

22. 49
    × 8

23. 76
    × 2

24. 43
    × 4

25. 86
    × 5

Copy and multiply.

26. 52×6

27. 9×68

28. 43×6

29. 8×26

30. 75×3

31. 40×9

32. 9×17

33. 7×88

34. 5×34

35. 7×48

36. 57×6

37. 84×8

Problem Solving

Solve each problem.

38. Apollo 16 orbited the Moon 64 times. Each orbit took 4 hours. How many hours did Apollo 16 orbit the Moon?

39. Soyuz 19 orbited the Earth 96 times. Apollo 18 orbited the Earth 136 times. How many more orbits did Apollo 18 make?

Lesson 9-5 • Multiplying by 1-Digit Factors, One Regrouping

Name _____

Multiplying by 1-Digit Factors, Two Regroupings

Mr. Harris made 4 round trips on business from Ellis to Washington. How many travel miles should Mr. Harris record on his expense report?

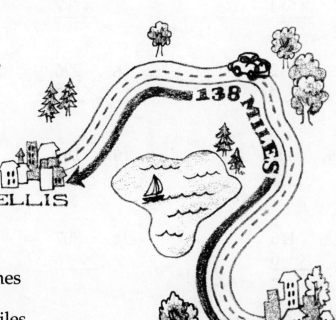

Mr. Harris wants to know how many miles he drove, so he can fill out his expense report.

The distance between Ellis and

Washington is ____ miles.

A round trip between the cities is 2 times

the distance between them, or ____ miles.

Mr. Harris made ____ round trips.

Multiply the ones. Regroup if needed.	Multiply the tens. Add any extra tens. Regroup if needed.	Multiply the hundreds. Add any extra hundreds.

$$\begin{array}{r} 2 \\ 27\textbf{6} \\ \times\ \ 4 \\ \hline 4 \end{array}$$

$$\begin{array}{r} 3\,2 \\ 27\textbf{6} \\ \times\ \ 4 \\ \hline 0\textbf{4} \end{array}$$

$$\begin{array}{r} 3 \\ 27\textbf{6} \\ \times\ \ 4 \\ \hline 1,1\textbf{0}4 \end{array}$$

Mr. Harris should record _____ miles on his expense report.

Getting Started

Multiply.

1. 246
   × 3

2. 508
   × 7

3. 621
   × 5

4. 835
   × 7

Copy and multiply.

5. 623 × 6   6. 290 × 4   7. 257 × 8   8. 399 × 9

Practice

Multiply.

1. 326×4

2. 845×7

3. 329×9

4. 334×6

5. 212×3

6. 296×8

7. 427×2

8. 725×5

9. 487×7

10. 183×2

11. 675×9

12. 526×3

13. 416×6

14. 807×6

15. 219×5

16. 438×7

Copy and multiply.

17. 157×8

18. 4×538

19. 175×9

20. 416×3

21. 239×7

22. 757×2

23. 5×919

24. 9×630

25. 4×212

26. 8×326

27. 808×3

28. 5×394

Problem Solving

Solve each problem.

29. Juanita started with $24.50. She spent $19.38. How much money did she have left?

30. Bill bought a sweater for $29.50 and a shirt for $16.37. How much did he spend?

31. Each weekday for one week, 146 lunches were served in the school cafeteria. How many lunches were served?

32. The custodian set up 8 rows of chairs, with 125 chairs in each row. How many chairs did the custodian set up?

Lesson 9-6 • Multiplying by 1-Digit Factors, Two Regroupings

Multiplying Money

Erica is starting a lawn-mowing service.
On one Saturday, she mows lawns for
5 hours. How much money does she earn?

*Lawn-mowing
Services
$3.75 an hour
call Erica Gordon
555-355-9612*

We want to know how much money
Erica earns for 5 hours of work.

Erica earns _____ per hour
for mowing lawns.

She works for _____ hours on Saturday.

To find the total amount of money Erica earns,

we multiply _____ by _____.

Multiply the pennies. Regroup if needed.	Multiply the dimes. Add any extra dimes. Regroup if needed. Write the decimal point in the product.	Multiply the dollars. Add any extra dollars. Write the dollar sign in the product.
$$\begin{array}{r} {}^{2}\\ \$3.75 \\ \times\quad 5 \\ \hline 5 \end{array}$$	$$\begin{array}{r} {}^{3\,2}\\ \$3.75 \\ \times\quad 5 \\ \hline .75 \end{array}$$	$$\begin{array}{r} {}^{3}\\ \$3.75 \\ \times\quad 5 \\ \hline \$18.75 \end{array}$$

Erica earns _____ .

Getting Started

Multiply.

1. $$\begin{array}{r} \$2.36 \\ \times\quad 4 \end{array}$$

2. $$\begin{array}{r} \$1.81 \\ \times\quad 6 \end{array}$$

3. $$\begin{array}{r} \$4.87 \\ \times\quad 3 \end{array}$$

4. $$\begin{array}{r} \$6.50 \\ \times\quad 7 \end{array}$$

Copy and multiply

5. $6.07 × 9

6. $5.43 × 8

7. $9.16 × 2

8. $7.68 × 5

Practice

Multiply.

1. $6.45 × 3	2. $4.57 × 9	3. $3.87 × 6	4. $4.81 × 4
5. $8.32 × 8	6. $2.79 × 5	7. $7.23 × 7	8. $9.10 × 2
9. $1.71 × 8	10. $5.39 × 4	11. $7.05 × 5	12. $6.21 × 8

Copy and multiply.

13. $2.76 × 2   14. $7.31 × 9   15. $1.89 × 7   16. $4.66 × 3

17. $8.96 × 6   18. $5.83 × 4   19. $3.29 × 5   20. $6.83 × 8

Now Try This!

A prime number is one having only two factors, itself and 1.
For example, 5 is a prime number because its only factors are 5 and 1.

$$5 × 1 = 5$$

Numbers that are not prime are called composites. For example, 6 is a composite because its factors include 1, 2, 3, and 6.

$$1 × 6 = 6 \qquad 2 × 3 = 6$$

List all the factors of the numbers below. Then tell whether each number is a prime or a composite.

Number	Factors	Prime or Composite
7	1, 7	prime
2		
9		
21		
17		
28		

Lesson 9-7 • Multiplying Money

Estimating Products

Sam collected acorns for a project.
Each bag contains about 219 acorns.
About how many acorns did
Sam collect?

We need to estimate how
many acorns Sam collected.

Sam collected _____ bags of acorns.

There are about _____ acorns in each bag.

To estimate, we round the number of
acorns in each bag to the nearest
hundred. Then we multiply by the
number of bags.

$$219 \xrightarrow{\text{rounds to}} \begin{array}{r} 200 \\ \times\ 5 \\ \hline \end{array}$$

Sam collected about _____ acorns.

Getting Started

Round to the nearest ten to estimate each product. Show your work.

1. $\begin{array}{r} 67 \\ \times\ 8 \\ \hline \end{array}$	2. $\begin{array}{r} 59 \\ \times\ 6 \\ \hline \end{array}$	3. $\begin{array}{r} 34 \\ \times\ 9 \\ \hline \end{array}$	4. $\begin{array}{r} 98 \\ \times\ 4 \\ \hline \end{array}$

Round to the nearest hundred or dollar to estimate each product.

5. $\begin{array}{r} 499 \\ \times\ 5 \\ \hline \end{array}$	6. $\begin{array}{r} 712 \\ \times\ 6 \\ \hline \end{array}$	7. $\begin{array}{r} \$1.97 \\ \times\ 2 \\ \hline \end{array}$	8. $\begin{array}{r} 149 \\ \times\ 3 \\ \hline \end{array}$

Practice

Round to the nearest ten to estimate each product. Show your work.

1. 95
    × 6

2. 27
    × 8

3. 43
    × 3

4. 58
    × 7

5. 12
    × 4

6. 35
    × 9

7. 67
    × 5

8. 89
    × 2

Round to the nearest hundred or dollar to estimate each product.

9. 138
    × 6

10. $3.27
    ×   9

11. 439
    × 4

12. 689
    × 8

13. 297
    × 6

14. 278
    × 4

15. $12.50
    ×   3

16. 115
    × 2

Problem Solving

Estimate each answer by rounding each amount to the nearest dollar.

Sports Equipment	
Dartboard $12.50	Golf balls $1.38
Tennis racket $29.15	Racquetball racket $28.15
Can of tennis balls $2.97	Basketballs $6.89

17. About what is the cost of a tennis racket and a can of tennis balls?

18. About how much less than the dartboard is the basketball?

19. About what is the cost of 8 golf balls?

20. About how much more is the tennis racket than the racquetball racket?

Lesson 9-8 • Estimating Products

Name _____

Problem Solving: Try, Check, Revise

Taro has 10 coins with a value of 80¢. He has dimes and nickels only. How many of each kind of coin does Taro have?

 SEE

Taro has _____ coins. The total amount is _____.

The coins are _____ and _____ only.

 PLAN

Try to guess the number of dimes and nickels.

Check your guess by adding the values of the dimes and nickels to see if the total is 80¢.

Revise your guess if it does not equal _____. Make a reasonable second guess. You can revise your guesses several times until you find the correct answer.

⭐ **DO**

Guess 1   5 dimes and 5 nickels

    $5 \times 10¢ =$ _____ and $5 \times 5¢ =$ _____

    _____ + _____ = _____   Too low!

Guess 2   6 dimes and 4 nickels

    $6 \times 10¢ =$ _____ and $4 \times 5¢ =$ _____

    _____ + _____ = _____   Correct!

Taro has _____ dimes and _____ nickels.

 **CHECK**

_____ dimes and _____ nickels is _____ coins.

Apply

**Try, check, and revise to solve each problem.
Use the dartboard to answer exercises 1, 2, and 3.**

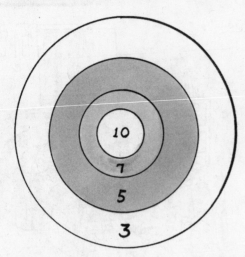

1. Katlyn played the dart game at the fair and scored exactly 24 points using 3 darts. Where might her darts have landed?

2. Dario played the dart game and scored exactly 8 points using 3 darts. Where did his darts land?

3. All 3 of your darts hit the dartboard. What are the highest and lowest scores you can get? Explain.

4. There are 8 bicycles and tricycles parked at a bike stand. There is a total of 18 wheels. How many bicycles and tricycles are there?

5. Bianca has 11 coins with a value of 70¢. All the coins are dimes and nickels. How many of each coin does she have?

6. Put each of the numbers from 1 to 6 in a circle so each side of the triangle has a sum of 9.

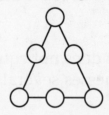

7. The sum of two numbers is 40. The numbers are 2 apart. What are the numbers?

8. Mary is twice as old as Joe. Lisa is 3 years older than Joe. The sum of all three ages is 23. How old is each child?

Calculator: Using the Equals Key

Mr. Roberts deposits $150 in his savings account each month. He has $300 in his account now. How much money will Mr. Roberts have in his account in 4 more months?

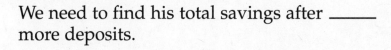

We need to find his total savings after _____ more deposits.

The current balance in Mr. Roberts' account is _____.

He will deposit _____ in his account each month. To find the total savings, we can use the calculator to add each deposit to the current balance.

300 $\boxed{+}$ 150 $\boxed{+}$ 150 $\boxed{+}$ 150 $\boxed{+}$ 150 $\boxed{=}$ $\overline{(\qquad)}$

Mr. Roberts will have _____ in his account in 4 months.

The equals key can be used to shorten the code for repeated addition or subtraction.

Every time we press the $\boxed{=}$ key, the number in front of the $\boxed{=}$ is added or subtracted. In this problem, we add the number 4 times, so we press the $\boxed{=}$ key 4 times.

300 $\boxed{+}$ 150 $\boxed{=}$ $\boxed{=}$ $\boxed{=}$ $\boxed{=}$ $\overline{(\qquad)}$

In the problem

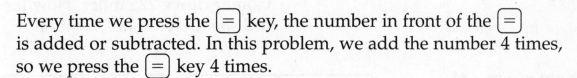

2 $\boxed{+}$ 3 $\boxed{+}$ 3 $\boxed{+}$ 3 $\boxed{+}$ 3 $\boxed{+}$ 3 $\boxed{=}$ $\overline{(\qquad)}$,

we add the number 5 times, so we press the $\boxed{=}$ key 5 times.

2 $\boxed{+}$ 3 $\boxed{=}$ $\boxed{=}$ $\boxed{=}$ $\boxed{=}$ $\boxed{=}$ $\overline{(\qquad)}$

Practice

1. 405 (+) 3 (+) 3 (+) 3 (=) ⬭

2. 405 (+) 3 (=) (=) (=) ⬭

3. 34 (+) 34 (=) (=) (=) ⬭

4. 34 (+) 34 (+) 34 (+) 34 (=) ⬭

5. 89 (+) 89 (+) 89 (+) 89 (=) ⬭

6. 89 (+) 89 (=) (=) (=) ⬭

7. 225 (−) 5 (−) 5 (−) 5 (−) 5 (=) ⬭

8. 225 (−) 5 (=) (=) (=) (=) ⬭

9. 49 (−) 7 (=) (=) (=) (=) ⬭

10. 975 (+) 975 (=) (=) (=) ⬭

11. 16 (−) 2 (=) (=) (=) (=) (=) ⬭

12. 720 (−) 240 (=) (=) (=) ⬭

Problem Solving

Use your calculator to solve each problem.

13. Heather bought a bike that costs $215. She gave a down payment of $40. She will pay $35 a month until the bike is paid for. How much will she still owe after 3 months?

14. Mrs. Gomez took a 7-day vacation. On the first day she drove 268 miles. On the second day she drove 196 miles. On each of the other days, Mrs. Gomez drove 225 miles. How far did she drive on her vacation?

15. At the right is a record of Maya's savings account. Add each deposit and subtract each withdrawal to find the balance.

Date	Deposit	Withdrawal	Balance
Nov. 1	$36		$36
Nov. 8	$68		
Nov. 13		$27	
Nov. 15	$49		
Nov. 20		$32	
Nov. 23	$75		
Nov. 28	$63		
Nov. 30		$115	

Lesson 9-10 • Calculator: Using the Equals Key

Multiply.

1.   32
   × 3

2.   24
   × 4

3.   13
   × 3

4.   34
   × 2

5.   122
   × 4

6.   333
   × 3

7.   214
   × 2

8.   221
   × 4

9.   48
   × 6

10.   37
    × 8

11.   59
    × 4

12.   86
    × 7

13.   138
    × 5

14.   376
    × 9

15.   529
    × 6

16.   862
    × 3

17. $1.86
    ×   7

18. $7.83
    ×   4

19. $6.39
    ×   8

20. $4.08
    ×   9

Solve each problem.

21. Penny worked out in the gym for 56 minutes every day. How many minutes did Penny work out each week?

22. Jack fills 138 crates of apples each day. He worked 5 days. How many crates of apples does Jack fill?

23. Ted works 8 hours on Saturday. He earns $5.26 each hour. How much does Ted make?

24. $5.62 × 3 = $16.86

$5.62 is a _____ and

$16.86 is a _____.

Circle the letter of the correct answer.

1 415 ◯ 216

    a. <
    b. >

2 What is the value of the 3 in 213,706?

    a. tens
    b. hundreds
    c. thousands
    d. NG

3
$$\begin{array}{r} \$16.27 \\ + \ \ 4.38 \end{array}$$

    a. $19.65
    b. $20.65
    c. $21.65
    d. NG

4
$$\begin{array}{r} 3,156 \\ 98 \\ + \ \ 574 \end{array}$$

    a. 3,718
    b. 3,728
    c. 3,828
    d. NG

5 Round to the nearest hundred to estimate the sum.
$$\begin{array}{r} 396 \\ + \ 238 \end{array}$$

    a. 400
    b. 500
    c. 600
    d. NG

6
$$\begin{array}{r} 602 \\ - \ 159 \end{array}$$

    a. 443
    b. 557
    c. 643
    d. NG

7
$$\begin{array}{r} \$28.15 \\ - \ \ 9.26 \end{array}$$

    a. $18.89
    b. $21.11
    c. $28.89
    d. NG

8 Round to the nearest hundred to estimate the difference.
$$\begin{array}{r} 815 \\ - \ 379 \end{array}$$

    a. 300
    b. 500
    c. 700
    d. NG

9

    a. 8:17
    b. 3:15
    c. 3:42
    d. NG

10 Find the perimeter.

36 cm
36 cm   36 cm
36 cm

    a. 72 cm
    b. 108 cm
    c. 144 cm
    d. NG

11 Choose the better estimate of volume.

    a. 2 milliliter
    b. 2 liters

12
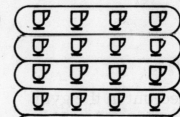

    a. $4 \times 4 = 16$
    b. $4 \times 5 = 20$
    c. $5 \times 4 = 20$
    d. NG

13
$$\begin{array}{r} 46 \\ \times \ \ 8 \end{array}$$

    a. 374
    b. 376
    c. 3,248
    d. NG

☐ **score**

Geometry

Plane Figures

Plane figures are shapes that appear on flat surfaces. Some plane figures, like squares and triangles, are called **polygons**. They have straight sides and corners. Other plane figures, like circles, have curved sides and no corners.

side → corner

square

triangle

circle

Study these plane figures. They are polygons.

rectangle   pentagon   hexagon   octagon

Getting Started

Write the name of the plane figure you see in each object.

1.

2.

3.

4. _____

_____   _____   _____   _____

Complete the table.

5.

Plane Figure	Name	Number of Straight Sides	Number of Corners	Is the figure a polygon?

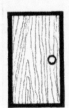				

Practice

Write the name of the plane figure you see in each object.

1.

_____

2.

_____

3.

_____

4.

_____

5.

_____

6.

_____

7.

_____

8.

_____

Complete the table.

9.

Plane Figure	Name	Number of Straight Sides	Number of Corners	Is the figure a polygon?

Now Try This!

A **diagonal** of a plane figure is a straight line connecting two corners that are not next to each other. Draw all possible diagonals in each figure. Then, fill in the number of sides, corners, and diagonals.

1.

Sides _____

Corners _____

Diagonals _____

2.

Sides _____

Corners _____

Diagonals _____

3.

Sides _____

Corners _____

Diagonals _____

4.

Sides _____

Corners _____

Diagonals _____

Lesson 10-1 • Plane Figures

It's Algebra!

Area of Plane Figures

Alan and his mom are tiling the top of a table. How many tiles will be on the table top when the job is completed?

It will take _____ tiles to cover the table.

We say the area of the table is _____ square units.

Area is the number of square units it takes to cover the surface of a plane figure. We count the number of units to find the area.

Getting Started

Write the number of square units in each plane figure.

1.

_____ square units

2.

_____ square units

3.

_____ square units

4.

_____ square units

Practice

Write the number of square units in each plane figure.

1. _____ square units

2. _____ square units

3. _____ square units

4. _____ square units

5. _____ square units

6. _____ square units

7. _____ square units

8. _____ square units

Lesson 10-2 • Area of Plane Figures

Solid Figures

Anna is the pitcher for the Madison
softball team. Which solid figure
will she use during each game?

Study each solid figure below.

    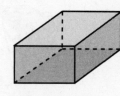

sphere   pyramid   cylinder   cone   cube   rectangular prism

Anna uses a _____ when she pitches softball.

Getting Started _____

Write the name of the solid figure under each item.

1.

_____

2.

_____

3.

_____

4.

_____

5.

_____

6.

_____

Write the name of the solid figure under each item.

1.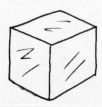

   _____

2.

   _____

3.

   _____

4.

   _____

5.

   _____

6.

   _____

7.

   _____

8.

   _____

9.

   _____

[Now Try This!]

A **line of symmetry** divides a figure into two parts so that both parts match exactly. Draw a line of symmetry through the symmetric figures. Tell whether each figure has symmetry. Write **yes** or **no**.

_____ _____ _____ _____ _____

Relating Solid and Plane Figures

The rectangular prism at the right is a solid figure.

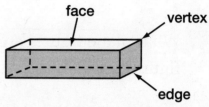

Look at the labels on the rectangular prism.

A **face** is a flat surface on a pyramid, cube, or prism.
Each face of the rectangular prism is a plane figure.
What plane figures are contained in the rectangular prism?

The rectangular prism has _____ as faces.

How many faces does the rectangular prism have?

The rectangular prism has _____ faces.

An **edge** is where two faces meet. How many edges
does the rectangular prism have?

The rectangular prism has _____ edges.

A **vertex** is where three or more edges meet. How many
vertices does the rectangular prism have?

The rectangular prism has _____ vertices.

The rectangular prism has _____ faces, _____ edges, and _____ vertices.

Getting Started

Use the figure at the right to answer each question.

1. What is the solid figure called? _____

2. What plane figures are contained in the solid

   figure? _____

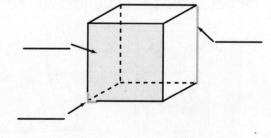

3. Use the words *face*, *edge*, and *vertex* to label
   each green part of the solid figure.

4. How many faces, edges, and vertices does the solid figure have?

_____

Practice

Use the figure at the right to answer each question.

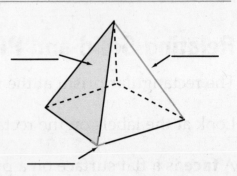

1. What is the solid figure called? _____

2. What plane figures are contained in the solid figure? _____

3. Use the words *face*, *edge*, and *vertex* to label each green part of the solid figure.

4. How many faces, edges, and vertices does the solid figure have?

_____

Complete the table.

	Solid Figure	Faces	Edges	Vertices
5.				
6.				
7.				
8.				

Now Try This!

Look at the top, front, and side view of each solid figure below. Write the name of the solid figure on the line. Then, write the names of the plane figure(s) on each side.

_____ _____ _____ _____

_____ _____ _____ _____

Lesson 10-4 • Relating Solid and Plane Figures

Volume of Solid Figures

Grant is packing gift boxes in a large carton. How many boxes will it take to fill the carton?

The carton will hold _____ boxes.

Volume is the number of cubic units it takes to fill a solid figure.

The volume of the solid figure below

is _____ cubic units.

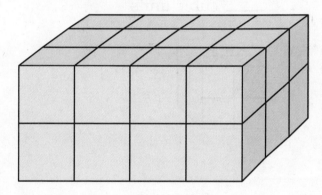

Getting Started

Write the number of cubic units in each solid figure.

1.

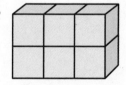

_____ cubic units

2.

_____ cubic units

3.

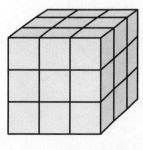

_____ cubic units

4.

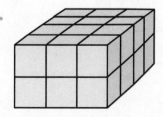

_____ cubic units

Practice

Write the number of cubic units in each solid figure.

1.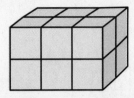

   _____ cubic units

2.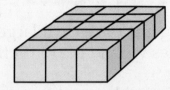

   _____ cubic units

3.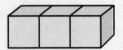

   _____ cubic units

4.

   _____ cubic units

5.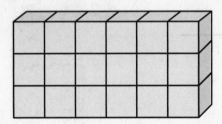

   _____ cubic units

6.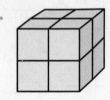

   _____ cubic units

7.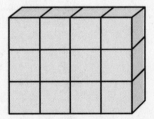

   _____ cubic units

8.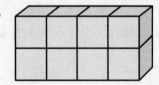

   _____ cubic units

9.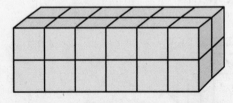

   _____ cubic units

10.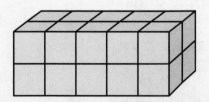

    _____ cubic units

Lesson 10-5 • Volume of Solid Figures

Name _____

Lines, Rays, and Line Segments

A **point** is a position in space.   •

A **line** is a set of points that go on indefinitely in both directions.

A **line segment** is part of a line. It has two endpoints.

A **ray** is part of a line. It has one endpoint.

A line that goes across is called a **horizontal line**.

A line that goes up and down is called a **vertical line**.

Lines that meet at one point are called **intersecting lines**.

Lines that do not intersect in the same plane, or flat surface, are called **parallel lines**.

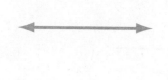

Getting Started

Write the name for each.

1.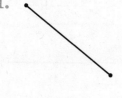

2.

3.

4.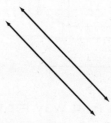

_____   _____   _____   _____

Practice

Write the name for each.

1.

2.

3.

4.

_____   _____   _____   _____

Draw each figure.

5. ray   6. horizontal line   7. parallel lines   8. line segment

Tell whether each pair of lines is intersecting or parallel.

9.

10.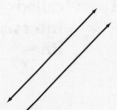

11.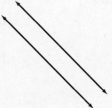

_____   _____   _____

Now Try This!

Use the words in this lesson to describe the green part of each cube.

1.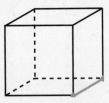

2.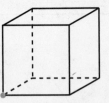

3.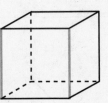

4.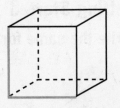

_____   _____   _____   _____

Here is a neat way for you to remember these words.
parallel   **intersect**

Angles

Two rays that have a common endpoint make an **angle**. The common endpoint is called the **vertex** of the angle.

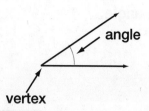

Angles are named according to the size of their openings. We can name angles by comparing the size of their openings to a right angle.

An angle that forms a square corner is called a **right angle**. The symbol used to show a right angle is ⌐.

An **acute angle** has less of an opening than a right angle.

An **obtuse angle** has a greater opening than a right angle but less than a straight line.

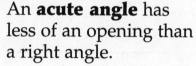

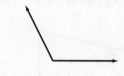

We say that lines, line segments, or rays that form right angles are **perpendicular**.

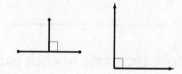

Getting Started

Write the name of each angle.

1.

2.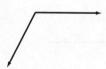

3.

4.

_____   _____   _____   _____

Write the number of right angles in each plane figure.

5.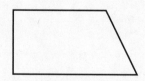

6.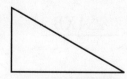

7.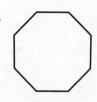

_____   _____   _____

Practice

Write the name of each angle.

1.

_____

2.

_____

3.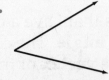

_____

4.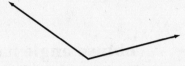

_____

5.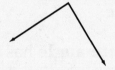

_____

6.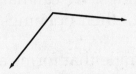

_____

Write the number of right angles in each plane figure.

7.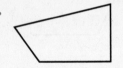

_____

8.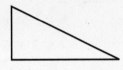

_____

9.

_____

Write the name of each pair of lines.

10.

_____

11.

_____

12.

_____

Now Try This!

Angles are named using 3 letters of the alphabet. The middle letter must always be the vertex of the angle. ∠ is a symbol for the word angle. In the figure below, ∠AXB is the name of the first angle on the left. Name the other angles.

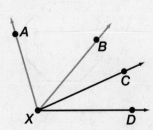

∠AXB _____   _____

_____   _____

_____

Triangles

Look at the flag for Guyana, a small country in South America. What kinds of angles are on the flag? There are _____ angles and _____ angles on the flag.

There are several different kinds of triangles on Guyana's flag. To name a triangle, we can look at the lengths of its sides.

equilateral triangle

isosceles triangle

scalene triangle

All sides are the same length.

At least two sides are the same length.

None of the sides are the same length.

On Guyana's flag, there are _____ triangles and _____ triangles.

Another way to name a triangle is by looking at the size of its angles.

right triangle

acute triangle

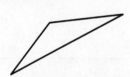

obtuse triangle

One angle is a right angle.

All three angles are acute angles.

One angle is an obtuse angle.

On Guyana's flag, there are _____ triangles and _____ triangles.

Getting Started

Write *equilateral*, *isosceles*, or *scalene* for each triangle.

1.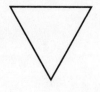

_____

2.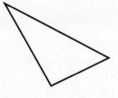

_____

3.

_____

Practice

Write _equilateral_, _isosceles_, or _scalene_ for each triangle.

1.

_____

2.

_____

3.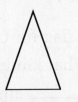

_____

Write _right_, _acute_, or _obtuse_ for each triangle.

4.

_____

5.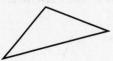

_____

6.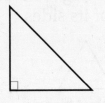

_____

Use two words to name each triangle by the size of its sides and angles.

7.

_____

8.

_____

9.

_____

Name the different triangles on each flag.

10.

_____

_____

11.

_____

_____

12.

_____

_____

Lesson 10-8 • Triangles

Quadrilaterals

All the figures Daria drew on the grid are quadrilaterals. Each figure is a polygon with 4 sides.

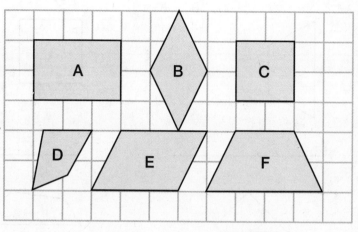

The figure labeled A is a _____.
Figure C is a square.

Quadrilaterals are named by their sides and angles.

quadrilateral

Quad- means "four"— four sides and four angles.

rectangle

Four right angles and opposite sides are the same length.

square

Four right angles and all sides are the same length.

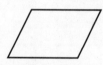

parallelogram

Opposite sides are parallel and the same length.

rhombus

Opposite sides are parallel and all sides are the same length.

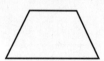

trapezoid

There is only one pair of parallel sides.

In Daria's drawings above, figure B is a _____ , figure D is a _____ , figure E is a _____ , and figure F is a _____ .

Getting Started

Write the name of each quadrilateral.

1.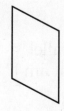

_____

2.

_____

3.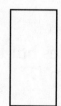

_____

4.

_____

Practice

Write the name of each quadrilateral.

1.

_____

2.

_____

3.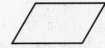

_____

4.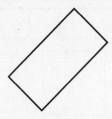

_____

5.

_____

6.

_____

Draw each of these quadrilaterals.

7. square

8. trapezoid

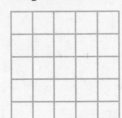

9. rectangle

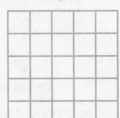

10. parallelogram

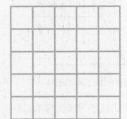

❲ Now Try This! ❳

Write the name of a quadrilateral to solve each riddle.

1. I have 4 sides but only one pair are parallel. What am I?

2. I have four sides of the same length but not four right angles. What am I?

3. I have four right angles but I'm not a square. What am I?

4. My opposite sides are parallel and the same length. What am I?

Lesson 10-9 • Quadrilaterals

Congruent Figures

Congruent means "the same." Plane figures that are the same size and shape are called **congruent figures**. Which of the triangles at the right are congruent?

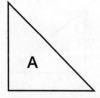 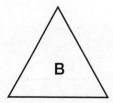 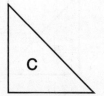

Congruent figures have the same _____ and _____.

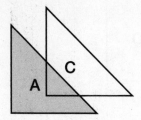

Triangle ____ and triangle ____ are congruent.

Getting Started _____

Circle the letters of the two congruent figures in each row.

1.

2.

3.

Practice

Circle the letters of the two congruent figures in each row.

1.

2.

3.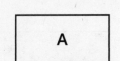

4.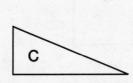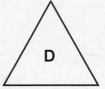

5.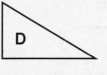

6.

Lesson 10-10 • Congruent Figures

Name _____

Transformations

You can move a figure three different ways from one place to another without changing its shape or size. You can slide, flip, or turn figures and they will remain congruent to each other. Each one of these moves is called a **transformation**.

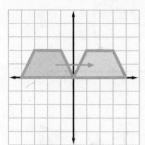 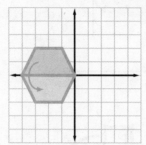 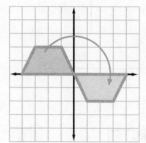

A **slide** moves a figure a given distance and a given direction. Another name for a slide is a **translation**.

A **flip** moves a figure over a line to get a mirror image. Another name for a flip is a **reflection**.

A **turn** rotates a figure clockwise or counterclockwise. Another name for a turn is a **rotation**.

What if each time a trapezoid moved, it did not change its _____ or _____?

The trapezoids in each movement would be _____ to each other.

Getting Started

Write *slide*, *flip*, or *turn* for each move.

1.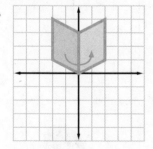

_____

2.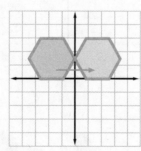

_____

3.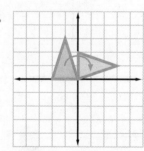

_____

4.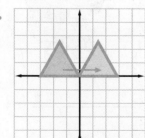

_____

5.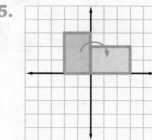

_____

6.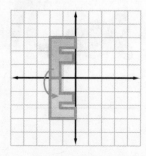

_____

Practice

Write *slide*, *flip*, or *turn* for each move.

1.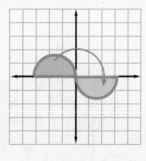

   _____

2.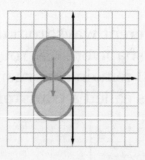

   _____

3.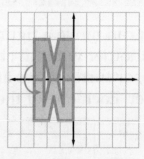

   _____

4.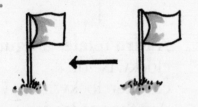

   _____

5.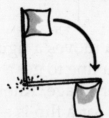

   _____

6.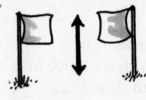

   _____

7.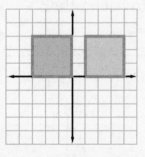

   _____

8.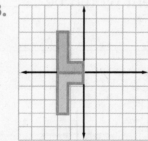

   _____

9.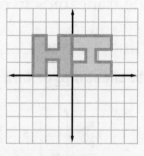

   _____

10.

    _____

11.

    _____

12.

    _____

Lesson 10-11 • Transformations

Name _____

Problem Solving: Draw a Picture

Mrs. Cox wants to cover the 8- by 6-foot floor in her kitchen with 1-foot square tiles. How many tiles does she need to buy?

 SEE

We want to know how many tiles Mrs. Cox needs to buy.

The kitchen floor measures _____ by _____.

Each tile is _____.

 PLAN

Draw a picture of the kitchen floor on grid paper.

Let each square on the grid paper stand for 1 square foot of tile.

DO

Count all the squares inside the rectangle.

There are _____ squares.

Mrs. Cox needs to buy _____ tiles to cover her kitchen floor.

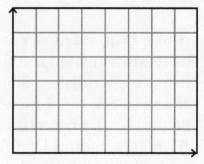

1 square = 1 square foot

CHECK

We can use multiplication to check.

There are _____ rows with _____ tiles in each row.

_____ × _____ = _____

Apply

Draw a picture to solve each problem. Make drawings on grid paper or another sheet of paper to show your work.

1. Kelly wants to put a fence around a play area for her dog. The dog's play area will be 10 feet long and 6 feet wide. How many feet of fencing will she need?

2. How many different ways can you cut a rectangular cake into 8 congruent pieces?

3. Andy, Dan, Ed, and Franco have just finished a 400-meter race. Andy finished 30 meters ahead of Ed, but 2 meters behind Dan. Franco finishes 10 meters behind Dan. What is the order of the four boys as they cross the finish line?

4. Katy moved her game piece 3 spaces to the right and 2 spaces up on a game board. Were the movements she made called flips, slides, or turns?

5. Terry hung her clothes in the closet so that a blouse is always between a dress and a skirt. What is the fourteenth garment?

6. The distance around a rectangle is 20 centimeters. The length of each of the two longer sides is 7 centimeters. What is the length of each of the two shorter sides?

7. Jordan wants to paint a corner of his bedroom red so that it looks like an isosceles right triangle. It will measure 4 feet on each side of the right angle of the corner of the room. How many square feet of floor space will he cover with red paint?

8. Janet made a triangle by arranging dimes in rows on a table. The first row has 1 dime, the second row has 2 dimes, and so on. How many dimes are in the sixth row? How much money is there in a 6-row triangle?

Name _____

Write the number of square units in each figure.

1.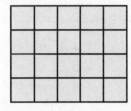

_____ square units

2.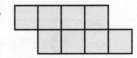

_____ square units

3.

_____ square units

Write the name of the solid figure under each item.

4.

_____

5.

_____

6.

_____

Write the number of cubic units in each figure.

7.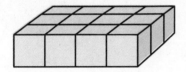

_____ cubic units

8.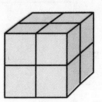

_____ cubic units

9.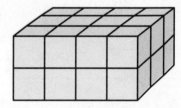

_____ cubic units

Circle the letters of the congruent figures.

10.

Write the name for each.

11.

_____

12.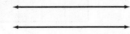

_____

13.

_____

14.

_____

Circle the letter of the correct answer.

① 187 ◯ 817

a. <
b. >

② What is the value of the 0 in 458,036?

a. ones
b. tens
c. hundreds
d. NG

③ $36.47
+ 9.56

a. $45.03
b. $45.93
c. $46.93
d. NG

④ 4,362
159
+ 87

a. 4,508
b. 4,606
c. 4,608
d. NG

⑤ 501
− 236

a. 335
b. 265
c. 737
d. NG

⑥ $52.37
− 18.58

a. $33.79
b. $34.79
c. $46.21
d. NG

⑦

a. 8:30
b. 6:40
c. 6:45
d. NG

⑧ Find the perimeter.

8 m   9 m
12 m

a. 17 m
b. 21 m
c. 29 m
d. NG

⑨ Choose the better estimate of the weight of a package of butter.

a. 1 oz
b. 1 lb

⑩ 32
× 5

a. 150
b. 160
c. 1,510
d. NG

⑪ 328
× 7

a. 2,294
b. 2,295
c. 2,296
d. NG

⑫ $3.09
× 4

a. $12. 36
b. $15. 05
c. $15. 06
d. NG

⑬ Find the area.

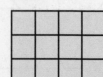

a. 3 sq units
b. 12 sq units
c. 15 sq units
d. NG

 score

STOP

Graphing

Name _____

Bar Graphs

Each of the students in Mr. Gray's class voted for his or her favorite color. The results of the vote are in the chart below.

Favorite Colors	
Colors	**Votes**
Yellow	Ben, Liza
Green	Sam, Martin, Nate, Andy
Red	Trudy, Dorothy, Kurt, Tabatha
Blue	Sonja, Juan, Rhea, Flo, Rex, Terry

Tally the number of student votes for each color.

Favorite Colors	
Colors	**Totals**
Yellow	
Green	
Red	
Blue	

Make a bar graph showing the total votes for each color.

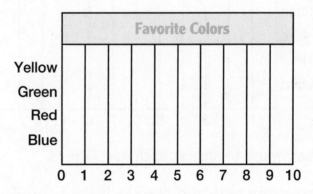

Getting Started

Use the bar graph to answer each question.

1. How many children voted for blue? _____

2. How many children voted for green? _____

3. Which color got the greatest number of votes? _____

4. Which color is the least favorite? _____

Practice

During their nature study, the students in Mr. Gray's class voted for their favorite birds. The results of that vote are in the chart below.

Favorite Birds	
Birds	**Votes**
Robin	Sam, Trudy, Dorothy, Liza, Nate, Terry
Bluebird	Ben, Flo, Tabatha
Cardinal	Martin, Juan, Kurt, Rex, Andy
Blackbird	Sonja, Rhea

Tally the number of student votes for each bird.

Favorite Birds		
Birds		**Totals**
Robin		
Bluebird		
Cardinal		
Blackbird		

Make a bar graph showing the total votes for each bird.

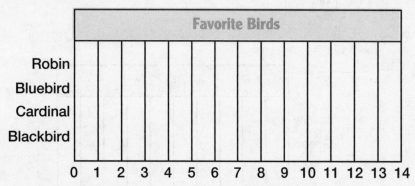

Use the bar graph to answer each question.

1. How many children voted for the robin? _____

2. How many children voted for the cardinal? _____

3. How many votes did the blackbird get? _____

4. How many more votes did the cardinal get than the blackbird? _____

5. Which bird is the favorite? _____

Pictographs

Roberto collects scallop shells. He made a pictograph to show the number of shells he had collected each month. How many shells did Roberto collect in July?

Shell Collection	
June	🐚 🐚
July	🐚 🐚 🐚
August	🐚 🐚 🐚 🐚 🐚 🐚
September	🐚 🐚

Each 🐚 stands for 5 shells.

We want to find the number of shells Roberto collected in July.

The graph shows ____ shells for July.

Each picture stands for ____ actual shells.

To find the number of shells collected

in July, we multiply ____ by ____.

July 🐚 🐚 🐚   ____ × ____ = ____

Roberto collected ____ scallop shells in July.

Getting Started _____

Use the pictograph to answer each question.

1. How many shells did Roberto collect in August? ____

2. How many shells did Roberto collect in June? ____

3. How many shells did he collect from June through September? ____

4. How many more shells did Roberto collect in July than in June? ____

5. In which months did Roberto collect the same number of

   shells? _____

6. In which month did Roberto collect the most shells? _____

Practice

Use the pictograph to answer each question.

1. How many students from Grade 3 attended the baseball game? ____

2. How many students from Grade 4 attended the baseball game? ____

3. Which class had the smallest attendance? _____

4. Which class had the largest attendance? _____

5. How many students from Grade 5 and Grade 6 attended the baseball game? ____

Baseball Game Attendance						
Grade 3	☺	☺	☺	☺		
Grade 4	☺	☺	☺			
Grade 5	☺	☺	☺	☺	☺	
Grade 6	☺	☺	☺	☺	☺	☺

Each ☺ stands for 3 students.

Use the pictograph to answer each question.

How many inches of snow fell:

6. in December? ____

7. in March? ____

8. in January? ____

9. in December and January? ____

10. How much more snow fell in November than in March? _____

11. How much less snow fell in February than in January? _____

12. How much snow fell in all 5 months? _____

Monthly Snow Fall						
November	❄	❄	❄			
December	❄	❄	❄	❄	❄	
January	❄	❄	❄	❄	❄	❄
February	❄	❄	❄	❄		
March	❄	❄				

Each ❄ stands for 6 inches.

Lesson 11-2 • Pictographs

Making and Using Line Graphs

A line graph is a good way to show changes in information over time. This line graph shows the rainfall for 2004. What was the greatest rainfall and when did it occur?

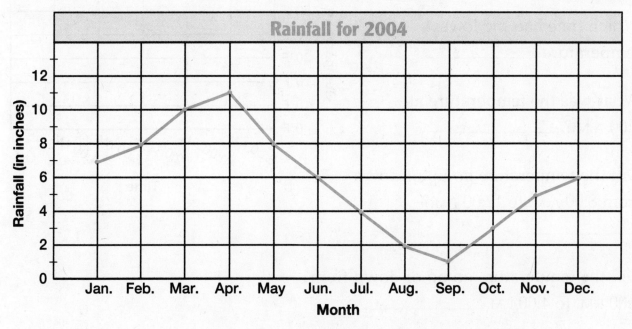

We want to find the greatest rainfall and the month it occurred.

The inches of rainfall go up the _____ side of the line graph.

The _____ goes across the _____ of the line graph.

To find the greatest rainfall amount, start with the lowest amount on the graph.

Follow the inches up the side of the chart to the highest dot, _____.

Then go down in a straight line to the bottom of the chart to _____.

The greatest rainfall was 11 inches and it occurred in _____.

Getting Started _____

Use the line graph above to answer these questions.

1. What was the rainfall in June?
_____

2. What was the least amount of rainfall? _____

3. In what month was the least rainfall? _____

4. Between which two months was there the greatest difference in rainfall? _____

Practice

Use the line graph on the right to answer each question.

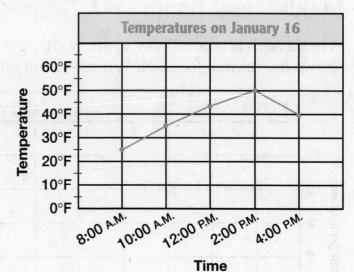

Temperatures on January 16

1. Which time had the highest temperature? _____

2. Which time had the lowest temperature? _____

3. What was the temperature at 8:00 A.M.? _____

4. Did the temperature go up or down from 8:00 A.M. to 12:00 P.M.?

   _____

5. Did the temperature go up or down from 2:00 P.M. to 4:00 P.M.? _____

6. How many degrees warmer was it at 2:00 P.M. than at 8:00 A.M.? _____

[Now Try This!]

Complete the line graph to show how many points the team scored during January.

Scores for January	
1st Week	45
2nd Week	38
3rd Week	25
4th Week	73
5th Week	55

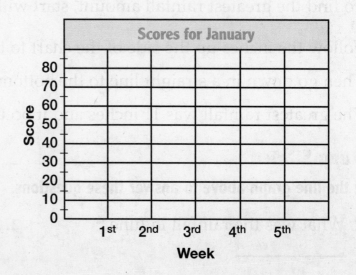

Scores for January

Lesson 11-3 • Making and Using Line Graphs

Ordered Pairs

It's Algebra!

Ordered pairs of numbers can be used to show points on a map, a graph, or a **coordinate grid**.

What ordered pair of numbers shows the location of the letter *B*?

To read the first number in an ordered pair, start at 0 and move your finger across the bottom of the graph until you reach the letter. To read the second number, go up the graph until you reach the letter.

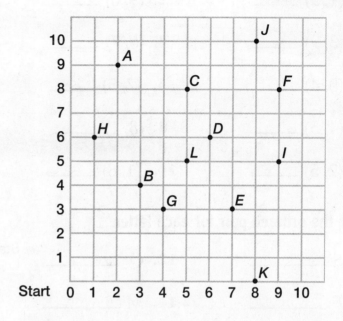

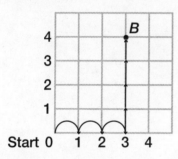

Count 3 units across the bottom.   **(3, 4)**   Count 4 units up the graph.

The letter *B* is named by the pair (3, ____).

Getting Started

Write the letter for each ordered pair. Use the graph above.

1. (2, 9) ____

2. (6, 6) ____

3. (9, 5) ____

4. (3, 4) ____

5. (5, 8) ____

6. (8, 10) ____

Write the ordered pair for each letter. Use the graph above.

7. *H* _____

8. *E* _____

9. *F* _____

10. *G* _____

11. *K* _____

12. *L* _____

Practice

Write the letter for each ordered pair.

1. (1, 2) _____
2. (9, 6) _____
3. (3, 9) _____
4. (6, 7) _____
5. (5, 4) _____
6. (7, 5) _____
7. (4, 5) _____
8. (8, 1) _____
9. (2, 5) _____
10. (1, 8) _____

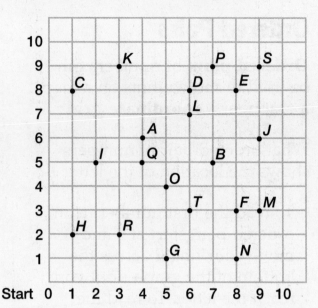

Write the ordered pair for each letter.

11. S _____
12. Q _____
13. F _____
14. M _____
15. J _____
16. A _____
17. B _____
18. O _____
19. P _____
20. H _____

Use the graph to find the letters to spell each word.

21. _____ _____ _____ _____
    (9, 3)   (4, 6)   (6, 3)   (1, 2)

22. _____ _____ _____ _____ _____ _____
    (7, 9)   (8, 8)   (8, 1)   (1, 8)   (2, 5)   (6, 7)

23. _____ _____ _____ _____ _____
    (5, 1)   (3, 2)   (4, 6)   (7, 9)   (1, 2)

24. _____ _____ _____ _____ _____
    (7, 9)   (4, 6)   (7, 9)   (8, 8)   (3, 2)

25. _____ _____ _____ _____ _____ _____ _____
    (2, 5)   (4, 6)   (9, 3)   (6, 8)   (5, 4)   (8, 1)   (8, 8)

Name _____

Problem Solving: Make a Graph

Lisa put 10¢ in her piggy bank. Next week, she will put in double that amount. The week after that, she will double that amount. If she continues this pattern, how many weeks will it take for Lisa to save more than a dollar a week?

 SEE

We want to know how long it will take for Lisa to save more than a dollar a week.

Lisa saves 10¢ the first week.

She always doubles the amount she saves from the week before.

 PLAN

We can make a bar graph of her savings.

 DO

In week number _____ , Lisa will save _____. This will be the first week her savings will be more than a dollar.

 CHECK

Week 1   10¢

Week 2   10¢ × 2 = 20¢

Week 3   _____ × 2 = _____

Week 4   _____ × 2 = _____

Week 5   _____ × 2 = _____

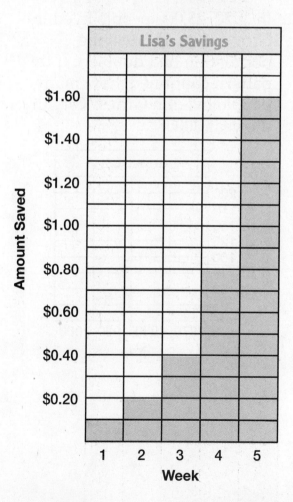

Lisa's Savings

Apply

Complete each graph to solve.

1. Fritz thinks about his day. He spends 8 hours sleeping, 2 hours eating, 6 hours studying, 4 hours playing, 1 hour reading, and 2 hours working. How many hours does Fritz spend watching television?

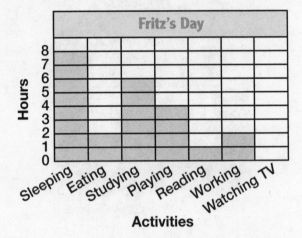

3. Sandi works for 15 hours each week at an ice cream store. This week, she worked 2 hours on Monday, 3 hours on Tuesday, 2 hours on Wednesday, and 4 hours on Thursday. How many hours does she need to work on Friday?

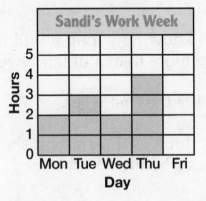

2. In 1970, 25,000 people lived in Grover City. By 1980 the population had doubled. If this pattern continued, how many people lived in Grover City in the year 2000?

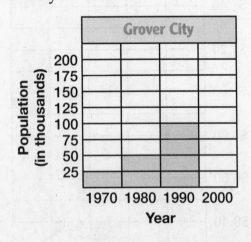

4. Ken rode 4 more miles than Wally. How many miles did Wally ride?

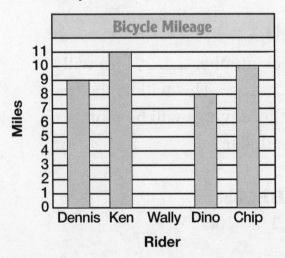

Make a graph to solve each problem.

5. In your class, what color eyes do most of the students have?

6. In your class, what kind of pet is the most popular and what kind is the least popular?

Name _____

Use the bar graph on the right to answer each question.

1. How many points did Linda score? _____

2. How many points did Angela score? _____

3. Who won the contest? _____

4. Who scored the least points? _____

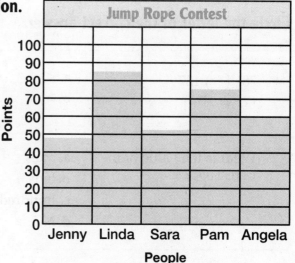

Use the bar graph on the right to answer each question.

5. How many aluminum cans did Tam collect? _____

6. How many more cans than Tam did Mary and Jan collect together? _____

7. How many cans did the three girls collect altogether? _____

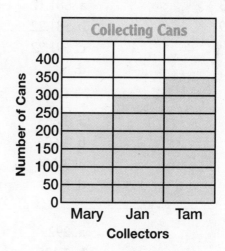

Make a bar graph to show the number of haircuts each child has had.

8.

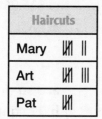

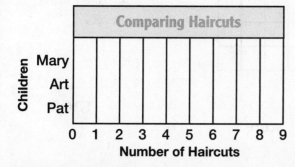

Write the ordered pair for each letter.

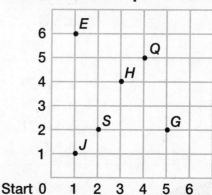

9. E _____

10. S _____

11. H _____

12. Q _____

13. G _____

14. J _____

Circle the letter of the correct answer.

1 781 ◯ 187

a. <
b. >

2 What is the value of the 0 in 630,854?

a. ones
b. tens
c. hundreds
d. NG

3
$74.63
+ 6.59

a. $81.12
b. $81.22
c. $91.22
d. NG

4
2,634
951
+ 78

a. 3,663
b. 4,606
c. 3,664
d. NG

5
632
− 493

a. 292
b. 1,135
c. 139
d. NG

6
$85.31
− 43.52

a. $41.79
b. $34.79
c. $46.21
d. NG

7

a. 8:30
b. 9:40
c. 6:45
d. NG

8 Find the perimeter.

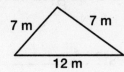

7 m   7 m
12 m

a. 17 m
b. 21 m
c. 26 m
d. NG

9 Choose the better estimate of the weight of a baby.

a. 7 oz
b. 7 lb

10
88
× 7

a. 150
b. 616
c. 1,510
d. NG

11
832
× 9

a. 7,380
b. 7,488
c. 6,498
d. NG

12
$9.03
× 6

a. $52.36
b. $54.15
c. $15.06
d. NG

13 Find the area.

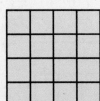

a. 3 sq units
b. 12 sq units
c. 16 sq units
d. NG

 score

 STOP

Division Facts Through Five

Understanding Division

Mary Lou's mother is giving her a surprise party. She has enough prizes to give each person an equal number. How many prizes will each person receive?

We want to know how many prizes each person will receive.
There are ____ people at the party.

Mary Lou's mother has ____ prizes to give away. To find the number of prizes for each person, we divide

____ into ____ equal groups.

We write: **12 ÷ 4 = ____**
We say: **twelve divided by 4 equals 3.**

Each person will receive ____ prizes.

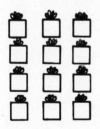

We can use division to find the number in each group, or the number of groups.

$$12 ÷ 4 = 3$$
dividend divisor quotient
$$12 ÷ 3 = 4$$

Getting Started

Answer the question and complete the number sentence.

15 in all
5 groups
How many in each group? ____

15 ÷ 5 = ____

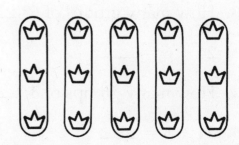

Practice

Answer each question and complete each number sentence.

1. 6 in all
    2 in each group
    How many groups? ____

    6 ÷ 2 = ____

2. 15 in all
    3 in each group
    How many groups? ____

    15 ÷ 3 = ____

3.

    16 in all
    8 in each group
    How many groups? ____

    16 ÷ 8 = ____

4.

    9 in all
    3 in each group
    How many groups? ____

    9 ÷ 3 = ____

5.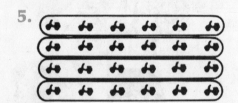

    24 in all
    6 in each group
    How many groups? ____

    24 ÷ 6 = ____

6.

    24 in all
    4 in each group
    How many groups? ____

    24 ÷ 4 = ____

Use the ribbons to answer each question and complete each number sentence.

7. How many ribbons? ____

8. How many groups of 4? ____

9. 24 ÷ 4 = ____

10. How many groups of 6? ____

11. 24 ÷ 6 = ____

12. How many groups of 3? ____

13. 24 ÷ 3 = ____

Lesson 12-1 • Understanding Division

Dividing by 2

After recess, Miss Crandle asked the students with wet gloves to hang them on hooks to dry. How many children had wet gloves?

We want to know how many children had wet gloves.

There are _____ gloves hanging on hooks.

Each child wore a pair, or _____ gloves.

To find the number of children, we divide _____ by _____.

$12 \div 2 =$ _____

There were _____ children with wet gloves.

Getting Started

Answer each question and complete each number sentence.

1.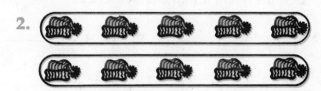

How many in all? _____

How many groups? _____

How many in each group? _____

$8 \div 2 =$ _____

2.

How many in all? _____

How many groups? _____

How many in each group? _____

$10 \div 2 =$ _____

Complete each number sentence.

3. $6 \div 2 =$ _____   4. $12 \div 2 =$ _____   5. $4 \div 2 =$ _____   6. $14 \div 2 =$ _____

Practice

Answer each question and complete each number sentence.

1.

How many in all? ____

How many groups? ____

How many in each group? ____

18 ÷ 2 = ____

2.

How many in all? ____

How many groups? ____

How many in each group? ____

14 ÷ 2 = ____

3.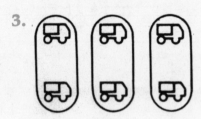

How many in all? ____

How many groups? ____

How many in each group? ____

6 ÷ 3 = ____

4.

How many in all? ____

How many groups? ____

How many in each group? ____

16 ÷ 2 = ____

Complete each number sentence.

5. 6 ÷ 2 = ____

6. 12 ÷ 2 = ____

7. 10 ÷ 2 = ____

8. 14 ÷ 2 = ____

9. 18 ÷ 2 = ____

10. 4 ÷ 2 = ____

11. 8 ÷ 2 = ____

12. 16 ÷ 2 = ____

[Now Try This!]

Write the letters of the two figures that, when put together, match each numbered figure.

1. ____ ____

2. ____ ____

3.  ____ ____

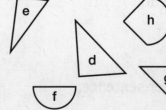

Name _____

Dividing by 3

George is cleaning out his closet. He finds
15 loose tennis balls.
How many cans will he need to pack
them all?

We want to know the number of cans
needed to hold all the tennis balls.

George finds _____ balls.

A can holds _____ balls.

To find the number of cans, we divide _____ by _____.

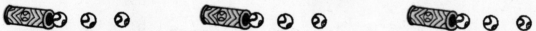

$15 \div 3 =$ _____

George will need _____ cans.

Getting Started

Answer each question and complete each number sentence.

1.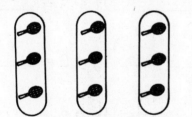

    How many in all? _____

    How many in each group? _____

    How many groups? _____

    $12 \div 3 =$ _____

2.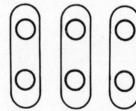

    How many in all? _____

    How many groups? _____

    How many in each group? _____

    $6 \div 3 =$ _____

Complete each number sentence.

3. $18 \div 3 =$ _____   4. $15 \div 3 =$ _____   5. $21 \div 3 =$ _____   6. $27 \div 3 =$ _____

Lesson 12-3 • Dividing by 3

two hundred nineteen   **219**

Practice

Answer each question and complete each number sentence.

1.

   How many in all? _____

   How many groups? _____

   How many in each group? _____

   24 ÷ 3 = _____

2. (triangles groups)

   How many in all? _____

   How many groups? _____

   How many in each group? _____

   21 ÷ 3 = _____

Complete each number sentence.

3. 15 ÷ 3 = _____   4. 16 ÷ 2 = _____   5. 12 ÷ 3 = _____   6. 8 ÷ 2 = _____

7. 10 ÷ 2 = _____   8. 18 ÷ 3 = _____   9. 6 ÷ 3 = _____   10. 14 ÷ 2 = _____

11. 27 ÷ 3 = _____   12. 9 ÷ 3 = _____   13. 18 ÷ 2 = _____   14. 4 ÷ 2 = _____

15. 8 ÷ 2 = _____   16. 24 ÷ 3 = _____   17. 16 ÷ 2 = _____   18. 21 ÷ 3 = _____

19. 10 ÷ 2 = _____   20. 12 ÷ 3 = _____   21. 6 ÷ 2 = _____   22. 15 ÷ 3 = _____

23. 14 ÷ 2 = _____   24. 6 ÷ 3 = _____   25. 24 ÷ 3 = _____   26. 18 ÷ 2 = _____

Problem Solving

Solve each problem.

27. Mickey wanted to invite his 24 classmates to his home for dinner. His father said they could only come 3 at a time. How many dinners will it take to invite the whole class?

28. The teacher divided 18 old magazines among 3 of her students for work on a project. How many magazines did each student have to work with?

Lesson 12-3 • Dividing by 3

Dividing by 4

Therese is using baskets of flowers to decorate the tables for a banquet. How many flowers will she put into each basket?

We want to know the number of flowers that Therese will put into each basket.

Therese has _____ baskets to make up.

She has _____ flowers to fill the baskets.

To find the number of flowers, we divide _____ by _____.

$24 \div 4 =$ _____

Therese will put _____ flowers into each basket.

Getting Started

Answer each question and complete each number sentence.

1.

How many in all? _____

How many groups? _____

How many in each group? _____

$20 \div 4 =$ _____

2.

How many in all? _____

How many groups? _____

How many in each group? _____

$12 \div 4 =$ _____

Complete each number sentence.

3. $24 \div 4 =$ _____   4. $16 \div 4 =$ _____   5. $8 \div 4 =$ _____   6. $32 \div 4 =$ _____

Practice

Answer each question and complete each number sentence.

1.

How many in all? ＿＿

How many groups? ＿＿

How many in each group? ＿＿

$28 \div 4 =$ ＿＿

2.

How many in all? ＿＿

How many groups? ＿＿

How many in each group? ＿＿

$32 \div 4 =$ ＿＿

Complete each number sentence.

3. $20 \div 4 =$ ＿＿   4. $21 \div 3 =$ ＿＿   5. $36 \div 4 =$ ＿＿   6. $12 \div 4 =$ ＿＿

7. $24 \div 3 =$ ＿＿   8. $24 \div 4 =$ ＿＿   9. $16 \div 2 =$ ＿＿   10. $28 \div 4 =$ ＿＿

11. $9 \div 3 =$ ＿＿   12. $40 \div 4 =$ ＿＿   13. $4 \div 4 =$ ＿＿   14. $18 \div 3 =$ ＿＿

15. $32 \div 4 =$ ＿＿   16. $10 \div 2 =$ ＿＿   17. $27 \div 3 =$ ＿＿   18. $30 \div 3 =$ ＿＿

19. $18 \div 2 =$ ＿＿   20. $12 \div 3 =$ ＿＿   21. $6 \div 3 =$ ＿＿   22. $8 \div 4 =$ ＿＿

23. $15 \div 3 =$ ＿＿   24. $16 \div 4 =$ ＿＿   25. $44 \div 4 =$ ＿＿   26. $14 \div 2 =$ ＿＿

Problem Solving

Solve each problem.

27. Nikki brought 36 fortune cookies to school. She shared them among her 4 friends. How many cookies did each friend receive?

28. Sal has 16 pages to study for a test on Friday. He has 4 days to prepare for the test. How many pages should he study each day?

Lesson 12-4 • Dividing by 4

Dividing by 5

The school district chess league has 20 players in all. How many chess players are on each team?

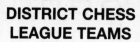

DISTRICT CHESS LEAGUE TEAMS

Blue Hills
Lincoln
Washington
Green
Oak

Each team has the same number of players. We want to know the number of players on each team.

There are ____ chess players.

The players are divided into ____ teams.

To find the number of players, we divide

____ by ____.

Blue Hills	Lincoln	Washington	Green	Oak
IIII	IIII	IIII	IIII	IIII

$$20 \div 5 = \underline{\quad}$$

There are ____ players on each team.

Getting Started

Answer each question and complete each number sentence.

1.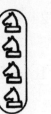

How many in all? ____

How many groups? ____

How many in each group? ____

$20 \div 5 = \underline{\quad}$

2.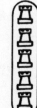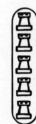

How many in all? ____

How many groups? ____

How many in each group? ____

$25 \div 5 = \underline{\quad}$

Complete each number sentence.

3. $15 \div 5 = \underline{\quad}$ 4. $10 \div 5 = \underline{\quad}$ 5. $30 \div 5 = \underline{\quad}$ 6. $25 \div 5 = \underline{\quad}$

Practice

Answer each question and complete each number sentence.

1.

How many in all? ____

How many groups? ____

How many in each group? ____

$40 \div 5 =$ ____

2.

How many in all? ____

How many groups? ____

How many in each group? ____

$45 \div 5 =$ ____

Complete each number sentence.

3. $40 \div 5 =$ ____   4. $20 \div 4 =$ ____   5. $20 \div 5 =$ ____   6. $24 \div 3 =$ ____

7. $9 \div 3 =$ ____   8. $45 \div 5 =$ ____   9. $10 \div 5 =$ ____   10. $32 \div 4 =$ ____

11. $30 \div 5 =$ ____   12. $10 \div 2 =$ ____   13. $50 \div 5 =$ ____   14. $25 \div 5 =$ ____

15. $35 \div 5 =$ ____   16. $15 \div 5 =$ ____   17. $24 \div 4 =$ ____   18. $21 \div 3 =$ ____

19. $36 \div 4 =$ ____   20. $60 \div 5 =$ ____   21. $16 \div 2 =$ ____   22. $55 \div 5 =$ ____

23. $16 \div 4 =$ ____   24. $27 \div 3 =$ ____   25. $5 \div 5 =$ ____   26. $35 \div 5 =$ ____

Problem Solving

Solve each problem.

27. Amanda is paring 45 apples to make tarts. She puts 5 apples into each tart. How many tarts will she make?

28. Morris arranges 40 dried seeds on a page of his science notebook. He puts 5 seeds in each row. How many rows of seeds does he have?

Writing Division Another Way

Lonnie needs quarters to play the computer game. How many times can Lonnie play the game with the money he has?

We want to know the number of quarters Lonnie can get for 40 nickels.

It takes ____ nickels to make a quarter.

Lonnie has ____ nickels.

To find the number Lonnie will have, we divide ____ by ____.

$40 \div 5 =$ ____

Lonnie will have ____ quarters.

This division can be written another way.

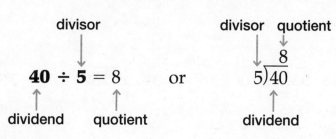

$$\overset{\text{divisor}}{\underset{\underset{\text{dividend}}{\uparrow}}{\mathbf{40}} \div \overset{}{\underset{\underset{\text{quotient}}{\uparrow}}{\mathbf{5}}} = 8} \qquad \text{or} \qquad \overset{\text{divisor}\quad\text{quotient}}{5\overline{)40}}$$

Getting Started

Divide.

1. $2\overline{)8}$
2. $4\overline{)36}$
3. $5\overline{)25}$
4. $3\overline{)18}$
5. $4\overline{)24}$

6. $3\overline{)27}$
7. $2\overline{)16}$
8. $4\overline{)16}$
9. $5\overline{)40}$
10. $4\overline{)32}$

11. $5\overline{)10}$
12. $2\overline{)18}$
13. $4\overline{)12}$
14. $4\overline{)28}$
15. $3\overline{)15}$

Practice

Divide.

1. $2\overline{)18}$
2. $4\overline{)20}$
3. $4\overline{)32}$
4. $2\overline{)6}$
5. $5\overline{)25}$

6. $4\overline{)8}$
7. $2\overline{)12}$
8. $3\overline{)12}$
9. $5\overline{)45}$
10. $4\overline{)12}$

11. $3\overline{)27}$
12. $2\overline{)16}$
13. $5\overline{)20}$
14. $3\overline{)24}$
15. $3\overline{)18}$

16. $5\overline{)40}$
17. $5\overline{)5}$
18. $2\overline{)14}$
19. $4\overline{)16}$
20. $4\overline{)40}$

21. $5\overline{)35}$
22. $4\overline{)36}$
23. $3\overline{)3}$
24. $5\overline{)50}$
25. $5\overline{)15}$

26. $3\overline{)30}$
27. $2\overline{)10}$
28. $4\overline{)24}$
29. $2\overline{)8}$
30. $2\overline{)20}$

31. $3\overline{)21}$
32. $3\overline{)6}$
33. $5\overline{)10}$
34. $3\overline{)15}$
35. $5\overline{)30}$

36. $4\overline{)4}$
37. $5\overline{)55}$
38. $4\overline{)36}$
39. $4\overline{)28}$
40. $4\overline{)44}$

Now Try This!

It's Algebra!

Write each missing number.

1. $5\overline{)}^{\,7}$
2. $3\overline{)}^{\,9}$
3. $4\overline{)}^{\,8}$
4. $2\overline{)}^{\,9}$

5. $^{\,5}\overline{)20}$
6. $^{\,9}\overline{)45}$
7. $^{\,8}\overline{)16}$
8. $^{\,6}\overline{)18}$

Lesson 12-6 • Writing Division Another Way

Name _____

Multiplying and Dividing

It's Algebra!

If we divide 24 by 6, we get 4.
If we multiply 4 by 6, we get 24
again. Let's think more about
this relationship.

$24 \div 6 = 4$
$4 \times 6 = 24$

We can find quotients by thinking of missing factors.

32 ÷ 8 = ___   ($4 \times 8 = 32$)

We can find missing factors by dividing.

___ × 7 = 35   ($35 \div 7 = 5$)

We can multiply to check division.

15 ÷ 3 = 5   ($5 \times 3 = 15$)

We can divide to check multiplication.

2 × 8 = 16   ($16 \div 8 = 2$)

Getting Started

Write each missing number. Use multiplication or division to check each answer.

1. $12 \div 3 =$ ___

2. $8 \times 5 =$ ___

3. $5\overline{)20}$

4. $2 \times$ ___ $= 8$

5. $3\overline{)18}$

6. ___ $\times 4 = 12$

7. $40 \div 5 =$ ___

8. $3 \times 7 =$ ___

9. ___ $\times 7 = 35$

10. $24 \div 4 =$ ___

11. $3\overline{)15}$

12. $4 \times 9 =$ ___

Practice

Write each missing number. Use multiplication or division to check your answers.

1. $15 \div 3 =$ ____

2. $4 \times 4 =$ ____

3. $5\overline{)40}$

4. $3 \times 8 =$ ____

5. $2 \times$ ____ $= 8$

6. $9 \div 3 =$ ____

7. $2\overline{)14}$

8. ____ $\times 5 = 30$

9. $4\overline{)24}$

10. $6 \times 3 =$ ____

11. $5 \times$ ____ $= 20$

12. $10 \div 2 =$ ____

13. $4\overline{)12}$

14. $2 \times$ ____ $= 16$

15. $12 \div 2 =$ ____

16. ____ $\times 4 = 32$

17. $5 \times$ ____ $= 35$

18. $5\overline{)25}$

19. $4 \times 3 =$ ____

20. $3\overline{)6}$

21. $6 \div 2 =$ ____

22. $3 \times$ ____ $= 15$

23. $4\overline{)36}$

24. $7 \times 3 =$ ____

25. $2\overline{)16}$

26. $10 \div 5 =$ ____

27. $9\overline{)27}$

28. $9 \times 5 =$ ____

29. $2 \times$ ____ $= 8$

30. ____ $\times 7 = 28$

31. $9\overline{)18}$

32. $35 \div 5 =$ ____

Problem Solving

Solve each problem.

33. There are 24 books divided evenly on 3 shelves. How many books are on each shelf?

34. There are 5 apples in each of 6 baskets. How many apples are there altogether?

35. Each package of cocoa contains 2 servings. How many servings are there in 7 packages?

36. A milk crate will hold 4 gallon containers of milk. How many crates are needed to hold 28 containers?

Lesson 12-7 • Multiplying and Dividing

Name _____

Problem Solving: Choose the Operation

Melanie needs to set up 20 chairs for the magic show she and her friends are having. If she only has room for 4 rows of chairs, how many chairs should she put in each row?

 SEE

Melanie has ____ chairs.

There is enough room for ____ rows of chairs.

 PLAN

To find how many chairs Melanie needs to put in each row, we _____.

We divide ____ chairs by 4 rows.

DO

Total number
of chairs
↓
20 ÷ 4 = 5
↑
Number of
rows

Melanie needs to put ____ chairs in each row.

 **CHECK**

We can check our answer by multiplying 4 by 5.

4 × ____ = ____

Apply

Choose an operation and solve each problem. Show your work.

Problem-Solving Strategy: Using the Four-Step Plan

★ **SEE** What do you need to find?

★ **PLAN** What do you need to do?

★ **DO** Follow the plan.

★ **CHECK** Does your answer make sense?

1. Alan arranged 36 photographs in a photo album. He put 4 photographs on each page. How many pages of the album did he use?

2. There are 16 tables in the school cafeteria. Each table can seat 8 students. How many students can eat in the cafeteria at one time?

3. Janice bought a jacket for $34.79. She paid for it with two $20-bills. How much change did she get?

4. Mr. Toner is tiling some floors in his house. He used 480 tiles in the bathroom and 644 tiles in the kitchen. How many tiles did he use?

5. Ken bought 9 cans of tennis balls. There are 3 balls in each can. How many tennis balls did he buy?

6. A car dealer has 365 cars to sell. The first week he sold 38 new cars and 66 used cars. How many cars does he have left to sell?

7. Kaisha took 8 pictures on Monday, 9 pictures on Tuesday, and 15 pictures on Wednesday. If she started with 36 pictures on the roll of film, did she use up the whole roll of film?

8. Darcy's stamp album has 8 pages. Each page can hold 6 rows of stamps with 5 stamps in each row. How many stamps can the album hold?

Divide.

1. $15 \div 3 =$ ____
2. $4\overline{)12}$
3. $2\overline{)10}$
4. $30 \div 5 =$ ____

5. $5\overline{)40}$
6. $21 \div 3 =$ ____
7. $14 \div 2 =$ ____
8. $2\overline{)6}$

9. $4\overline{)16}$
10. $45 \div 9 =$ ____
11. $6 \div 3 =$ ____
12. $18 \div 2 =$ ____

13. $3\overline{)24}$
14. $28 \div 4 =$ ____
15. $5\overline{)15}$
16. $3\overline{)27}$

17. $9 \div 3 =$ ____
18. $25 \div 5 =$ ____
19. $4 \div 2 =$ ____
20. $3\overline{)18}$

21. $2\overline{)16}$
22. $20 \div 4 =$ ____
23. $24 \div 4 =$ ____
24. $5\overline{)10}$

Write each missing number. Use multiplication or division. Check your answers with multiplication or division.

25. $15 \div 5 =$ ____
26. $9 \times 4 =$ ____
27. $6\overline{)36}$
28. $3 \times$ ____ $= 24$

29. $4\overline{)28}$
30. ____ $\times 8 = 40$
31. $32 \div 4 =$ ____
32. $9 \times 3 =$ ____

33. ____ $\times 9 = 18$
34. $4 \times 4 =$ ____
35. $3 \times 6 =$ ____
36. $50 \div 5 =$ ____

37. $12 \div 3 =$ ____
38. $2\overline{)8}$
39. $4\overline{)36}$
40. $35 \div 5 =$ ____

41. $4\overline{)8}$
42. $12 \div 2 =$ ____
43. $4\overline{)32}$
44. $5\overline{)20}$

Circle the letter of the correct answer.

1 642 ◯ 646

    a. <
    b. >

2 What is the value of the 7 in 739,201?

    a. hundred thousands
    b. ten thousands
    c. thousands
    d. NG

3
$$3,265 + 1,868$$

    a. 4,023
    b. 5,033
    c. 5,123
    d. NG

4
$$3,041 \quad 986 \quad + \quad 53$$

    a. 3,980
    b. 4,080
    c. 4,180
    d. NG

5
$$673 - 259$$

    a. 314
    b. 324
    c. 426
    d. NG

6
$$\$37.00 - 12.56$$

    a. $24.44
    b. $25.54
    c. $25.56
    d. NG

7

    a. 2:15
    b. 3:10
    c. 3:15
    d. NG

8 Find the perimeter.
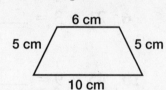

    a. 10 cm
    b. 16 cm
    c. 20 cm
    d. NG

9 Choose the better estimate of height.

    a. 30 feet
    b. 30 yards

10
$$73 \times 6$$

    a. 428
    b. 438
    c. 4,218
    d. NG

11
$$\$4.26 \times 8$$

    a. $3.40
    b. $33.08
    c. $34.08
    d. NG

12 Find the area.
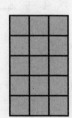

    a. 3 sq units
    b. 15 sq units
    c. 16 sq units
    d. NG

 score

STOP

Division Facts Through 9

Dividing by 6

Ronnie sees a sale on fishing bobbers at his favorite sporting goods store. How much will he pay for 1 bobber?

We want to find the cost of 1 bobber.

The bobbers are on sale at 6 for ____.

To find the cost of 1, we divide ____ by ____.

54¢ ÷ 6 = ____ (9¢ × 6 = 54¢)

Ronnie will pay ____ for 1 bobber.

Getting Started

Complete each number sentence.

1. 36 ÷ 6 = ____   2. 12 ÷ 6 = ____   3. 40 ÷ 5 = ____   4. 18 ÷ 6 = ____

5. 12 ÷ 3 = ____   6. 24 ÷ 6 = ____   7. 32 ÷ 4 = ____   8. 30 ÷ 6 = ____

Divide.

9. 6)42   10. 5)25   11. 6)48   12. 6)12

13. 3)18   14. 6)30   15. 6)54   16. 4)28

Practice

Complete each number sentence.

1. $18 \div 6 =$ _____
2. $36 \div 6 =$ _____
3. $32 \div 4 =$ _____
4. $20 \div 5 =$ _____

5. $24 \div 3 =$ _____
6. $48 \div 6 =$ _____
7. $15 \div 3 =$ _____
8. $54 \div 6 =$ _____

9. $36 \div 6 =$ _____
10. $14 \div 2 =$ _____
11. $24 \div 6 =$ _____
12. $18 \div 6 =$ _____

Divide.

13. $6\overline{)30}$
14. $4\overline{)28}$
15. $6\overline{)48}$
16. $6\overline{)54}$
17. $3\overline{)9}$

18. $3\overline{)27}$
19. $6\overline{)48}$
20. $4\overline{)36}$
21. $6\overline{)12}$
22. $5\overline{)10}$

Problem Solving

Solve each problem.

23. Ruth earned $10 babysitting for 5 hours. How much did she earn per hour?

24. Alicia bought 4 sweaters for $32. How much did each sweater cost?

Now Try This!

A number is divisible by 3 if the sum of its digits is divisible by 3. For example, 237 is divisible by 3, because $2 + 3 + 7 = 12$, and 12 is divisible by 3. Find the sum of the digits for each number and check to see if it is divisible by 3.

Number	Sum of the Digits	Divisible by 3
51	$5 + 1 = 6$	yes
29	_____	____
234	_____	____
1,633	_____	____
4,044	_____	____

Lesson 13-1 • Dividing by 6

Dividing by 7

Naomi is counting the days until summer vacation. She has 56 days to wait. How many weeks are there until Naomi's vacation begins?

We are looking for the number of weeks before Naomi's vacation starts.

There are _____ days until vacation begins.

In one week there are _____ days.

To find the total number of weeks, we divide _____ by _____.

56 ÷ 7 = _____ $\left(\text{8 × 7 = 56}\right)$

Naomi has _____ weeks to wait.

Getting Started

Complete each number sentence.

1. 21 ÷ 7 = _____   2. 14 ÷ 7 = _____   3. 18 ÷ 6 = _____   4. 63 ÷ 7 = _____

5. 25 ÷ 5 = _____   6. 49 ÷ 7 = _____   7. 28 ÷ 4 = _____   8. 42 ÷ 7 = _____

Divide.

9. 7)28   10. 7)56   11. 3)27   12. 5)45

13. 2)18   14. 7)35   15. 4)36   16. 6)42

Practice

Complete each number sentence.

1. $42 \div 6 =$ _____ 2. $32 \div 4 =$ _____ 3. $18 \div 3 =$ _____ 4. $36 \div 6 =$ _____

5. $35 \div 7 =$ _____ 6. $21 \div 7 =$ _____ 7. $16 \div 4 =$ _____ 8. $40 \div 5 =$ _____

9. $15 \div 3 =$ _____ 10. $63 \div 7 =$ _____ 11. $18 \div 2 =$ _____ 12. $21 \div 3 =$ _____

13. $49 \div 7 =$ _____ 14. $24 \div 6 =$ _____ 15. $42 \div 7 =$ _____ 16. $20 \div 4 =$ _____

Divide.

17. $3\overline{)15}$ 18. $7\overline{)63}$ 19. $5\overline{)10}$ 20. $7\overline{)49}$ 21. $4\overline{)24}$

22. $7\overline{)14}$ 23. $2\overline{)8}$ 24. $6\overline{)42}$ 25. $5\overline{)35}$ 26. $6\overline{)24}$

27. $5\overline{)40}$ 28. $7\overline{)28}$ 29. $7\overline{)56}$ 30. $3\overline{)27}$ 31. $7\overline{)21}$

32. $3\overline{)12}$ 33. $6\overline{)54}$ 34. $7\overline{)21}$ 35. $4\overline{)36}$ 36. $7\overline{)49}$

37. $3\overline{)9}$ 38. $7\overline{)56}$ 39. $7\overline{)63}$ 40. $6\overline{)30}$ 41. $4\overline{)28}$

42. $7\overline{)14}$ 43. $7\overline{)35}$ 44. $6\overline{)48}$ 45. $5\overline{)25}$ 46. $7\overline{)42}$

Problem Solving

Solve each problem.

47. Rachel's kitten is 49 days old. How many weeks old is her kitten?

48. Ben practiced piano 21 days in a row. How many weeks did Ben practice without missing a day?

49. Pat bought 9 pencils. Each pencil costs 7¢. How much did Pat pay for the pencils?

50. Vince paid 56¢ for 7 decals. How much did each decal cost?

Dividing by 8

Rhonda is making wooden plaques as gifts for her family. She wants to divide her piece of wood into 8 equal lengths. How long will each piece be?

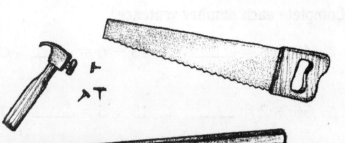

We want to know the length of each piece of wood.

The board is ____ inches long.

Rhonda needs ____ pieces for her plaques.

To find the length of each piece, we divide

____ by ____.

48 ÷ 8 = ____   (6 × 8 = 48)

Each plaque will be ____ inches long.

Getting Started

Complete each number sentence.

1. 24 ÷ 8 = ____   2. 35 ÷ 7 = ____   3. 48 ÷ 8 = ____   4. 27 ÷ 3 = ____

5. 32 ÷ 8 = ____   6. 40 ÷ 8 = ____   7. 36 ÷ 6 = ____   8. 16 ÷ 8 = ____

Divide.

9. $8\overline{)72}$ 10. $5\overline{)45}$ 11. $8\overline{)64}$ 12. $6\overline{)42}$

13. $4\overline{)28}$ 14. $6\overline{)48}$ 15. $8\overline{)56}$ 16. $3\overline{)24}$

Practice

Complete each number sentence.

1. 40 ÷ 8 = _____   2. 48 ÷ 6 = _____   3. 35 ÷ 7 = _____   4. 28 ÷ 7 = _____

5. 56 ÷ 7 = _____   6. 15 ÷ 5 = _____   7. 32 ÷ 4 = _____   8. 16 ÷ 8 = _____

Divide.

9. $8\overline{)56}$ 10. $8\overline{)24}$ 11. $4\overline{)24}$ 12. $8\overline{)32}$ 13. $8\overline{)72}$

14. $7\overline{)49}$ 15. $8\overline{)56}$ 16. $8\overline{)16}$ 17. $8\overline{)48}$ 18. $6\overline{)12}$

19. $5\overline{)45}$ 20. $8\overline{)72}$ 21. $3\overline{)21}$ 22. $8\overline{)32}$ 23. $7\overline{)56}$

24. $8\overline{)40}$ 25. $2\overline{)14}$ 26. $7\overline{)42}$ 27. $6\overline{)36}$ 28. $8\overline{)64}$

Problem Solving

Solve each problem.

29. Angie is making award badges from a piece of ribbon 64 centimeters long. She wants 8 badges. How long should she make each ribbon?

30. A square has 4 equal sides. Each side of the square is 8 inches long. What is the perimeter of the square?

31. Erasers cost 5¢ each. Amy bought 8 of them to use at home. How much did the erasers cost?

32. Ricky earned $40 this fall raking leaves. He had 8 customers. How much did Ricky charge each customer?

Dividing by 9

Mr. Edward bought a robot for each of his 9 grandchildren. He spent $72 in all. How much did each robot cost?

We are looking for the cost of one robot.

Mr. Edward has _____ grandchildren.

He spent _____ for all the robots.

To find the cost of one robot, we divide

_____ by _____.

$72 ÷ 9 = _____ $8 × 9 = $72

Mr. Edward paid _____ for each robot.

Getting Started

Complete each number sentence.

1. 36 ÷ 9 = ____   2. 45 ÷ 9 = ____   3. 42 ÷ 7 = ____   4. 27 ÷ 9 = ____

5. 35 ÷ 5 = ____   6. 72 ÷ 9 = ____   7. 32 ÷ 8 = ____   8. 36 ÷ 6 = ____

Divide.

9. $9\overline{)54}$ 10. $7\overline{)28}$ 11. $9\overline{)18}$ 12. $8\overline{)72}$

13. $9\overline{)63}$ 14. $4\overline{)20}$ 15. $7\overline{)56}$ 16. $9\overline{)81}$

Practice

Complete each number sentence.

1. $40 \div 5 =$ _____
2. $18 \div 9 =$ _____
3. $49 \div 7 =$ _____
4. $24 \div 6 =$ _____

5. $63 \div 9 =$ _____
6. $21 \div 3 =$ _____
7. $15 \div 5 =$ _____
8. $54 \div 6 =$ _____

9. $18 \div 6 =$ _____
10. $81 \div 9 =$ _____
11. $27 \div 9 =$ _____
12. $14 \div 7 =$ _____

13. $45 \div 9 =$ _____
14. $64 \div 8 =$ _____
15. $30 \div 6 =$ _____
16. $72 \div 9 =$ _____

Divide.

17. $9\overline{)63}$
18. $9\overline{)27}$
19. $7\overline{)42}$
20. $6\overline{)36}$
21. $9\overline{)45}$

22. $8\overline{)56}$
23. $5\overline{)35}$
24. $9\overline{)72}$
25. $9\overline{)54}$
26. $4\overline{)12}$

27. $8\overline{)32}$
28. $9\overline{)36}$
29. $6\overline{)24}$
30. $9\overline{)81}$
31. $9\overline{)18}$

32. $9\overline{)54}$
33. $7\overline{)49}$
34. $9\overline{)18}$
35. $3\overline{)21}$
36. $2\overline{)12}$

37. $8\overline{)40}$
38. $9\overline{)81}$
39. $9\overline{)72}$
40. $8\overline{)72}$
41. $3\overline{)27}$

42. $9\overline{)63}$
43. $6\overline{)48}$
44. $9\overline{)36}$
45. $9\overline{)45}$
46. $7\overline{)35}$

Problem Solving

Solve each problem.

47. There are 8 baseball teams in the league. Each team has 9 players. How many players are in the league?

48. There are 36 children in the third grade who want to play volleyball. Each team has 9 players. How many teams can the third grade make up?

49. Pretzels cost 9¢ each. Aaron spends 54¢ buying some for his friends. How many pretzels does he buy?

50. Joan is buying 9 books that cost $5 each. What will she pay for all the books?

Lesson 13-4 • Dividing by 9

1 and 0 in Division

Study these important ideas about 1 and 0 in division.

Dividing any number by 1 does not change the number.

$5 \div 1 = 5$ or $1\overline{)5}^{5}$ because $5 \times 1 =$ _____

Dividing any number by itself equals 1.

$8 \div 8 = 1$ or $8\overline{)8}^{1}$ because $1 \times 8 =$ _____

Dividing 0 by any number always equals 0.

$0 \div 7 = 0$ or $7\overline{)0}^{0}$ because $0 \times 7 =$ _____

Dividing a number by 0 doesn't make sense.

$6 \div 0 = ?$ $0 \times ? = 6$ There is no number that, multiplied by 0, would make 6.

Never divide by zero.

Getting Started

Divide.

1. $6\overline{)6}$ 2. $3\overline{)0}$ 3. $1\overline{)4}$ 4. $9\overline{)9}$ 5. $1\overline{)1}$

6. $3\overline{)3}$ 7. $7\overline{)0}$ 8. $1\overline{)8}$ 9. $2\overline{)0}$ 10. $1\overline{)6}$

11. $7\overline{)7}$ 12. $9\overline{)0}$ 13. $5\overline{)5}$ 14. $4\overline{)4}$ 15. $5\overline{)0}$

Practice _____

Divide.

1. $9\overline{)27}$ $7\overline{)42}$ $8\overline{)40}$ $6\overline{)42}$ $4\overline{)0}$ $9\overline{)81}$ $4\overline{)36}$ $5\overline{)0}$

2. $8\overline{)48}$ $8\overline{)32}$ $3\overline{)6}$ $6\overline{)24}$ $3\overline{)24}$ $6\overline{)6}$ $2\overline{)6}$ $2\overline{)12}$

3. $1\overline{)5}$ $1\overline{)9}$ $8\overline{)0}$ $9\overline{)36}$ $3\overline{)9}$ $2\overline{)14}$ $5\overline{)30}$ $1\overline{)6}$

4. $4\overline{)28}$ $2\overline{)0}$ $5\overline{)40}$ $1\overline{)0}$ $2\overline{)2}$ $8\overline{)64}$ $3\overline{)18}$ $5\overline{)35}$

5. $4\overline{)20}$ $4\overline{)8}$ $1\overline{)7}$ $4\overline{)4}$ $3\overline{)27}$ $7\overline{)56}$ $7\overline{)14}$ $2\overline{)8}$

6. $8\overline{)8}$ $9\overline{)18}$ $4\overline{)24}$ $2\overline{)18}$ $9\overline{)63}$ $7\overline{)35}$ $5\overline{)45}$ $2\overline{)10}$

7. $1\overline{)8}$ $5\overline{)15}$ $7\overline{)49}$ $5\overline{)10}$ $5\overline{)25}$ $7\overline{)0}$ $7\overline{)63}$ $3\overline{)12}$

8. $4\overline{)16}$ $2\overline{)4}$ $8\overline{)24}$ $6\overline{)36}$ $8\overline{)16}$ $3\overline{)15}$ $5\overline{)5}$ $3\overline{)21}$

9. $6\overline{)54}$ $4\overline{)32}$ $5\overline{)20}$ $1\overline{)3}$ $9\overline{)54}$ $9\overline{)0}$ $7\overline{)28}$ $3\overline{)0}$

10. $2\overline{)16}$ $6\overline{)0}$ $4\overline{)12}$ $1\overline{)4}$ $8\overline{)56}$ $9\overline{)45}$ $6\overline{)18}$ $1\overline{)1}$

11. $7\overline{)7}$ $6\overline{)12}$ $7\overline{)21}$ $8\overline{)72}$ $1\overline{)2}$ $3\overline{)3}$ $6\overline{)48}$ $6\overline{)30}$

Lesson 13-5 • 1 and 0 in Division

Name _____

Estimating Quotients

Towne Square Butcher Shop is having a sale. About how much does 1 pound of sirloin steak cost?

We want to know about how much 1 pound of sirloin steak costs.

Sirloin steak sells at 3 pounds for _____.

We need to round the amount to the nearest dollar and

divide by _____.

$8.75
↓ rounds to

_____ ÷ 3 = _____

One pound of sirloin steak costs about _____.

Getting Started

Round the amounts to the nearest dollar and estimate your answers.

1. $8.25 ÷ 2
2. $15.95 ÷ 4
3. $4.36 × 5
4. $53.80 ÷ 9
5. $21.25 ÷ 7
6. $6.27 + $3.48
7. $45.35 ÷ 5
8. $55.90 ÷ 8
9. $34.23 × 3
10. $16.21 ÷ 8
11. $11.98 ÷ 3
12. $9.26 − $3.75
13. $35.75 ÷ 6
14. $23.60 ÷ 3
15. $41.63 ÷ 7
16. $23.85 ÷ 6

Practice

Round each amount to the nearest dollar and solve each exercise.

1. $8.31 ÷ 4
2. $7.38 × 5
3. $35.19 ÷ 7
4. $9.52 − $3.87

5. $4.79 × 9
6. $53.86 ÷ 9
7. $9.95 ÷ 2
8. $7.57 + $8.86

9. $24.16 ÷ 8
10. $23.59 ÷ 6
11. $16.51 − $7.83
12. $8.50 × 6

13. $4.21 × 7
14. $27.09 ÷ 3
15. $48.75 ÷ 7
16. $4.39 + $8.05

17. $8.75 ÷ 9
18. $14.25 − $8.21
19. $5.68 − $1.39
20. $21.12 ÷ 3

21. $17.12 − $9.15
22. $7.83 × 5
23. $11.83 ÷ 4
24. $32.19 ÷ 8

25. $7.50 + $9.82
26. $42.15 ÷ 6
27. $10.20 ÷ 5
28. $6.21 × 9

29. $34.61 ÷ 7
30. $12.37 ÷ 2
31. $12.75 − $7.95
32. $4.51 × 3

Problem Solving

Solve each problem. Use estimation.

33. One plant stand costs $7.85. About how much will 5 plant stands cost?

34. Four bicycle tires cost $27.65. About how much does 1 bicycle tire cost?

35. Drinking glasses are on sale at 6 for $24.25. About how much does 1 glass cost?

36. A beach towel costs $8.43. Sun tan lotion costs $5.65. About how much do they cost together?

37. Tapes cost $8.98 each. Tad bought 6 tapes and Marcy bought 9 tapes. About how much more did Marcy spend?

38. Ties cost $9.75 each. Walter bought 7 ties. He gave the clerk $100. About how much change did Walter receive?

Lesson 13-6 • Estimating Quotients

Name _____

Problem Solving:
Solve a Simpler Problem

Some figures show shapes within shapes. How many triangles are in this figure?

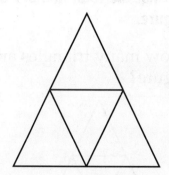

⭐ SEE

We want to know how many triangles are in the figure. There are large and small triangles in the figure.

⭐ PLAN

Sometimes you can solve a difficult problem by first solving a simpler problem. Break apart or change the problem into parts that are easier to solve.

Solve the simpler problems.

Look for small triangles.

There are _____ small triangles.

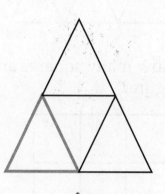

Look for large triangles.

There is _____ large triangle.

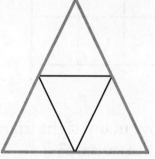

⭐ DO

Use the answers to the simpler problems to solve the original problem.

4 + 1 = _____

There is a total of _____ triangles in the figure.

⭐ CHECK

Count all the possible triangles to check your answer.

There are _____ triangles.

Apply

Draw or list the total number of shapes for each figure.

1. How many triangles are in this figure?

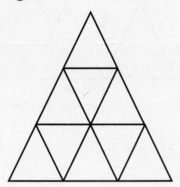

2. How many squares are in this figure?

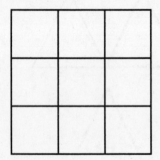

3. How many right triangles are in this square?

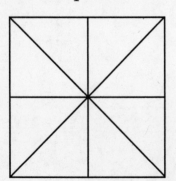

4. Gary had an orange. He cut it in half. Then he cut each half piece in half and cut each of those pieces in half again. He ate one piece of the orange. How many pieces did he have left?

5. One face of a cube looks like this. How many small green squares are there in the entire cube?

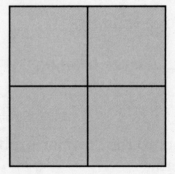

6. How many rectangles are in the figure in Problem 2?

Lesson 13-7 • Problem Solving: Solve a Simpler Problem

Calculator: The Division Key

Division is a shortcut for repeated subtraction. Division tells us how many times a number can be subtracted from another number.

$12 \div 4 = \square$

Notice that 12 $\div$ 4 $=$ 3 is a shortcut way of writing that 4 can be subtracted from 12 three times before we get 0.

$12 - 4 - 4 - 4 = \square$

Complete each code.

1. 12 $-$ 4 $-$ 4 $-$ 4 $=$ [____]

2. 12 $\div$ 4 $=$ [____]

3. 25 $-$ 5 $-$ 5 $-$ 5 $-$ 5 $-$ 5 $=$ [____]

4. 25 $\div$ 5 $=$ [____]

5. 12 $-$ 12 $=$ [____]

6. 12 $\div$ 12 $=$ [____]

7. 36 $-$ 6 $-$ 6 $-$ 6 $-$ 6 $-$ 6 $-$ 6 $=$ [____]

8. 36 $\div$ 6 $=$ [____]

9. 56 $-$ 8 $-$ 8 $-$ 8 $-$ 8 $-$ 8 $-$ 8 $-$ 8 $=$ [____]

10. 56 $\div$ 8 $=$ [____]

Complete each shortcut code. Write each answer in the screen.

11. 9 $\div$ 3 $=$ [____]   12. 14 $\div$ 2 $=$ [____]

13. 8 $\div$ 4 $=$ [____]   14. 5 $\div$ 5 $=$ [____]

15. 18 $\div$ 3 $=$ [____]   16. 28 $\div$ 7 $=$ [____]

17. 63 $\div$ 9 $=$ [____]   18. 8 $\div$ 1 $=$ [____]

19. 54 $\div$ 6 $=$ [____]   20. 72 $\div$ 8 $=$ [____]

Use your calculator to complete the cross-number puzzle.

<table>
<tr><td>

Across

1. 9×7
2. $35 + 18$
3. $427 + 486$
5. $1,276 - 639$
7. $91 - 38$
8. $6 \div 3$
9. $968 - 509$
11. $3,426 - 3,385$
15. $20 \div 4 \times 5$
17. $28 \div 7$
18. 7×7
19. $96 + 85 - 138$
20. $168 - 79 - 46$
24. $4 \times 3 \div 6 \times 35$
25. $196 + 77 - 28$
26. $6 \div 3 \times 18$

</td><td>

Down

1. $953 - 285$
2. 7×8
4. $5 \times 5 \times 5$
6. $2,988 + 4,563$
10. $18 \div 9 \times 486$
12. 36×4
13. $4 \div 1$
14. $486 + 278$
16. 6×9
21. $(43 + 65) \times 3$
22. $(75 \times 6) + 216$
23. $45 \div 5$
24. $38 + 47 + 89 - 98$

</td></tr>
</table>

Lesson 13-8 • Calculator: The Division Key

Divide.

1. $12 \div 6 =$ _____   2. $40 \div 8 =$ _____   3. $28 \div 4 =$ _____   4. $10 \div 5 =$ _____

5. $9 \div 9 =$ _____   6. $42 \div 7 =$ _____   7. $16 \div 2 =$ _____   8. $18 \div 3 =$ _____

9. $64 \div 8 =$ _____   10. $18 \div 6 =$ _____   11. $27 \div 9 =$ _____   12. $6 \div 1 =$ _____

13. $0 \div 3 =$ _____   14. $14 \div 2 =$ _____   15. $72 \div 8 =$ _____   16. $56 \div 7 =$ _____

17. $24 \div 3 =$ _____   18. $32 \div 4 =$ _____   19. $30 \div 5 =$ _____   20. $81 \div 9 =$ _____

21. $6\overline{)48}$ 22. $7\overline{)49}$ 23. $2\overline{)6}$ 24. $3\overline{)21}$

25. $4\overline{)4}$ 26. $4\overline{)16}$ 27. $5\overline{)45}$ 28. $9\overline{)72}$

29. $8\overline{)24}$ 30. $6\overline{)42}$ 31. $3\overline{)27}$ 32. $4\overline{)32}$

33. $1\overline{)9}$ 34. $5\overline{)35}$ 35. $9\overline{)63}$ 36. $4\overline{)28}$

37. $2\overline{)18}$ 38. $4\overline{)36}$ 39. $8\overline{)0}$ 40. $6\overline{)54}$

Solve each problem. Use estimation for problems 41 and 43.

41. Michelle buys 3 pumpkins as gifts for her teachers. If she pays $2.74 for each pumpkin, about how much money does she need?

42. Manuel spent 15 hours this week working on his computer. If he worked 5 days, how long did he work each day?

43. Scott bought 5 computer games for $34.75. About how much did he pay for each game?

44. Victoria is reading a book that is 81 pages long. How long will it take her to finish the book if she reads 9 pages a day?

Circle the letter of the correct answer.

1 912 ◯ 921

a. <
b. >

2 What is the value of the 5 in 320,510?

a. tens
b. ones
c. hundreds
d. NG

3
```
  5,396
+ 2,085
```
a. 7,381
b. 7,371
c. 7,481
d. NG

4
```
  2,365
     86
+   194
```
a. 2,545
b. 2,635
c. 2,745
d. NG

5
```
  703
- 285
```
a. 988
b. 582
c. 418
d. NG

6
```
  $43.20
-  8.98
```
a. $34.38
b. $45.78
c. $52.18
d. NG

7

a. 3:40
b. 3:45
c. 10:15
d. NG

8 Find the perimeter.

12 m
12 m [square] 12 m
12 m

a. 48 m
b. 24 m
c. 144 m
d. NG

9 Choose the better estimate for the weight of a pair of sneakers.

a. 6 oz
b. 1 lb

10
```
  48
×  7
```
a. 334
b. 336
c. 2,856
d. NG

11
```
  $6.37
×     4
```
a. $24.28
b. $25.28
c. $25.48
d. NG

12 Find the area.

a. 7 units
b. 7 sq units
c. 14 sq units
d. NG

13 Find the volume.

a. 4 cu units
b. 6 cu units
c. 12 cu units
d. NG

[ ] score

 STOP

Division

Understanding Division

Ed works in a nursery. His job today is to fill flats with 25 begonias. Each flat must contain the same number of plants. How many begonias will go into each flat? How many plants will Ed have left over?

We want to know the number of plants in each flat and the number left over.

Ed has _____ flats to fill.

He has _____ begonias to put into the flats.

To find the number of begonias in each flat, we

separate the _____ plants into _____ equal groups.

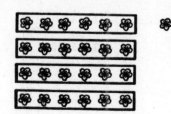

We divide 25 by 4 and get _____, with _____ left over.

Ed can put _____ plants into each flat and have _____ left over.

Getting Started

Use the pictures to solve each problem.

1. 19 flowers
    3 flats

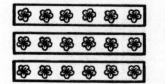

    _____ in each flat
    _____ left over

2. 27 packs of seeds
    5 rows planted

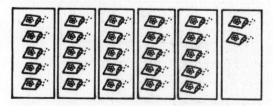

    _____ packs in each row
    _____ left over

Practice

Use the pictures to solve each problem.

1. 11 books
   2 shelves

   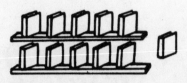

   _____ books on a shelf
   _____ left over

2. 17 sheets of paper
   4 paper clips

   _____ sheets clipped together
   _____ left over

3. 19 tennis balls
   3 balls to a can

   _____ cans
   _____ ball left over

4. $15 to spend
   $4 for each kite

   _____ kites bought
   _____ left over

[Now Try This!]

A number that is divisible by 2, with no leftovers, is an **even** number.
If there is a leftover of 1, then the number is **odd**.

Find the sum for each pair of addends. Then write **odd** or **even** below
each number.

	Addend	Addend	Sum
1.	7	9	16
	odd	odd	even
2.	6	5	
3.	8	6	

	Addend	Addend	Sum
4.	3	4	
5.	7	5	
6.	4	8	

Dividing, 1-Digit Quotients

Lana helps her father in the produce department of his grocery store. He needs her to put 6 apples into each plastic bag. How many bags of apples can she pack? How many apples will be left over?

We want to know the number of bags Lana packs and how many apples are left over.

Lana has ____ apples to pack.

She packs ____ apples in each bag.

To see how many bags can be packed, we need to

divide ____ by ____. The number of apples left over is called the **remainder**.

☐ × 6 = 20 or a number less than, but close to 20.	Multiply. 3 × 6 = 18	Subtract. 20 − 18 = 2 Compare. 2 < 6	Write the remainder after R in the quotient.

$$\begin{array}{r} 3 \\ 6\overline{)20} \end{array}$$ $$\begin{array}{r} 3 \\ 6\overline{)20} \\ \underline{18} \end{array}$$ $$\begin{array}{r} 3 \\ 6\overline{)20} \\ \underline{18} \\ 2 \end{array}$$ $$\begin{array}{r} 3\ \text{R2} \\ 6\overline{)20} \\ \underline{18} \\ 2 \end{array}$$

20 divided by 6 is ____ with a remainder of ____.

Lana will pack ____ bags of apples with ____ apples left over.

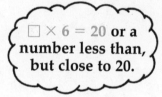
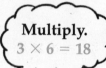
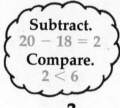

quotient
3 R2 ← remainder
6)20
divisor ↑ ↑ dividend

Getting Started

Divide. Show your work.

1. 5)27   2. 3)19   3. 7)25   4. 6)34   5. 8)40

Practice

Divide. Show your work.

1. $6\overline{)19}$ 2. $4\overline{)25}$ 3. $7\overline{)32}$ 4. $8\overline{)27}$ 5. $2\overline{)9}$

6. $5\overline{)40}$ 7. $9\overline{)43}$ 8. $3\overline{)17}$ 9. $4\overline{)19}$ 10. $7\overline{)56}$

11. $8\overline{)44}$ 12. $9\overline{)59}$ 13. $2\overline{)15}$ 14. $5\overline{)43}$ 15. $6\overline{)46}$

16. $4\overline{)25}$ 17. $3\overline{)27}$ 18. $8\overline{)31}$ 19. $6\overline{)45}$ 20. $2\overline{)13}$

21. $9\overline{)35}$ 22. $7\overline{)50}$ 23. $5\overline{)45}$ 24. $3\overline{)22}$ 25. $4\overline{)15}$

26. $8\overline{)43}$ 27. $9\overline{)72}$ 28. $6\overline{)29}$ 29. $2\overline{)17}$ 30. $5\overline{)34}$

Problem Solving

Solve each problem.

31. Tom has 56 empty bottles to put into cases. Each case holds 6 bottles. How many full cases will he have? How many bottles will be left over?

32. Rhoda takes stickers to school to give to her 23 classmates. Rhoda gives each student 3 stickers. How many stickers does she give away?

33. One store is selling Good Glassware at 6 glasses for $48. Another store is selling the same brand at 8 glasses for $56. Which is the better buy?

34. Mr. Harris is buying tires for his lawnmower. The tires he wants to buy are priced at 4 for $50. Another store will sell Mr. Harris 5 tires for $59. Which is the better buy?

Checking Division

Roy is making necklaces for gifts. He is
stringing 5 beads on each necklace. How
many necklaces can he make? How many
beads will he have left over?

We want to find the number of necklaces
Roy can make and the number of beads
left over.

Roy has _____ beads.

Each necklace needs _____ beads.

To find the number of necklaces and the

beads left over, we divide _____ by _____.

$$\underset{\text{divisor}\longrightarrow}{} 5\overline{)37} \begin{array}{l} \xleftarrow{\quad} \text{quotient} \\ 7 \text{ R2} \xleftarrow{} \text{remainder} \\ \xleftarrow{} \text{dividend} \\ \underline{35} \\ 2 \end{array}$$

| To check division, we multiply the divisor by the quotient and then add any remainder. The sum should be the same as the dividend. |

$$\begin{array}{c} 7 \\ \times\ 5 \\ \hline 35 \end{array} \nearrow \begin{array}{c} 35 \\ +\ 2 \\ \hline 37 \end{array}$$

Roy can make _____ necklaces.

He will have _____ beads left over.

Getting Started

Divide. Check each division.

1. $4\overline{)17}$
2. $7\overline{)60}$
3. $9\overline{)86}$

Practice

Divide. Check each division.

1. $7\overline{)44}$ 2. $6\overline{)53}$ 3. $8\overline{)49}$ 4. $9\overline{)40}$

5. $5\overline{)41}$ 6. $4\overline{)14}$ 7. $7\overline{)53}$ 8. $8\overline{)70}$

9. $9\overline{)49}$ 10. $4\overline{)31}$ 11. $5\overline{)18}$ 12. $6\overline{)50}$

Problem Solving

Solve each problem.

13. In your school, 26 students sign up for the chess tournament. There will be 4 players on each team. How many teams will there be? How many extra players will there be?

14. The principal wants to write directions. He knows there are 6 teams with 4 players on each team. He knows that there are also 2 extra players. Show how he knows that he needs 26 copies of directions.

Now Try This!

What are the chances that the chosen square will be

white? _____ in _____   black? _____ in _____

black or white? _____ in _____   black, white, or green? _____ in _____

Dividing, 2-Digit Quotients

Rolando has 48¢ left in the club's treasury. He wants to divide it equally among all the club's members. How much money will each member receive?

We want to know the amount of money each member will receive if the treasury is divided equally.

The club's treasury has _____ in it.

The club has _____ members.

To find the amount in one share, we divide

_____ by _____.

Divide. $3\overline{)4}$ with 1 above
Multiply. $3 \times 1 = 3$
Subtract. $4 - 3 = 1$
Compare. $1 < 3$

Bring down the ones digit. There are now 18 pennies.

Divide. $3\overline{)18}$ with 6 above
Multiply. $3 \times 6 = 18$
Subtract. $18 - 18 = 0$
Compare. $0 < 3$
No remainder.

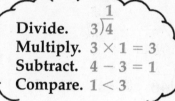

$$3\overline{)48¢}$$ quotient 1, $\frac{3}{1}$

$$3\overline{)48¢}$$ quotient 1, $\frac{3}{18}$

$$3\overline{)48¢}$$ quotient 16¢, $\frac{3}{18}$, $\frac{18}{0}$

Each member will receive _____.

Getting Started

Divide. Show your work.

1. $2\overline{)36}$ 2. $4\overline{)92}$ 3. $8\overline{)80}$ 4. $2\overline{)78}$ 5. $7\overline{)84}$

Practice

Divide. Show your work.

1. $3\overline{)48}$
2. $5\overline{)65}$
3. $8\overline{)96}$
4. $4\overline{)96}$
5. $7\overline{)70}$

6. $9\overline{)99}$
7. $6\overline{)84}$
8. $2\overline{)56}$
9. $3\overline{)72}$
10. $8\overline{)80}$

11. $5\overline{)70}$
12. $4\overline{)88}$
13. $9\overline{)90}$
14. $2\overline{)76}$
15. $3\overline{)87}$

16. $7\overline{)91}$
17. $5\overline{)75}$
18. $8\overline{)88}$
19. $6\overline{)72}$
20. $7\overline{)84}$

21. $3\overline{)81}$
22. $2\overline{)48}$
23. $5\overline{)60}$
24. $2\overline{)46}$
25. $3\overline{)90}$

26. $5\overline{)85}$
27. $7\overline{)77}$
28. $2\overline{)90}$
29. $6\overline{)78}$
30. $4\overline{)80}$

Problem Solving

Solve each problem.

31. Quan has 98¢. He wants to divide the money among his 7 brothers and sisters. How much will each person get?

32. Toni bought a top for 79¢. Lois bought one for 87¢. How much more did Lois pay for her top?

33. Alexi collected 95 pine cones to make fall wreaths. Each wreath takes 5 pine cones. How many wreaths can he make?

34. Corey bought 3 birthday cards. Each card cost $1.25. How much did Corey pay for the cards?

Lesson 14-4 • Dividing, 2-Digit Quotients

Dividing, 2-Digit Quotients With Remainders

Jill baked 71 gingerbread cookies to give her 3 neighbors as gifts. She wants to give each neighbor the same number of cookies. How many cookies will each neighbor receive? How many cookies will be left over?

We are looking for the number of cookies each neighbor will receive, and the number left over.

Jill baked ____ gingerbread cookies.

She wants to give gift boxes to ____ neighbors.

To find how many cookies go in each gift box, we divide ____ by ____.

The remainder is the number of leftovers.

How many 3s are in 7? Multiply. $2 \times 3 = 6$	Subtract. $7 - 6 = 1$ Compare. $1 < 3$ Bring down the 1.	How many 3s are in 11? Multiply. $3 \times 3 = 9$	Subtract. $11 - 9 = 2$ Compare. $2 < 3$ The remainder is 2.

$$\begin{array}{r} 2 \\ 3\overline{)71} \\ 6 \\ \hline \end{array}$$

$$\begin{array}{r} 2 \\ 3\overline{)71} \\ 6 \\ \hline 11 \end{array}$$

$$\begin{array}{r} 23 \\ 3\overline{)71} \\ 6 \\ \hline 11 \\ 9 \\ \hline \end{array}$$

$$\begin{array}{r} 23 \text{ R2} \\ 3\overline{)71} \\ 6 \\ \hline 11 \\ 9 \\ \hline 2 \end{array}$$

Jill can put ____ gingerbread cookies in each gift box.

She will have ____ cookies left over to eat.

Getting Started _____

Divide. Show your work.

1. $4\overline{)65}$ 2. $6\overline{)81}$ 3. $7\overline{)90}$ 4. $5\overline{)43}$ 5. $9\overline{)97}$

Practice

Divide. Show your work.

1. $5\overline{)68}$ 2. $7\overline{)93}$ 3. $6\overline{)87}$ 4. $3\overline{)55}$ 5. $8\overline{)98}$

6. $7\overline{)75}$ 7. $5\overline{)88}$ 8. $8\overline{)83}$ 9. $4\overline{)74}$ 10. $3\overline{)86}$

11. $2\overline{)91}$ 12. $9\overline{)93}$ 13. $4\overline{)64}$ 14. $6\overline{)71}$ 15. $3\overline{)49}$

16. $6\overline{)78}$ 17. $2\overline{)67}$ 18. $5\overline{)53}$ 19. $8\overline{)97}$ 20. $4\overline{)83}$

21. $3\overline{)71}$ 22. $7\overline{)84}$ 23. $9\overline{)86}$ 24. $5\overline{)99}$ 25. $2\overline{)63}$

26. $6\overline{)68}$ 27. $3\overline{)96}$ 28. $8\overline{)88}$ 29. $7\overline{)79}$ 30. $4\overline{)94}$

Problem Solving

Solve each problem.

31. The 8 pandas at the zoo were fed 48 pounds of food in one week. How many pounds of food did each panda eat?

32. Each of the school buses can carry 72 passengers. How many passengers can ride in 4 buses?

33. The school bus holds 72 passengers. Each seat holds 2 people. How many seats are in the bus?

34. Fifty-eight shirts need to be packed in boxes. Only 4 shirts fit in a box. How many boxes are needed? How many shirts are left over?

Lesson 14-5 • Dividing, 2-Digit Quotients With Remainders

Understanding Remainders

Stacey has 98¢ to spend on barrettes for her hair. Each costs 8¢. How many barrettes can she buy?

We want to know how many barrettes Stacey can buy.

Stacey has ____ to spend on barrettes.

One barrette costs ____.

To find the number she can buy, we divide

____ by ____.

$$\begin{array}{r} 12\ \textbf{R2} \\ 8¢\overline{)98¢} \\ 8 \\ \hline 18 \\ 16 \\ \hline 2 \end{array}$$

To check: multiply and add.

$$\Box \times 8¢ \quad \Box¢$$

$$+ \quad 2¢ \text{ remainder}$$

$$\Box¢ \qquad \Box¢$$

Stacey can buy ____ barrettes. The remaining 2¢ is not enough to buy another barrette, so the remainder does not affect the answer.

REMEMBER Sometimes the remainder will affect the answer.

Getting Started

Divide and check your answers.

1. 4)93

2. 6)75

3. 7)91

4. 5)87

Solve each problem.

5. Susan has 92 oranges to put into bags. Each bag holds 8 oranges. How many bags will Susan need?

6. There are 53 children riding floats in the parade. Only 4 children can ride on each float. How many floats will be needed to hold all the children?

Practice

Divide. Show your work.

1. $5\overline{)63}$ 2. $4\overline{)97}$ 3. $2\overline{)83}$

4. $7\overline{)84}$ 5. $6\overline{)88}$ 6. $3\overline{)76}$

7. $9\overline{)95}$ 8. $2\overline{)57}$ 9. $8\overline{)80}$

10. $3\overline{)91}$ 11. $5\overline{)79}$ 12. $4\overline{)95}$

13. $6\overline{)76}$ 14. $2\overline{)89}$ 15. $5\overline{)97}$

Problem Solving

Solve each problem.

16. Mr. Frank is building a split-rail fence around his yard. He has 39 split rails. It takes 4 rails for each section. How many sections can Mr. Frank build?

17. Mrs. Granski's class of 23 students is going on a field trip. A school rule allows only 4 students in a car. How many cars will be needed?

18. Dean is making sandwiches for the class picnic. He has 35 slices of bread. How many full sandwiches can he make?

19. Roberta bought 80 ounces of juice for the picnic. Each paper cup holds 6 ounces. How many cups will she need to use all the juice?

Lesson 14-6 • Understanding Remainders

Name _____

Problem Solving: Make a Table

Eric's mother was 30 when he was born. How old will Eric be when his mother is 4 times his age?

⭐ SEE

We want to find Eric's age when his mother's age is 4 times his age.

When Eric was 0 years old, his mother was 30.

⭐ PLAN

We can make a table comparing Eric's age with his mother's age. We begin with Eric's birth.

⭐ DO

Eric's Age	0	1	2	3		5	6		8	9	
Mother's Age	30	31	32	33		35	36		38	39	

When Eric is _____, his mother will be _____.

She will be 4 times his age.

⭐ CHECK

$4 \times 10 = 40$

This is the first age combination that solves the problem.

Apply

Make a table on a sheet of paper to solve each problem.

Problem-Solving Strategy: Using the Four-Step Plan

★ **SEE** What do you need to find?
★ **PLAN** What do you need to do?
★ **DO** Follow the plan.
★ **CHECK** Does your answer make sense?

1. How many months have only 30 days? How many have a total of 31?

2. How many brothers and sisters of your classmates are between 0 and 5 years of age? How many are between 6 and 10?

3. What numbers between 75 and 100 are evenly divisible by both 2 and 3?

4. What numbers between 20 and 40 can be divided by 3, 6, and 9?

5. Ask each of your classmates their favorite color, day of the week, and season. Record each student's response.

6. Make up three questions that can be answered by yes or no. Ask each of your classmates the questions and record each student's answers.

7. There are 9 equal groups of birds in a tree. The total number of birds is less than 100 and greater than 9. What is the greatest possible number of birds in each group, and what is the least possible number of birds in each group?

8. Molly is the manager for the Blue Birds Baseball Team. She tries to put the bats in equal rows. When she makes 3 equal rows, she has 1 bat left over. When she makes 4 equal rows, she has 1 bat left over. If she has fewer than 20 bats, exactly how many bats does she have?

9. Suppose a stationery store sells a package of 4 notepads for $1.68. Explain how to find the cost of 24 notepads.

Divide. Show your work.

1. $7\overline{)71}$ 2. $5\overline{)86}$ 3. $9\overline{)81}$ 4. $2\overline{)57}$ 5. $3\overline{)72}$

6. $6\overline{)53}$ 7. $8\overline{)98}$ 8. $4\overline{)83}$ 9. $5\overline{)35}$ 10. $7\overline{)86}$

11. $5\overline{)82}$ 12. $4\overline{)76}$ 13. $7\overline{)99}$ 14. $3\overline{)97}$ 15. $2\overline{)80}$

16. $7\overline{)43}$ 17. $9\overline{)99}$ 18. $6\overline{)87}$ 19. $5\overline{)88}$ 20. $3\overline{)71}$

Solve each problem.

21. Rodney is sewing 26 badges on his scout uniform. How many badges will be on each sleeve?

22. Mr. Springer has 50 extra math worksheets to hand out to 8 students. How many worksheets will he have left over if he gives each student the same number?

23. If there are 4 cups in 1 quart and I have 80 cups, how many quarts do I have?

24. Last week, Larry bought 8 pounds of birdseed for 65¢. This week he saw a sign that said a pound of birdseed is on sale for 10¢. Do you think this sign is correct or incorrect? Why?

Circle the letter of the correct answer.

1   346 ◯ 643

- **a.** <
- **b.** >

---

2   What is the value of the 0 in 940,681?

- **a.** tens
- **b.** hundreds
- **c.** thousands
- **d.** NG

3

$$\begin{array}{r} 39 \\ 78 \\ +\ 56 \\ \hline \end{array}$$

- **a.** 163
- **b.** 173
- **c.** 183
- **d.** NG

4

$$\begin{array}{r} \$16.47 \\ +\ 34.95 \\ \hline \end{array}$$

- **a.** $40.32
- **b.** $50.42
- **c.** $51.42
- **d.** NG

5

$$\begin{array}{r} 638 \\ -\ 257 \\ \hline \end{array}$$

- **a.** 421
- **b.** 481
- **c.** 895
- **d.** NG

6

$$\begin{array}{r} \$82.36 \\ -\ 29.78 \\ \hline \end{array}$$

- **a.** $52.58
- **b.** $62.58
- **c.** $67.42
- **d.** NG

7

- **a.** 4:00
- **b.** 12:27
- **c.** 5:00
- **d.** NG

---

8   Find the perimeter.

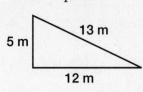

- **a.** 17 m
- **b.** 18 m
- **c.** 25 m
- **d.** NG

---

9   Choose the better estimate.

- **a.** 1 mL
- **b.** 1 L

10

$$\begin{array}{r} 25 \\ \times\ 9 \\ \hline \end{array}$$

- **a.** 34
- **b.** 225
- **c.** 1,845
- **d.** NG

11

$$\begin{array}{r} \$3.68 \\ \times\ \ \ 7 \\ \hline \end{array}$$

- **a.** $25.26
- **b.** $25.74
- **c.** $25.76
- **d.** NG

---

12   Find the area.

- **a.** 3 sq units
- **b.** 6 sq units
- **c.** 18 sq units
- **d.** NG

---

13   7)‾42‾

- **a.** 6
- **b.** 7
- **c.** 8
- **d.** NG

[   ]   **score**

STOP

Fractions and Probability

Understanding Fractions

Art and Phil are planting seeds. They have finished planting one section. What part of the job is finished?

When an object is separated into equal parts, each part is called a fraction.

_____ equal parts
Each part is $\frac{1}{2}$.

_____ equal parts
Each part is $\frac{1}{3}$.

_____ equal parts
Each part is $\frac{1}{4}$.

_____ equal parts
Each part is $\frac{1}{5}$.

_____ equal parts
Each part is $\frac{1}{6}$.

_____ equal parts
Each part is $\frac{1}{7}$.

The garden has _____ equal parts. Each part of the garden is $\frac{1}{4}$.

Art and Phil have finished $\frac{\boxed{}}{\boxed{}}$ of the garden.

Getting Started

Write the number of equal parts. Write the fraction for each part.

1.

_____ parts

Each part is _____.

2.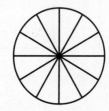

_____ parts

Each part is _____.

Practice

Write the number of equal parts. Write the fraction for each part.

1.  ____ parts

   Each part is ____.

2. 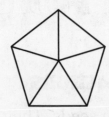 ____ parts

   Each part is ____.

3. 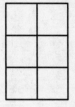 ____ parts

   Each part is ____.

4.  ____ parts

   Each part is ____.

5. 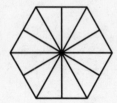 ____ parts

   Each part is ____.

6. 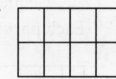 ____ parts

   Each part is ____.

7.  ____ parts

   Each part is ____.

8. 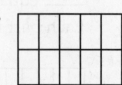 ____ parts

   Each part is ____.

Now Try This!

1. Divide each square into 4 equal parts a different way.

2. Divide each square into 6 equal parts a different way.

Lesson 15-1 • Understanding Fractions

Name _____

Naming Parts of a Whole

Rosita is making a quilt for her bed. She has finished 3 of the quilt's 4 squares. What part of the quilt has Rosita completed?

We want to write a number that shows the part of the quilt that is finished.

Rosita has finished _____ squares of the quilt.

The finished quilt will have _____ squares.

We use a fraction to show what part is finished.

finished parts → **3** ← numerator
parts in the → **4** ← denominator
whole quilt

Three-fourths or ▭/▭ of the quilt is finished.

Getting Started

Write each as a fraction.

1. five-twelfths _____   2. one-eighth _____   3. three-hundredths _____

Write the fraction of each figure that is green.

4. 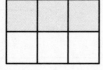   5. 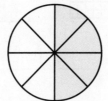   6.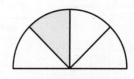
_____   _____   _____

Write the fraction of each figure that is *not* green.

7. 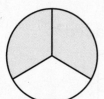   8.    9.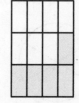
_____   _____   _____

Practice

Write each as a fraction.

1. nine-hundredths _____
2. three-fourths _____
3. five-eighths _____

4. ten-twelfths _____
5. four-fifths _____
6. seven-tenths _____

Write the fraction of each figure that is green.

7. _____

8.  _____

9. 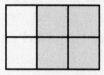 _____

10. 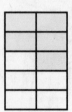 _____

11. 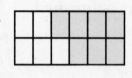 _____

12. _____

Write the fraction of each figure that is _not_ green.

13. 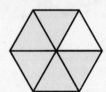 _____

14. 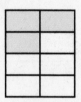 _____

15. _____

16. 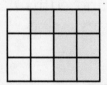 _____

17. _____

18. 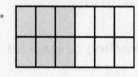 _____

Problem Solving

Solve each problem.

19. Shade $\frac{5}{6}$ of the circle.
What part is not shaded?

 _____

20. Shade $\frac{1}{8}$ of the figure.
Shade another $\frac{3}{8}$.
What part is not shaded?

_____

Lesson 15-2 • Naming Parts of a Whole

Naming Parts of a Set

Tina fills 3 of the glasses in the set with milk. What part of all the glasses are filled with milk?

We want to know what part of all the glasses contains milk.

Tina pours milk into ____ glasses.

There are ____ glasses in the set.

We use a fraction to show what part of the set of glasses is filled.

glasses filled → **3** ← numerator

number in → **5** ← denominator
the set

Tina fills ⬜/⬜ of the set with milk.

Getting Started

Write a fraction to answer each question.

1. What part of all the cars are green?

____

2. What part of all the pets are puppies?

____

3. What part of the set of coins are pennies?

____

4. What part of the set of figures are *not* squares?

△ △ ⬜ △ ⬜
⬜ ⬜ ⬜ ⬜ ⬜
____

Practice

Write a fraction to answer each question.

1. What fraction of all the triangles are green?

_____

2. What fraction of all the squares are not green?

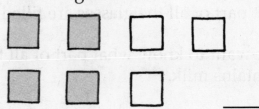

_____

3. What fraction of all the bowls are full?

_____

4. What fraction of all the vases have flowers?

_____

5. What fraction of the set of dishes are not broken?

_____

6. What fraction of the set of coins are quarters?

_____

7. What fraction of the week has already passed?

_____

8. What fraction of the set of candles are lit?

_____

Problem Solving

Solve each problem.

9. What fraction of all of the days of the week starts with the letter *S*?

_____

10. What fraction of all of the months of the year start with the letter *J*?

_____

Lesson 15-3 • Naming Parts of a Set

Name _____

Probability

The spinner is divided into five equal sections. There are five possible **outcomes**. The pointer can land on 1, 2, 3, or 4. What is the probability that the pointer will land on 3?

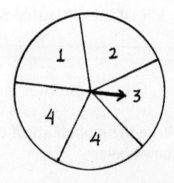

Probability is the chance that something will happen. The spinner has ____ sections. It has one 3. The probability that the pointer will land on 3 is 1 out of 5. We can write this as a fraction: $\frac{1}{5}$.

What is the probability that the pointer will land on 4? There are two 4s. The probability that the pointer will land on 4 is 2 out of 5 or $\frac{2}{5}$.

Some events are more likely to happen than others. An event that cannot happen is **impossible**. The pointer cannot land on 0.

Some events are **certain**. They are sure to happen. The pointer is sure to land on 1, 2, 3, or 4.

Getting Started _____

Use the spinner on the right. Write the probability of the pointer landing on each number given.

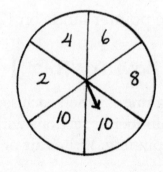

1. 2 ____

2. 10 ____

3. A number less than 10 ____

Write the word *certain* or *impossible* to show the likeliness of each event.

4. The pointer lands on 12. _____

5. The pointer lands on an even number. _____

Practice

Use the spinner at the right to answer the questions.

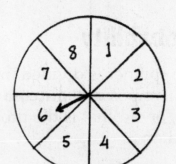

1. List all the outcomes for this spinner.

   _____

2. Can the pointer land on 10? _____

Write the probability of the pointer landing on each number shown below.

3. 3 _____

4. A number greater than 5 _____

5. A number less than 3 _____

Write the word *certain* or *impossible* to show the likeliness of each event.

6. The pointer lands on 9. _____

7. The pointer lands on a number less than 9. _____

8. The pointer lands on 0. _____

9. The pointer lands on a number greater than 0. _____

10. The pointer lands on 12. _____

(Now Try This!)

A **fair game** is when each section of a spinner is the same size and there is an equal number of sections with the same label. Everyone has an equal chance when spinning. Write **fair** or **unfair** for each spinner.

1.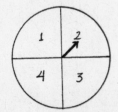

   _____

2.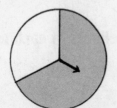

   _____

3.

   _____

4.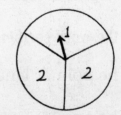

   _____

Lesson 15-4 • Probability

Finding a Fraction of a Number

Martina is polishing her mother's shoes to earn her allowance this week. She has polished $\frac{1}{2}$ of all the shoes so far. How many shoes has she polished?

We want to know the number of shoes Martina has polished.

Martina has ____ shoes to polish.

She has shined $\frac{\square}{\square}$ of them.

To find the number of shoes, we find $\frac{1}{2}$ of 12. This is the same as dividing 12 by 2.

12 ÷ ____ = ____

Martina has polished ____ shoes so far.

Getting Started

Write the fraction of each number.

1. $\frac{1}{3}$ of 6 = ____
2. $\frac{1}{2}$ of 8 = ____
3. $\frac{1}{5}$ of 10 = ____
4. $\frac{1}{3}$ of 12 = ____

5. $\frac{1}{6}$ of 18 = ____
6. $\frac{1}{9}$ of 27 = ____
7. $\frac{1}{7}$ of 49 = ____
8. $\frac{1}{4}$ of 64 = ____

Write the fraction of each number.

9. Pat has 60¢. She gave her brother $\frac{1}{4}$ of the money. How much money did Pat give her brother?

10. Dick has 85 marbles. He gave $\frac{1}{5}$ of the marbles to Jim. How many marbles does Dick still have?

Practice

Write the fraction of each number.

1. $\frac{1}{2}$ of 16 = ____   2. $\frac{1}{3}$ of 18 = ____   3. $\frac{1}{5}$ of 25 = ____   4. $\frac{1}{7}$ of 28 = ____

5. $\frac{1}{4}$ of 32 = ____   6. $\frac{1}{6}$ of 30 = ____   7. $\frac{1}{8}$ of 64 = ____   8. $\frac{1}{9}$ of 72 = ____

9. $\frac{1}{7}$ of 56 = ____   10. $\frac{1}{4}$ of 60 = ____   11. $\frac{1}{3}$ of 69 = ____   12. $\frac{1}{8}$ of 72 = ____

13. $\frac{1}{2}$ of 76 = ____   14. $\frac{1}{6}$ of 72 = ____   15. $\frac{1}{5}$ of 85 = ____   16. $\frac{1}{9}$ of 27 = ____

17. $\frac{1}{6}$ of 36 = ____   18. $\frac{1}{4}$ of 96 = ____   19. $\frac{1}{3}$ of 81 = ____   20. $\frac{1}{8}$ of 40 = ____

Problem Solving

Solve each problem.

21. Rene buys 18 cans of cat food. She wants $\frac{1}{2}$ of the cans to be tuna. How many cans of tuna does she buy?

22. Mr. Campana buys 48 cans of vegetables. He wants $\frac{1}{4}$ of the cans to be corn. How many cans of corn does Mr. Campana buy?

23. Hal has 36 fish in his tank. He says $\frac{1}{3}$ of them are goldfish. How many of Hal's fish are goldfish?

24. Lori has 75¢. She gives $\frac{1}{5}$ of her money to her best friend Jo. How much does Lori give Jo?

25. Ellen has 24 stamps. She uses $\frac{1}{4}$ of them to mail a package. How many stamps does Ellen have left?

26. Eduardo buys a jacket for $96. His father agrees to pay $\frac{1}{6}$ of the price. How much does Eduardo pay?

Lesson 15-5 • Finding a Fraction of a Number

Writing Equivalent Fractions

Jeff and Nadia are cutting pies to serve at the PTA social. Jeff cuts his pies into thirds, and serves $\frac{1}{3}$ of a pie to each person. Nadia cuts her pies into sixths. How many sixths does Nadia have to serve to each person to equal Jeff's serving?

We want to know how many of Nadia's pieces equal one of Jeff's.

Each of Jeff's pieces is $\frac{\square}{\square}$ of a pie.

Nadia cuts her pie into _____ equal pieces.

We can draw a picture and compare the pies.

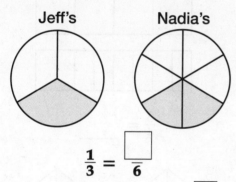

Jeff's   Nadia's

$\frac{1}{3} = \frac{\square}{6}$

One-third of Jeff's pie equals $\frac{\square}{\square}$ of Nadia's pie.

Fractions that are equal are called **equivalent fractions.**

Getting Started

Write the equivalent fractions.

1. $\frac{1}{2} =$ _____

2. $\frac{1}{3} =$ _____

Draw a picture to help you complete each number sentence.

3. $\frac{1}{2} = \frac{\square}{6}$

4. $\frac{3}{4} = \frac{\square}{8}$

Practice _____

Write the equivalent fractions.

1.

$\frac{1}{3} =$ _____

2.

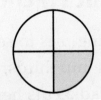

$\frac{1}{4} =$ _____

3.

$\frac{2}{6} =$ _____

4.

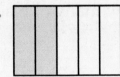 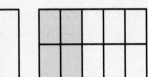

$\frac{2}{5} =$ _____

5.

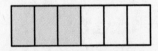

$\frac{3}{6} =$ _____

6.

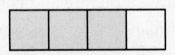
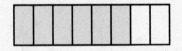

$\frac{3}{4} =$ _____

7.

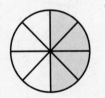

$\frac{4}{8} =$ _____

8.

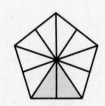 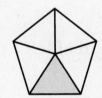

$\frac{2}{10} =$ _____

Draw a picture to help you complete each number sentence.

9. $\frac{8}{10} = \frac{\Box}{5}$

10. $\frac{\Box}{9} = \frac{1}{3}$

11. $\frac{3}{6} = \frac{\Box}{12}$

12. $\frac{4}{8} = \frac{\Box}{2}$

Lesson 15-6 • Writing Equivalent Fractions

Comparing and Ordering Fractions

Cathy used $\frac{2}{3}$ yard of ribbon to decorate a hat. Miko used $\frac{5}{6}$ yard of ribbon to wrap a gift. Lane used $\frac{1}{2}$ yard of ribbon to make a necklace. Who used more ribbon, Cathy or Lane? Which girl used the most ribbon?

We need to compare the ribbon Cathy and Lane used.

Cathy used _____ yard and Lane used _____ yard.

We can use fraction strips to compare fractions.

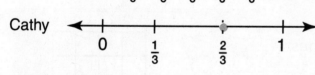

$\frac{2}{3} >$ _____

Because $\frac{2}{3}$ _____ $\frac{1}{2}$, Cathy used more ribbon than Lane.

To find out which girl used the most ribbon, we put all three fractions in order.

Miko

Cathy

Lane

$\frac{5}{6} > \frac{2}{3}$ and $\frac{2}{3} > \frac{1}{2}$

The lengths of ribbon from least to greatest are: $\frac{1}{2}$, _____, and _____.

Miko used the most ribbon.

Getting Started

Compare. Write <, >, or = in the circle.

1.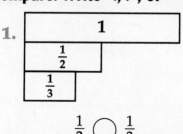

$\frac{1}{2} \bigcirc \frac{1}{3}$

2.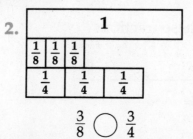

$\frac{3}{8} \bigcirc \frac{3}{4}$

3.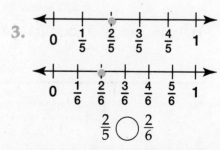

$\frac{2}{5} \bigcirc \frac{2}{6}$

Practice _____

Compare. Write <, >, or = in the circle.

1.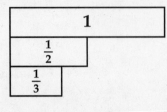

$\dfrac{1}{2}$ ◯ $\dfrac{1}{3}$

2.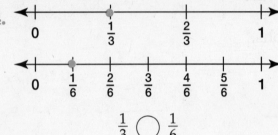

$\dfrac{2}{6}$ ◯ $\dfrac{2}{4}$

3.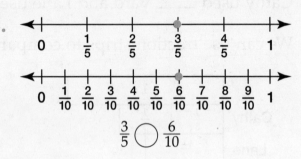

$\dfrac{6}{8}$ ◯ $\dfrac{3}{4}$

Compare fractions. Write <, > or = in the circle.

4.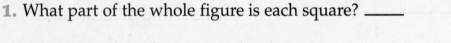

$\dfrac{1}{3}$ ◯ $\dfrac{1}{6}$

5.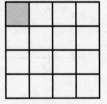

$\dfrac{3}{5}$ ◯ $\dfrac{6}{10}$

Order each set of fractions from least to greatest.

6. $\dfrac{1}{2}, \dfrac{1}{3}, \dfrac{3}{4}$ _____

7. $\dfrac{3}{8}, \dfrac{1}{2}, \dfrac{2}{3}$ _____

8. $\dfrac{4}{8}, \dfrac{1}{3}, \dfrac{5}{6}$ _____

9. $\dfrac{1}{6}, \dfrac{2}{3}, \dfrac{3}{8}$ _____

[Now Try This!]

Use the picture to help you answer the questions.

1. What part of the whole figure is each square? _____

2. What part of the figure is each column? _____

3. What part is each row? _____   4. What part is each half-row? _____

5. What part is 2 rows? _____   6. What part is 2 columns? _____

7. Why is it easy to compare all these fractions?

_____

Lesson 15-7 • Comparing and Ordering Fractions

Adding Fractions

On Monday, Beth's father told her he had worked $\frac{1}{5}$ of his workweek already. On Wednesday, he said he had worked another $\frac{2}{5}$ of his week. What part of the week had her father worked?

We want to find what part of the week Beth's father worked so far.

By Monday evening he had worked $\frac{\square}{\square}$ of a week.

Tuesday and Wednesday he had worked another $\frac{\square}{\square}$ of a week.

To find the part of the week that he had worked, we add $\frac{1}{5}$ and $\frac{2}{5}$.

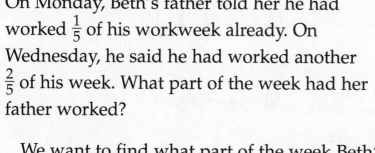

$$\frac{1}{5} + \frac{2}{5} = \frac{\square}{5}$$

$\frac{1}{5}$ Monday

$+ \frac{2}{5}$ Tuesday and Wednesday

$\frac{\square}{5}$ Monday through Wednesday

Beth's father had worked $\frac{\square}{\square}$ of his workweek.

REMEMBER When the denominators are the same, only the numerators are added. The denominator remains the same.

Getting Started

Shade the figures. Add the fractions.

1.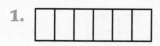

Shade $\frac{3}{6}$.

Shade another $\frac{1}{6}$. $\frac{3}{6} + \frac{1}{6} = $ _____

2.

Shade $\frac{2}{8}$.

Shade another $\frac{3}{8}$.

$$\begin{array}{r} \frac{2}{8} \\ + \frac{3}{8} \\ \hline \end{array}$$

Practice

Shade the figures. Add the fractions.

1.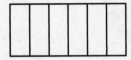

    Shade $\frac{1}{6}$.

    Shade another $\frac{2}{6}$. $\frac{1}{6} + \frac{2}{6} =$ _____

2.

    Shade $\frac{2}{5}$.

    Shade another $\frac{2}{5}$.

    $\frac{2}{5}$
    $+ \frac{2}{5}$

3.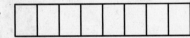

    Shade $\frac{3}{8}$.

    Shade another $\frac{2}{8}$. $\frac{3}{8} + \frac{2}{8} =$ _____

4.

    Shade $\frac{3}{10}$.

    Shade another $\frac{2}{10}$.

    $\frac{3}{10}$
    $+ \frac{2}{10}$

5.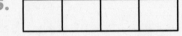

    Shade $\frac{1}{4}$.

    Shade another $\frac{2}{4}$. $\frac{1}{4} + \frac{2}{4} =$ _____

6.

    Shade $\frac{3}{7}$.

    Shade another $\frac{4}{7}$.

    $\frac{3}{7}$
    $+ \frac{4}{7}$

7.

    Shade $\frac{4}{9}$.

    Shade another $\frac{3}{9}$. $\frac{4}{9} + \frac{3}{9} =$ _____

8.

    Shade $\frac{5}{8}$.

    Shade another $\frac{2}{8}$.

    $\frac{5}{8}$
    $+ \frac{2}{8}$

9.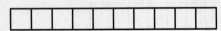

    Shade $\frac{5}{10}$.

    Shade another $\frac{3}{10}$. $\frac{5}{10} + \frac{3}{10} =$ _____

10.

    Shade $\frac{2}{6}$.

    Shade another $\frac{3}{6}$.

    $\frac{2}{6}$
    $+ \frac{3}{6}$

Subtracting Fractions

Daphne is making instant pudding. She needs $\frac{1}{4}$ cup of milk. How much milk will she have left in her measuring cup?

We want to know how much milk Daphne will have left.

Daphne starts with $\frac{\square}{\square}$ cup of milk.

She uses $\frac{\square}{\square}$ cup of milk for pudding.

To find the part left over, we subtract $\frac{1}{4}$ from $\frac{3}{4}$.

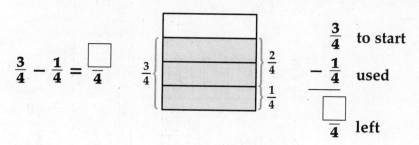

$$\frac{3}{4} - \frac{1}{4} = \frac{\square}{4}$$

$\frac{3}{4}$ to start

$-\frac{1}{4}$ used

$\frac{\square}{4}$ left

Daphne has $\frac{\square}{\square}$ or $\frac{1}{2}$ of a cup of milk left.

REMEMBER When the denominators are the same, only the numerators are subtracted. The denominator remains the same.

Getting Started

Shade the figures. Subtract the fractions.

1.

Shade $\frac{5}{6}$.

Cross out $\frac{3}{6}$. $\frac{5}{6} - \frac{3}{6} =$ _____

2.

Shade $\frac{6}{7}$.

Cross out $\frac{5}{7}$.

$\begin{array}{r} \frac{6}{7} \\ -\frac{5}{7} \\ \hline \end{array}$

Practice _____

Shade the figures. Subtract the fractions.

1.

   Shade $\frac{3}{8}$.

   Cross out $\frac{1}{8}$.　　$\frac{3}{8} - \frac{1}{8} =$ ___

2.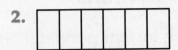

   Shade $\frac{5}{6}$.

   Cross out $\frac{3}{6}$.

   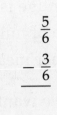
   $\frac{5}{6}$
   $- \frac{3}{6}$
   ___

3.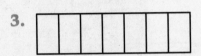

   Shade $\frac{5}{7}$.

   Cross out $\frac{2}{7}$.　　$\frac{5}{7} - \frac{2}{7} =$ ___

4.

   Shade $\frac{2}{3}$.

   Cross out $\frac{1}{3}$.

   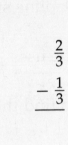
   $\frac{2}{3}$
   $- \frac{1}{3}$
   ___

5.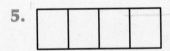

   Shade $\frac{3}{4}$.

   Cross out $\frac{1}{4}$.　　$\frac{3}{4} - \frac{1}{4} =$ ___

6.

   Shade $\frac{7}{10}$.

   Cross out $\frac{5}{10}$.

   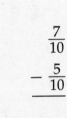
   $\frac{7}{10}$
   $- \frac{5}{10}$
   ___

7.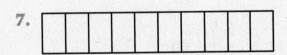

   Shade $\frac{9}{10}$.

   Cross out $\frac{6}{10}$.　　$\frac{9}{10} - \frac{6}{10} =$ ___

8.

   Shade $\frac{4}{5}$.

   Cross out $\frac{3}{5}$.

   $\frac{4}{5}$
   $- \frac{3}{5}$
   ___

9.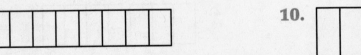

   Shade $\frac{5}{9}$.

   Cross out $\frac{3}{9}$.　　$\frac{5}{9} - \frac{3}{9} =$ ___

10.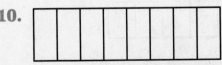

   Shade $\frac{7}{8}$.

   Cross out $\frac{3}{8}$.

   $\frac{7}{8}$
   $- \frac{3}{8}$
   ___

Mixed Numbers

When a fraction amount is greater than 1, you can write a **mixed number** to name the amount. A mixed number is a number written as a whole number and a fraction.

Darcy baked two pies. Her family ate 3 pieces of one pie. How much pie was left?

There was _____ whole pie and _____ of another pie.

We say: **one and five-eighths**.

Darcy has _____ pies left.

Getting Started _____

Write a mixed number for each picture.

1.
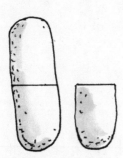

_____

2.

_____

3.

_____

4.

_____

Write a mixed number for each picture.

1.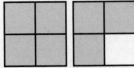

_____

2.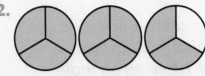

_____

3.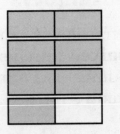

_____

4.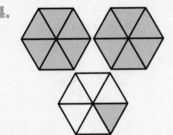

_____

5.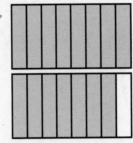

_____

6.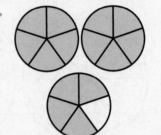

_____

Draw a picture to show each mixed number.

7. $2\frac{1}{8}$

8. $1\frac{3}{4}$

9. $3\frac{1}{2}$

Now Try This!

You can use number lines to show mixed numbers.
Write the missing fractions and mixed numbers to
finish labeling each number line.

1.

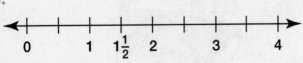

2.

3.

4.

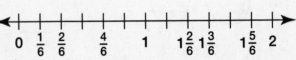

Lesson 15-10 • Mixed Numbers

Name _____

Problem Solving: Use Logical Reasoning

Anna, Randy, Cindy, and Dan are four friends, each with one pet. There are four pets: a cat, a dog, a pig, and a horse. Anna has the largest pet. Randy does not have a cat or a pig. Cindy is allergic to cats. What kind of pet does each friend have?

 SEE

We want to find out what kind of pet each friend has.
Clues: Anna has the largest pet.
        Randy does not have a cat or a pig.
        Cindy is allergic to cats.

⭐ **PLAN**

We can use **logical reasoning**. Organize the information in a table. Read each clue one at a time. Use the information in each clue to write *Yes* or *No* under as many pets as you can.

⭐ **DO**

Anna has the largest pet. The largest

pet is a _____. Randy does not

have a _____ or a _____.

Cindy is allergic to _____.

Anna's pet is a _____.

Randy's pet is a _____.

Cindy's pet is a _____. Dan's pet is a _____.

	Cat	Dog	Pig	Horse
Anna	No	No	No	
Randy		Yes		
Cindy		No	Yes	
Dan		No	No	

⭐ **CHECK**

Reread each clue to make sure you have chosen the correct pet.

Is the horse the largest pet of all the pets? _____

Is Randy's pet a cat or a pig? _____

Is Cindy's pet a cat? _____

Apply

Use logical reasoning to solve each problem. Make a table, if needed.

1. Lauren, Mia, Nancy, and Rosa are almost the same height. Their heights are 50 inches, 52 inches, 53 inches, and 54 inches. Nancy is the tallest. Mia is 52 inches tall. Rosa is taller than Lauren. How tall is each girl?

2. Mike, Nicole, Pedro, and Salim are friends. Each friend is either 6, 7, 8, or 9 years old. Pedro is older than Mike. Nicole is the youngest. Salim is 8 years old. How old is each friend?

3. The hundreds digit is equal to the thousands digit. The ones digit is 6. The sum of the ones and thousands digits is the tens digit. The ones digit is twice the size of the thousands digit. What is the mystery number?

4. The tens digit is equal to the thousands digit. The sum of the tens digit and the ten-thousands digit is 3. The sum of the tens digit and the hundreds digit is 5. The thousands digit is 2. The sum of all the digits is 13. What is the mystery number?

5. Gary, Mark, Abdul, and Yoshi were in a race. Mark finished ahead of Gary. Abdul also finished ahead of Gary but did not win the race. Mark finished in third place. Who won the race?

6. Sam is less than 20 years old. The sum of the two digits of his age is even. The difference of the two digits is 0. How old is Sam?

7. The mystery number is less than 30. It can be divided by 6 and 8. What is the mystery number?

8. Use the numbers 5 through 9 to fill in the empty spaces in this square. The sum of each row and column is 15.

2		4
		3
	1	

Write the fraction of each figure that is green.

1.  ___

2. 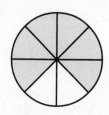 ___

3. 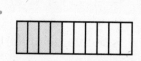 ___

Write the fraction that tells what part of each set of figures are squares.

4.

5. ___

6. ___

Write the fraction of each number.

7. $\frac{1}{3}$ of 12 = ____

8. $\frac{1}{5}$ of 60 = ____

9. $\frac{1}{8}$ of 56 = ____

Write the equivalent fractions.

10.

$\frac{2}{3}$ = ____

11.

$\frac{5}{8}$ > ____

Shade each figure. Add or subtract the fractions.

12.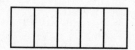

Shade $\frac{2}{5}$. $\frac{2}{5} + \frac{1}{5}$ = ____

Shade another $\frac{1}{5}$.

13.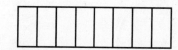

Shade $\frac{7}{8}$. $\frac{7}{8}$

Cross out $\frac{4}{8}$. $-\frac{4}{8}$

Circle the letter of the correct answer.

1 What is the value of the 3 in 536,296?

    a. thousands
    b. ten thousands
    c. hundred thousands
    d. NG

2
    42
    78
  + 57

    a. 167
    b. 177
    c. 187
    d. NG

3
    $27.48
  + 58.18

    a. $85.66
    b. $85.67
    c. $75.66
    d. NG

4
    803
  − 658

    a. 157
    b. 252
    c. 1,461
    d. NG

5
    $17.46
  − 2.99

    a. $14.47
    b. $15.53
    c. $20.45
    d. NG

6

    a. 5:45
    b. 9:25
    c. 9:38
    d. NG

7 Find the perimeter.

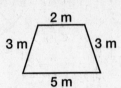

    a. 6 m
    b. 7 m
    c. 13 m
    d. NG

8
    36
  × 8

    a. 248
    b. 288
    c. 2,448
    d. NG

9
    $4.50
  ×   9

    a. $5.05
    b. $36.50
    c. $40.50
    d. NG

10 Find the area.

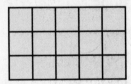

    a. 3 sq units
    b. 5 sq units
    c. 16 sq units
    d. NG

11 $3\overline{)48}$

    a. 12
    b. 14
    c. 16
    d. NG

12 $4\overline{)97}$

    a. 20 R1
    b. 24
    c. 24 R1
    d. NG

    score

STOP

Decimals

Understanding Tenths

Lorinda's job is to paint the fence on the east side of Mayfield Street. It started to rain before she could finish it. What decimal part of the fence did she get painted?

We want to write the part of the fence Lorinda painted as a decimal.

She painted _____ sections of the fence.

There are _____ sections in a fence.

We can write this part as a fraction.

Lorinda has painted **two tenths** or $\frac{2}{10}$ of the fence.

We can also write two tenths as a decimal.

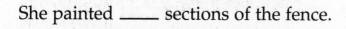

whole number $\rightarrow$ **0.2** $\leftarrow$ decimal

↑
**decimal
point**

Study this place value chart.

ones	tenths
0	2

Lorinda has painted _____ of the fence.

REMEMBER The decimal point always separates the ones place from the tenths place.

Getting Started

Write each as a decimal.

1. five tenths _____

2. $\frac{1}{10}$ _____

3. seven tenths _____

Practice

Write each as a decimal.

1. $\frac{3}{10}$ _____

2. four tenths _____

3. nine tenths _____

4. $\frac{5}{10}$ _____

5. two tenths _____

6. $\frac{8}{10}$ _____

7. six tenths _____

8. one tenth _____

9. $\frac{7}{10}$ _____

10. What part is painted? _____

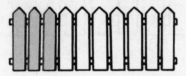

11. What part is *not* painted? _____

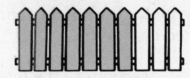

12. What part is *not* painted? _____

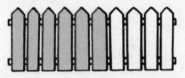

13. What part is painted? _____

14. What part is painted? _____

15. What part is painted? _____

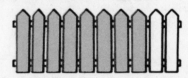

16. What part is *not* painted? _____

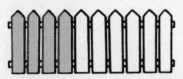

17. What part is painted? _____

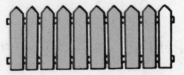

18. What part is painted? _____

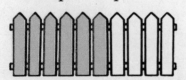

19. What part is *not* painted? _____

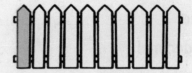

Lesson 16-1 • Understanding Tenths

Understanding Mixed Decimals

Lorinda is still painting fences at the end of the week. How many fences has she completed?

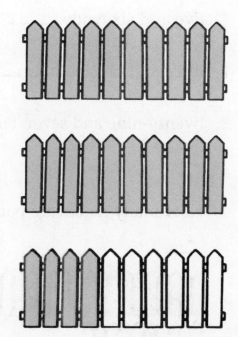

We want to write a decimal number that tells the number of fences Lorinda has painted.

She has painted _____ complete fences and _____ sections of another fence.

There are _____ sections in a fence.

We can write this as a **mixed number.**

two full → **2.4** ← four tenths of
fences   another fence

We write this as **two and four tenths.**

Study this place-value chart.

ones	tenths
2	4

Lorinda has painted _____ fences.

Getting Started

Write each as a mixed decimal.

1. three and six tenths _____

2. four and eight tenths _____

3. twelve and one tenth _____

4. thirty-six and two tenths _____

5. How many fences are painted?

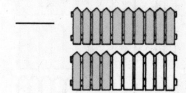

_____

6. How many fences are *not* painted?

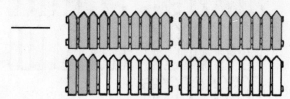

_____

Practice

Write each as a mixed decimal.

1. five and six tenths _____

2. nine and five tenths _____

3. three and one tenth _____

4. fifteen and three tenths _____

5. twenty-nine and seven tenths

   _____

6. seventy-five and two tenths

   _____

7. How many fences are painted?

   _____

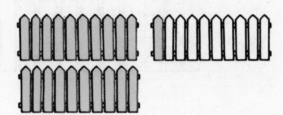

8. How many fences are *not* painted?

   _____

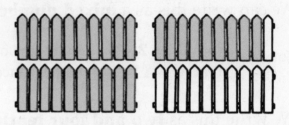

9. How many fences are painted?

   _____

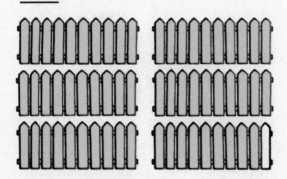

10. How many fences are *not* painted?

    _____

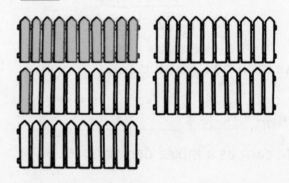

11. How many fences are painted?

    _____

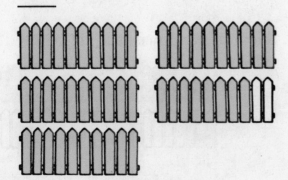

12. How many fences are *not* painted?

    _____

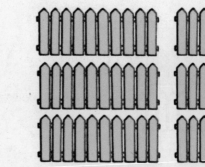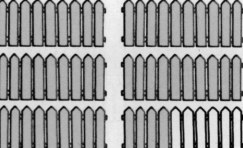

Lesson 16-2 • Understanding Mixed Decimals

Name _____

Comparing Decimals

The third grade raised money for charity in a walk-a-thon. Those who walked the farthest also earned prizes. Who won the top prize?

John	2.7 km
Dave	2.2 km
Sue	2.9 km
Polly	2.8 km

We want to know which third grader won the prize for walking the farthest.

John walked _____ kilometers, Dave _____ kilometers, Sue _____ kilometers, and Polly _____ kilometers.

To find which student went the farthest, we can draw pictures to compare the distances.

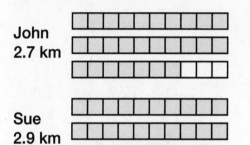

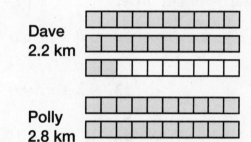

We can also compare the distances on a number line.

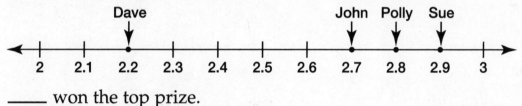

_____ won the top prize.

Getting Started

Use the number line to answer Exercises 1 and 2.

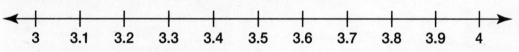

1. Circle the number that is less.

    3.3   3.8   3.5

2. Circle the number that is greater.

    3.6   3.9

Compare. Write < or > in the circle.

3. 5.7 ◯ 5.9

4. 0.7 ◯ 0.3

5. 12.3 ◯ 15.3

Practice

Use the number line to help you circle the number that is less.

1.

```
<──┼──┼──┼──┼──┼──┼──┼──┼──┼──┼──┼──>
   8  8.1 8.2 8.3 8.4 8.5 8.6 8.7 8.8 8.9  9
```

   8.6   8.2   8.8

Use the picture to help you circle the greater number.

2.

   3.8   3.6

Circle the greater number.

3. 6.4   6.8

4. 9.1   9.0

5. 1.6   1.7

6. 2.7   2.4

7. 4.3   4.2

8. 9.5   9.6

Compare. Write < or > in the circle.

9. 6.4 ◯ 6.7

10. 8.8 ◯ 8.9

11. 2.5 ◯ 2.3

12. 0.6 ◯ 0.8

13. 9.3 ◯ 9.6

14. 12.2 ◯ 12.3

15. 28.5 ◯ 28.1

16. 17.6 ◯ 17.8

17. 30.2 ◯ 30.4

18. 94.8 ◯ 94.6

19. 27.3 ◯ 72.3

20. 48.4 ◯ 48.5

Problem Solving

Solve each problem.

21. Jan ran 4.2 kilometers. Sid ran 4.7 kilometers. Who ran farther?

22. Roberto weighs 68.6 kilograms. Raul weighs 68.7 kilograms. Who is lighter?

Now Try This!

Compare. Write <, >, or = in the circle.

1. 0.6 ◯ $\frac{7}{10}$

2. $\frac{5}{10}$ ◯ 0.4

3. $\frac{8}{10}$ ◯ 0.8

4. 0.4 ◯ $\frac{2}{10}$

5. $\frac{3}{10}$ ◯ 0.3

6. 0.7 ◯ $\frac{6}{10}$

Lesson 16-3 • Comparing Decimals

Name _____

Understanding Hundredths

Jaime's goal is to do 100 situps. He charts his progress on a grid of 100 squares. Each square stands for a situp. The shaded squares in this grid show the number of situps Jaime has done. What part of his goal has he reached in decimals?

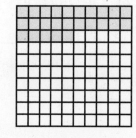

We want to write in decimals the part of Jaime's goal that he has reached.

Jaime wants to do _____ situps.

So far he has done _____ situps.

We can write this as the fraction $\frac{25}{100}$ or **twenty-five hundredths**.

As a decimal, $\frac{25}{100}$ is written as **0.25**.

whole number → **0.25** ← decimal
↑
decimal point

Study this place-value chart.

ones	tenths	hundredths
0	2	5

Jaime has reached _____ of his goal.

Getting Started

Write each as a decimal.

1. fourteen hundredths _____

2. $\frac{19}{100}$ _____

3. five hundredths _____

4. What part is green? _____

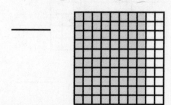

5. What part is *not* green? _____

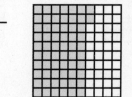

Practice

Write each as a decimal.

1. twelve hundredths _____

2. six hundredths _____

3. $\frac{14}{100}$ _____

4. sixteen hundredths _____

5. $\frac{3}{100}$ _____

6. thirty-six hundredths _____

7. ninety-nine hundredths _____

8. $\frac{1}{100}$ _____

9. four hundredths _____

10. $\frac{25}{100}$ _____

What part is green?

11.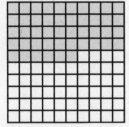
_____

12.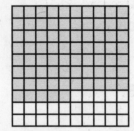
_____

13.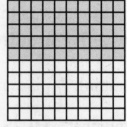
_____

14.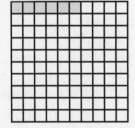
_____

15.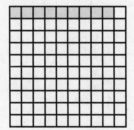
_____

16.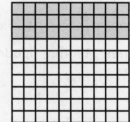
_____

What part is *not* green?

17.
_____

18.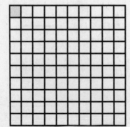
_____

19.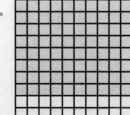
_____

Lesson 16-4 • Understanding Hundredths

Adding Decimals

Pablo, the weatherman, will report the amount
of rain that fell on Thursday and Friday in his weekly
wrap-up. How much rain fell on those two days?

Rainfall for the Week	
Monday	None
Tuesday	2.08 cm
Wednesday	None
Thursday	4.57 cm
Friday	2.36 cm

We want the total amount of rainfall for both days.

On Thursday, _____ centimeters of rain fell.

The rainfall for Friday was _____ centimeters.

To find the total rainfall, we add _____ and _____.

REMEMBER Always line up the decimal points in
the addends.

Add hundredths. Regroup, if needed.	Add tenths. Regroup, if needed. Bring down and line up the decimal point.	Add ones.
$\overset{1}{4}.5\,7$ $+\ 2.3\,6$ ___ 3	$\overset{1}{4}.5\,7$ $+\ 2.3\,6$ ___ $.93$	4.57 $+\ 2.36$ ___ 6.93

It rained _____ centimeters on Thursday and Friday.

Getting Started

Add.

1. 3.6
    $+\ 5.9$

2. 7.85
    $+\ 8.60$

3. 0.87
    $+\ 5.39$

4. 2.08
    4.57
    $+\ 2.36$

Copy and add.

5. $2.08 + 4.57$

6. $3.24 + 6.93$

7. $7.4 + 8.9$

Practice

Add.

1.	4.6 + 2.3	2.	6.6 + 1.2	3.	8.4 + 3.3	4.	7.3 + 6.5
5.	5.6 + 4.7	6.	9.7 + 3.8	7.	6.4 + 8.9	8.	4.8 + 0.6
9.	2.43 + 3.16	10.	5.18 + 1.30	11.	2.48 + 7.35	12.	4.27 + 5.76
13.	1.6 4.3 + 5.9	14.	4.7 8.2 + 7.5	15.	2.39 1.64 + 0.86	16.	5.48 3.25 + 1.07

Copy and add.

17. 2.35 + 9.16   18. 8.06 + 7.28   19. 3.79 + 0.85

20. 9.39 + 6.87   21. 4.52 + 7.79   22. 8.56 + 9.70

23. 8.13 + 3.23   24. 6.39 + 5.82   25. 7.34 + 3.69

26. 39.8 + 12.3   27. 59.9 + 60.7   28. 35.1 + 42.9

Problem Solving

Solve each problem.

29. It is 3.5 kilometers from Steve's house to the market. It is 2.3 kilometers farther to the library. What is the distance from Steve's house to the library?

30. One jar holds 1.45 liters of juice. Another jar holds 3.76 liters. How many liters will both jars hold?

Subtracting Decimals

Pablo's snowfall reports are of special interest to the weekend skiers. How much more snow fell on Friday than on Thursday?

Snowfall for the Week	
Monday	None
Tuesday	None
Wednesday	1.11 cm
Thursday	2.45 cm
Friday	6.73 cm

We want to know how much more snow fell on Friday than on Thursday.

On Thursday, _____ centimeters of snow fell.

Friday's snowfall was _____ centimeters.

To to find out how much more snow fell on Friday than on Thursday, we subtract _____ from _____.

Subtract hundredths. Regroup, if needed.	Subtract tenths. Regroup, if needed. Bring down and line up the decimal point.	Subtract ones.
$$\begin{array}{r} {\scriptstyle 6\ 13} \\ 6.7\cancel{3} \\ -\ 2.45 \\ \hline 8 \end{array}$$	$$\begin{array}{r} {\scriptstyle 6} \\ 6.\cancel{7}3 \\ -\ 2.45 \\ \hline .28 \end{array}$$	$$\begin{array}{r} 6.73 \\ -\ 2.45 \\ \hline 4.28 \end{array}$$

It snowed _____ centimeters more on Friday than on Thursday.

Getting Started

Subtract.

1. $\begin{array}{r} 6.9 \\ -\ 2.5 \\ \hline \end{array}$ 2. $\begin{array}{r} 7.36 \\ -\ 2.56 \\ \hline \end{array}$ 3. $\begin{array}{r} 8.02 \\ -\ 5.46 \\ \hline \end{array}$ 4. $\begin{array}{r} 6.30 \\ -\ 2.52 \\ \hline \end{array}$

Copy and subtract.

5. $5.21 - 2.57$ 6. $9.20 - 5.84$ 7. $6.24 - 5.88$

Practice

Subtract.

1. 7.4
   − 2.3

2. 8.7
   − 5.6

3. 9.2
   − 3.2

4. 8.3
   − 8.1

5. 5.3
   − 2.6

6. 7.2
   − 3.7

7. 8.1
   − 4.8

8. 9.3
   − 2.9

9. 4.64
   − 2.32

10. 7.75
    − 5.61

11. 8.57
    − 1.53

12. 6.68
    − 2.48

13. 7.96
    − 4.58

14. 8.15
    − 2.58

15. 6.21
    − 5.96

16. 9.85
    − 2.86

Copy and subtract.

17. 8.06 − 2.88

18. 9.00 − 5.29

19. 6.18 − 2.09

20. 3.89 − 2.96

21. 7.08 − 3.65

22. 6.24 − 3.86

23. 7.95 − 4.36

24. 9.74 − 2.84

25. 6.11 − 1.29

26. 5.20 − 2.29

27. 7.24 − 7.13

28. 2.22 − 1.66

Problem Solving

Solve each problem.

29. Keith pours 2.6 liters of milk from a new jug that holds 4.0 liters. How much milk is left in the jug?

30. The American record for the women's indoor high hurdles is 8.07 seconds. The world record is 7.86 seconds. How much difference is there between the two records?

Estimating With Decimals

Barry and Peter ran their turtles in the annual fundraiser for the protection of reptiles. About how far did Barry's turtle go in the race?

	Barry's Turtle	Peter's Turtle
Heat 1	32.4 cm	28.9 cm
Heat 2	43.3 cm	35.2 cm
Heat 3	31.5 cm	39.6 cm

We want to know how far Barry's turtle raced altogether.

It ran heats of _____, _____, and

_____ centimeters.

To find how far Barry's turtle went, we can add the length of each heat.

We can check by rounding the distance of each heat to a whole number, and adding.

> To round a decimal number to the nearest whole number, look at the tenths digit.

If the tenths digit is 0, 1, 2, 3, or 4, the ones digit remains the same and all the digits to the right are dropped.

32.4 is rounded to **32.**

If the tenths digit is 5, 6, 7, 8 or 9, the ones digit is raised one and all the digits to the right are dropped.

31.5 is rounded to **32.**

$$\underline{\quad} + \underline{\quad} + \underline{\quad} = \underline{\quad}$$
$$\uparrow \qquad \uparrow \qquad \uparrow$$
$$32.4 \qquad 43.3 \qquad 31.5$$

Barry's turtle raced about _____ centimeters in the three heats.

Getting Started

Round each decimal number to the nearest whole number.

1. 4.6 ____

2. 7.2 ____

3. 1.46 ____

4. 18.9 ____

Add or subtract. Use rounding to check each answer.

5.
```
  16.4
+ 12.7
```

6.
```
  5.91
- 2.57
```

7.
```
  42.3
  18.6
+  5.5
```

8.
```
  53.2
   7.4
+ 16.9
```

Practice

Round each decimal number to the nearest whole number.

1. 5.3 ____

2. 4.9 ____

3. 2.16 ____

4. 3.87 ____

5. 12.5 ____

6. 19.7 ____

7. 3.56 ____

8. 4.39 ____

9. 17.6 ____

10. 18.1 ____

11. 88.9 ____

12. 1.25 ____

Add or subtract. Use rounding to check each answer.

13.	9.63	14.	4.27	15.	34.6
	− 2.47		+ 3.16		+ 18.4

16.	26.8	17.	4.27	18.	25.9
	− 10.9		− 2.35		+ 18.9

Copy and add or subtract.

19. 26.5 + 7.3 + 8.2

20. 49.7 − 28.9

21. 8.54 − 1.87

22. 6.91 − 5.95

23. 2.56 + 4.29

24. 5.77 + 1.89 + 2.01

[Now Try This!]

Zero can be written at the end of a decimal number without changing its value. For example, 3.7 = 3.70. Use this idea to help find a number between the two given numbers.

1. 2.5 < 2.6   __2.50__ < __2.55__ < __2.60__

2. 1.9 < 2.0   ____ < ____ < ____

3. 1.3 < 1.4   ____ < ____ < ____

4. 3.2 < 3.3   ____ < ____ < ____

5. 3.1 < 3.2   ____ < ____ < ____

6. 2.05 < 2.1   ____ < ____ < ____

Lesson 16-7 • Estimating With Decimals

Name _____

Problem Solving: Too Much or Too Little Information

The Maestro family is taking a vacation trip along the eastern coast of the state of Florida. How many kilometers will they drive to get from Jacksonville, Florida to Miami Beach, Florida?

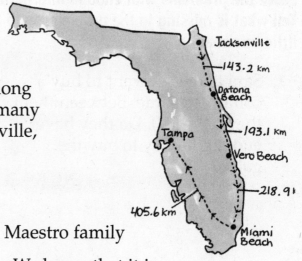

⭐ **SEE**

We need to find out how many kilometers the Maestro family

will drive from _____ to _____. We know that it is _____

kilometers from Jacksonville to Daytona Beach, _____ kilometers from

Daytona Beach to Vero Beach, _____ kilometers from Vero Beach to

Miami Beach, and _____ kilometers from Miami Beach to Tampa.

⭐ **PLAN**

Like a word problem, a map can also give too much or too little information. Find the information on the map that is needed to solve the problem.

Is there too much information? _____

To get the total number of kilometers, we add the mileages from

Jacksonville to _____ , from _____ to

Vero Beach, and from Vero Beach to _____ .

⭐ **DO**

From Jacksonville to Daytona Beach	143.2 km
From Daytona Beach to Vero Beach	km
From Vero Beach to Miami Beach	+ 218.9 km
	km

⭐ **CHECK**

Use subtraction to check the answer.

km	km
− 218.9 km	− 193.1 km

Apply

Solve the problems with enough information. Tell what is missing in the problems with too little information.

1. Sara and Max want to buy a computer game. Between them, they have $20. Do they have enough money to buy the game?

2. Kaitlyn poured 1.6 liters of juice from a container. The container held 5.0 liters. How much juice was left in the container?

3. Jake earns $5 an hour for mowing lawns. He mowed 3 lawns on Friday and 5 lawns on Saturday. How much money did Jake earn?

4. Mrs. Foster's car averages 25 miles per gallon on one tank of gas. The tank holds 10 gallons of gas. She bought the car 3 years ago and has driven 37,245 miles so far. Can Mrs. Foster travel 270 miles on one tank of gas?

5. A circus came to town and is having 3 shows a day, starting at 10:00 A.M. An adult ticket costs $12 and children's tickets cost $8. Each show lasts for 105 minutes. Can Andy's father buy tickets for himself, his wife, 2 daughters, and Andy with $50?

6. Jenny and her friend went to the museum of art on Wednesday. There are more than 4,000 pieces of art in the museum. Some paintings are worth as much as $10,000. The museum is free to visitors on Monday. How much did it cost for Jenny and her friend to go to the museum?

Lesson 16-8 • Problem Solving: Too Much or Too Little Information

Name _____

Write a decimal for the parts that are green.

1.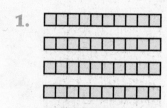

_____

2.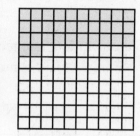

_____

Compare. Write < or > in the circle.

3. 0.3 $\bigcirc$ 0.6

4. 15.1 $\bigcirc$ 15.6

5. 4.7 $\bigcirc$ 4.3

6. 5.9 $\bigcirc$ 7.9

7. 9.5 $\bigcirc$ 9.2

8. 27.8 $\bigcirc$ 27.7

Add.

9.   13.3
    + 26.5

10.   27.5
    + 14.8

11.   39.7
    + 11.9

12.   7.24
    + 1.18

13.   4.96
    + 2.37

14.   3.26
    + 5.84

Subtract.

15.   7.6
     − 1.4

16.   86.8
     − 43.9

17.   73.2
     − 36.8

18.   8.46
     − 2.29

19.   6.17
     − 4.38

20.   9.41
     − 8.65

Circle the letter of the correct answer.

1 What is the value of the 4 in 932,450?
- **a.** tens
- **b.** hundreds
- **c.** thousands
- **d.** NG

2
```
   38
   47
 + 76
```
- **a.** 141
- **b.** 151
- **c.** 161
- **d.** NG

3
```
  $38.42
+ 46.59
```
- **a.** $75.01
- **b.** $84.01
- **c.** $85.01
- **d.** NG

4
```
  627
- 428
```
- **a.** 201
- **b.** 209
- **c.** 1,055
- **d.** NG

5
```
  8,246
- 3,198
```
- **a.** 4,048
- **b.** 5,048
- **c.** 5,148
- **d.** NG

6 Find the perimeter.

18 cm / 18 cm / 18 cm

- **a.** 36 cm
- **b.** 54 sq cm
- **c.** 54 cm
- **d.** NG

7
```
   42
 ×  9
```
- **a.** 368
- **b.** 378
- **c.** 3,618
- **d.** NG

8
```
  $3.75
×    4
```
- **a.** $13.00
- **b.** $14.00
- **c.** $14.80
- **d.** NG

9 Find the area.

- **a.** 20 units
- **b.** 20 sq units
- **c.** 21 sq units
- **d.** NG

10 $4\overline{)72}$
- **a.** 13
- **b.** 15
- **c.** 17
- **d.** NG

11 $6\overline{)70}$
- **a.** 11
- **b.** 11 R4
- **c.** 12
- **d.** NG

12 $\frac{1}{3}$ of 54
- **a.** 18
- **b.** 19
- **c.** 20
- **d.** NG

score

Glossary

A

acute angle an angle that has less of an opening than a right angle (p. 189)

acute triangle a triangle with three acute angles (p. 191)

addend a number that is added to another number (p. 1)

In 3 + 4 = 7, 3 and 4 are both addends.

angle a figure formed by two rays that have the same endpoint; the endpoint is called the vertex. (p. 189)

area the number of square units needed to cover a region (p. 179)

Associative Property When the grouping of three or more addends or factors is changed, the sum or product remains the same. (pp. 9, 147)

B

bar graph a graph that uses columns or bars to show data (p. 203)

C

calculator codes symbols that name the keys to be pressed on a calculator (p. 79)

Celsius scale a metric temperature scale naming 0° as the freezing point of water and 100° as its boiling point (p. 115)

centimeter (cm) a metric unit of length (p. 107)

100 centimeters = 1 meter

certain event an event that is sure to happen (p. 273)

Commutative Property The order of addends or factors does not change the sum or product. (pp. 9, 147)

5 + 7 = 7 + 5

cone a solid figure with a circle for its base and a curved surface forming a point (p. 181)

congruent figures figures that have the same shape and size (p. 195)

cube a solid figure with six equal, square sides (p. 181)

cubic units units used to measure the volume of solid figures (p. 185)

customary units standard measures of length, weight, volume, and capacity (pp. 91, 95, 97, 99)

Inches, miles, pounds, cubic feet, and ounces are examples of customary units.

cylinder a solid figure with two bases that are congruent circles (p. 181)

D

decimal a fractional part that uses place value and a decimal point to show tenths, hundredths, and so on (p. 291)

0.6 is the decimal equivalent for the fraction $\frac{3}{5}$.

decimal point a point or dot used to separate dollars from cents and ones from tenths in a number (p. 19)

denominator the number below the line in a fraction (p. 269)

In $\frac{3}{5}$, 5 is the denominator.

difference the answer in a subtraction problem (p. 5)

In 14 − 2 = 12, 12 is the difference.

digit any of the symbols used to write numbers (p. 33)

0, 1, 2, 3, 4, 5, 6, 7, 8, and 9 are digits

dividend the number that is being divided in a division problem (p. 215)

In 42 ÷ 7 = 6, 42 is the dividend.

divisor the number that is being divided into the dividend (p. 215)

In 42 ÷ 7 = 6, 7 is the divisor.

E

edge a line segment where two faces of a solid figure meet (p. 183)

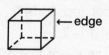

elapsed time total amount of time that passes from the starting time to the ending time (p. 87)

equilateral triangle a triangle with three equal sides (p. 191)

equivalent fractions fractions that name the same number (p. 277)

$\frac{3}{4}$ and $\frac{9}{12}$ are equivalent fractions because both name $\frac{3}{4}$.

estimate to give an answer that is close to the correct answer (pp. 55, 57, 75, 169, 243, 303)

even number a whole number with 0, 2, 4, 6, or 8 in the ones place (p. 252)

event a possible outcome of an experiment (p. 273)

F

face a plane figure making up part of a solid figure (p. 183)

face

factor a number to be multiplied (p. 121)

In $2 \times 3 = 6$, both 2 and 3 are factors.

Fahrenheit scale a temperature scale naming 32° as the freezing point of water and 212° as its boiling point (p. 101)

flip the change in the position of a figure that is the result of picking up and turning it over; a flip is also called a reflection. (p. 197)

fraction a number that names a part of a whole (p. 267)

$\frac{1}{2}$ is a fraction.

G

greater than a comparison of two numbers with the number of greater value written first (p. 35)

$10 > 5$

H

hexagon a plane figure with six sides and six angles (p. 177)

horizontal line a line that goes across (p. 187)

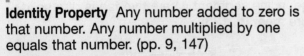

I

Identity Property Any number added to zero is that number. Any number multiplied by one equals that number. (pp. 9, 147)

$7 + 0 = 7 \quad 7 \times 1 = 7$

impossible event an event that will never happen (p. 273)

intersecting lines lines that meet at one point (p. 187)

inverse operations operations that undo each other (pp. 9, 227)

isosceles triangle a triangle with two equal sides (p. 191)

K

kilogram (kg) a metric unit of weight (p. 113)

1 kilogram = 1,000 grams

kilometer (km) a metric unit of length (p. 109)

1 kilometer = 1,000 meters

L

less than a comparison of two numbers with the number of lesser value written first (p. 35)

$3 < 10$

line a set of points that go on indefinitely in both directions (p. 187)

line graph a graph that shows a change in data over time (p. 207)

line of symmetry a line that equally divides a figure to produce a mirror image (p. 182)

line segment a part of a line that has two endpoints (p. 187)

liter (L) a basic metric unit of capacity (p. 111)

1 liter = 1, 000 milliliters

M

meter a metric unit of length (p. 109)

1 meter = 100 centimeters

metric units measures of length, weight, volume, and capacity based on the decimal system; meters, grams, and liters are basic metric units. (pp. 107, 109, 111, 113)

mile a customary unit of length (p. 93)

1 mile = 5,280 feet

milliliter (mL) a metric unit of capacity (p. 111)

minuend a number or quantity from which another is subtracted (p. 5)

In $18 - 5 = 13$, 18 is the minuend.

mixed decimal a number containing both a whole number and a decimal (p. 293)

3.4 is a mixed decimal.

mixed number a fractional number greater than 1 that is written as a whole number and a fraction (p. 285)

$5\frac{2}{3}$ is a mixed number.

N

numerator the number above the line in a fraction (p. 269)

In $\frac{3}{5}$, 3 is the numerator.

O

obtuse angle an angle that has a greater opening than a right angle but less than a straight line (p. 189)

obtuse triangle a triangle with one obtuse angle (p. 191)

octagon a plane figure with eight sides and eight angles (p. 177)

odd number a whole number with 1, 3, 5, 7, or 9 in the ones place (p. 252)

ordered pair two numbers that define one point on a grid; the first number names the distance across, and the second names the distance up. (p. 209)

ordinal number a number that shows the position of things in order; first, second, third (p. 33)

ounce (oz) a customary unit of weight (p. 99)

outcome a possible result of an experiment or a game (p. 273)

P

parallel lines lines in the same plane that do not intersect (p. 187)

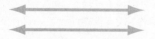

parallelogram a quadrilateral whose opposite sides are parallel and the same length (p. 193)

pentagon a plane figure with five straight sides and five angles (p. 177)

perimeter the distance around a shape that is the sum of the lengths of all of its sides (p. 95)

perpendicular lines lines that form right angles where they intersect (p. 189)

pictograph a way to show numbers or amounts using symbols or pictures (p. 205)

place value the value of the place where a digit appears in a number (pp. 15, 17, 29, 31)

In 137,510, the 7 is in the thousands place and stands for 7,000.

plane figure a shape that appears on a flat surface (p. 177)

point an exact position in space, usually shown by a dot (p. 187)

polygon a closed plane figure having three or more angles or sides (p. 177)

probability the chance an event will happen (p. 273)

product the answer to a multiplication problem (p.121)

In $4 \times 5 = 20$, 20 is the product.

pyramid a solid figure whose base is a polygon and whose faces are triangles with a common vertex (p. 181)

Q

quadrilateral a polygon with four sides and four angles (p. 193)

quotient the answer to a division problem (p. 215)

In $63 \div 7 = 9$, 9 is the quotient.

R

ray a part of a line that has one endpoint (p. 187)

rectangle a quadrilateral with four right angles in which pairs of opposite sides are the same length (p. 173)

rectangular prism a solid figure with six rectangular sides (p. 181)

reflection moving a plane figure over a line to get a mirror image (p. 197)

regroup to rename a number value so that an operation can be performed (pp. 41, 63, 161)

remainder the number left over in a division problem (p. 259)

```
      16 R4
  6)100
   − 6
    40
   − 36
      4
```

In this problem, 4 is the remainder.

rhombus a quadrilateral whose opposite sides are parallel and all sides are the same length (p. 193)

right angle an angle that makes a square corner; the symbol used to show a right angle is ⌐. (p. 189)

rotation turning a plane figure around a point (p. 197)

rounding estimating a number's value by raising or lowering any of its place values (pp. 25, 27)

S

scalene triangle a triangle with no sides the same length (p. 191)

slide a move that slides a figure a given distance in a given direction; a slide is also called a translation. (p. 197)

solid figure a figure with three dimensions—length, width, and height—such as a cube or a pyramid (p. 181)

sphere a solid figure in the shape of a ball (p. 181)

square a rectangle with four sides equal in length (p. 193)

standard form a number written using the symbols 0 through 9 in place-value form (pp. 15, 17, 29, 31)

4,036 is in standard form.

subtrahend the number that is subtracted from the minuend (p. 5)

In 18 − 5 = 13, 5 is the subtrahend.

sum the answer to an addition problem (p. 1)

In 8 + 9 = 17, 17 is the sum.

T

tally marks used to count by fives (p. 203)

transformation a slide, a flip, and a rotation (p. 197)

translation sliding a plane figure (p. 197)

trapezoid a quadrilateral with only one pair of parallel sides (p. 193)

triangle a polygon with three sides (p. 177)

turn a move that rotates a figure clockwise or counterclockwise and at a certain angle around a point; a turn is also called a rotation. (p. 197)

V

vertex (pl. vertices) the point where two sides of an angle, two sides of a plane figure, or three or more sides of a solid figure meet (p. 189)

vertical line a line that goes up and down (p. 187)

volume the number of cubic units needed to fill a solid figure (p. 185)

W

whole numbers those numbers used in counting and zero (p. 299)

Z

Zero Property of Multiplication If a factor is zero, the product will be zero. (p. 147)